The
Modem Reference

4th Edition

The Modem Reference

4th Edition

The Complete Guide to PC Communications

Michael A. Banks

CyberAge Books

Information Today, Inc.
Medford, New Jersey

First printing, 2000

The Modem Reference, 4th Edition
The Complete Guide to PC Communications

Library of Congress Cataloging-in-Publication Data

Banks, Michael A.
    The modem reference guide : the complete guide to PC communications / Michael A. Banks.—4th ed.
        p. cm.
    Includes bibliographical references and index.
    ISBN 0-910965-36-6
1. Modems. I. Title.

    TK5103 .B36 2000
    004.6'16—dc21

                                                                00-029487

Printed and bound in the United States of America.

Publisher: Thomas H. Hogan, Sr.
Editor-in-Chief: John B. Bryans
Managing Editor: Janet M. Spavlik
Copy Editor: Kimberly Mestrow
Production Manager: M. Heide Dengler
Cover Design: Jacqueline Walter
Book Design: Jeremy M. Pellegrin
Indexer: Laurie Andriot

This book is dedicated to the pioneering members
and staff at BIX and DELPHI, where I put so much
of it to the test over the past 16 years

Table of Contents

Figures and Tables

FIGURES

TABLES

Acknowledgments

As always, special thanks are due to those who helped make this book what it is.

John Bryans, Janet Spavlik, Kim Mestrow, Heide Dengler, and Jeremy Pellegrin at Information Today have my appreciation for their professionalism and their patience.

Thanks also to Larry Judy, Amy Forrester, Wayne Hall, Laura Kelly, Becky Lasater, and Debra Morner for support and assistance rendered.

Introduction

As a child in the late 1950s, I read a lot of science fiction. Robots, space travel, and many other wonders assailed my senses, but most of all I marveled at the idea of people being able to carry computers in their pockets. And even as I marveled, I told myself that one day this would be real—that I would be able to carry a computer in my pocket.

Today, pocket computers are a rather unremarkable fact of life to most of us. This is also the case with space stations, men on the moon, and a veritable cornucopia of other "wild ideas" that I first encountered in the pages of science fiction magazines and novels.

Among the more interesting of those wild ideas was something called a "home terminal," a handy little device that could deliver news, letters from friends, and more—including photos—right into your living room. This wonder could also tap vast databanks of knowledge, and a user could even "chat" with friends from around the world by typing and reading! This was quite a mind-expanding concept in 1958. (Actually, it's quite a mind-expanding concept for a lot of people in 2000.) Save for the databanks, the "home terminal" might be a contemporary fax machine. Add a PC with fax capability and a printer, and you have the complete package.

When I was young, most adults of my acquaintance regarded this sort of thing as pure nonsense. (I suppose their parents and teachers had put the same label on TV in the 1930s.) But I—and thousands of other science fiction fans, young and old—knew it would one day be a reality.

Obviously, however, the science fiction predictions were not as nonsensical as they seemed. Anyone with a PC can dial up his or her Internet service provider (ISP) and scan headline news stories, check stock prices, look up "science fiction" in an online encyclopedia, read and reply to a dozen electronic mail messages, or chat in a real-time conference with friends from around the country or across the sea.

Computer telecommunications (or "telecomputing," as I prefer to call it) is no longer the exclusive province of techies, hackers, and professional engineers. The only physical requirements are a modem-equipped PC, the appropriate software, and a telephone line—nothing that's beyond those of at least average means these days. The level of technical sophistication required is little more than that necessary to operate an automatic bank teller or your own computer, for that matter. This is to say that if you can operate a personal computer you can telecompute.

The social, cultural, and other implications of this ease of telecomputing are staggering and won't be completely realized for decades. Entire electronic subcultures have been evolving on and across computer bulletin boards and online services for a decade and more, and I have no doubt we'll see still more science fiction concepts realized via telecomputing in coming years.

The same is true of using fax machines (and PC-based fax) to transmit documents and images across town or across the world. Moreover, fax is an even more common technological tool than PC telecomputing is in the personal and business lives of hundreds of millions of people. It is so common that contracts are signed and financial transfers are routinely conducted by fax.

But even the current reality of telecomputing is something more than what was imagined by the science fiction writers who first introduced the concept. Certainly the information and communications elements of telecomputing reflect what science fiction foresaw, but telecomputing is so much more than just exchanging information. Formal education is now conducted via online services, as are shopping, banking, and stock trading. And, as you'll learn from this book and through your online explorations, there is much, much more happening online. The applications of this marvelous tool—this conglomeration of modems and PCs and host mainframe computers and telephone lines—are virtually limitless.

Still, the complete home terminal of science fiction lore is not yet mundane to us, nor is it likely to be for some time to come. Telecomputing today is as new as tomorrow and has only recently begun to find its place in our civilization's infrastructure. The directions it will take in the future may be even more fascinating than contemporary speculations about global computer networks. Although telecomputing is fast achieving the status of a "legitimized" technological application, it will continue to grow and evolve as technology—and imagination—create new applications for it.

At the same time, there is a need to understand the technology behind fax and PC telecommunications. Those who design, build, and repair telecomputing systems must of course understand the technology. But the need for knowledge isn't restricted to engineers and technicians. Those people who specify and buy systems, administrators, and even business and personal end users ought to know more about what connects them with the world. Why? The answer is because even a little knowledge is a grand thing when it comes to telecomputing, which is not the case in many other fields. To understand how a system works is to be able to use it better.

Whether you are an engineer or technician-in-training, an accomplished professional, or a curious buyer or user, this book has something for you. I show you how and why telecomputing technology works, and how to apply it. I also show you the inner workings of the world's telecomputing infrastructure and a little bit of how we got where we are in terms of data telecommunications.

If you're not well versed in things technical, you can still learn from this book. All explanations and examples are designed to be understandable in context, which means that even those who know nothing more than how to turn on a computer can learn quite a bit about the workings of PC and fax communications. At the same time, students or professionals in the electronics and data communications fields will find that they can quickly isolate needed knowledge or easily study the entire book.

So, approach reading this book in any fashion you feel is appropriate. Of course this book will also serve as a continuing resource on all aspects of PC and fax communications.

See you online!

—Michael A. Banks
Oxford, Ohio
June 2000

CHAPTER 1

A Survey of PC Communications Activities

In this chapter I'll provide an overview of telecomputing activities and applications, and introduce concepts and terms used throughout this book. If you're completely new to telecomputing, it's especially important that you read this chapter.

We'll examine the major online activities by category:

■ Messaging

■ Real-time conferencing

■ File transfer

■ Online research

■ Online transactions

Then we'll take an introductory look at your major links to the online world—the Internet and online services—and wrap up with a discussion of the potential benefits of telecomputing.

MESSAGING

Electronic messaging is easily the most-used feature of any online system. (A message in this context is a note, letter, announcement, or other private or public textual communication.) Messages are exchanged online in a number of ways. The main distinction, however, is in whether messages are private or public.

Public Messages

Public messages are posted on what are usually called bulletin boards but are sometimes referred to as conferences in certain venues.

GETTING THE WORDS RIGHT

Having introduced those two terms in this context, I think it would be best take a few lines to distinguish their meanings from those in other contexts.

First, the term "electronic mail," or "e-mail," is erroneously used by some to refer to public message areas. This can be confusing, so try to read (and use) these terms in context.

Strictly speaking, a bulletin board is a public area where messages, announcements, and comments of general interest are posted—in short, a public system for written communications.

Unfortunately (in linguistic terms), certain types of small-scale computer systems are called "bulletin boards" too, and most of these offer far more than just message reading and posting. (You'll find more information on these systems at the end of this chapter and in Chapter 6.) The appropriate terminology for such a dial-up system is *computer bulletin board system* (usually shortened to the acronym BBS). To avoid confusion, I'll use "bulletin board" only when I'm referring to an area on a BBS, online service, or Web site where public messages are posted.

Similarly, *conference* has two meanings in the lexicon of the online world. As mentioned a few paragraphs back, the term sometimes refers to an area where public messages are posted. This is archaic usage. (Yes, I can hear the mainframe computer users screaming, but it's still archaic. The term came into use when message bases and e-mail were the only common means of communication via computer. Hanging the "conference" tag on such communication was very shortsighted, indeed.) In contemporary telecomputing, conference usually means real-time, face-to-face (or, keyboard-to-keyboard) online chatting, or typing and reading in lieu of talking and listening. To simplify matters, I'll usually use the word conference to mean real-time chatting. You should be aware, however, that certain systems use the term conference to refer to a public-bulletin-board-type message area. Actually, when used in this context, conference usually refers to a very specific and sophisticated type of public messaging system in which messages are organized and linked for access by subjects. Fortunately, you'll know which kind of conference I'm referring to by context (ditto for any services or Web sites that mention conference).

Finally, if you note anomalies involving these terms later in the book, remember that I follow the usage of the Web site, online service, or BBS. In other words, if a system calls a message base a conference, I'll discuss it as such.

Now, back to the topic at hand …

BULLETIN BOARDS

Bulletin boards are found on BBSs as well as on Web sites and online services. They may go by any of several different names, such as "forum," "conference," "board," "classified ads," and "post," to name a few.

The idea behind bulletin boards is the same as that behind the cork boards found in laundromats, apartment complex common rooms, meeting halls, or other public areas: to share information. Messages are grouped in categories or subjects, such as "For Sale," "Jokes," "News," or "Wanted." There may be subcategories or topics as well, such as "Automobiles" and "Rockets" under a "For Sale" subject.

Public messages can be read and (usually) replied to by anyone with access to the system on which they are found. Replies are normally public, unless the system offers a "Private" option.

You can read and post messages by category, but the more sophisticated online bulletin boards allow even greater control and definition of messages. For instance, you may be able to view messages based on any combination of the parameters of subject, sender, addressee, and date, if you wish. Some bulletin boards allow for the division of each subject into various subtopics and for some subtopics to be limited-access areas.

Public messages may or may not be addressed to individuals. Usually, if a message is addressed to you, you have the privilege of deleting it. You can also delete messages you have posted. A system may also allow you the option of making a message readable only by the addressee, providing, in effect, a private messaging service.

As you'll learn, a typical bulletin board message is brief—a couple hundred words long at the most—and to the point. This is because the length of a bulletin board message is limited on some systems (to conserve storage space), and, I suspect, because so many computer users are poor typists.

Private Messaging

Private messaging is commonly called *electronic mail* or *e-mail* and exists quite apart from bulletin boards. In e-mail, text messages are stored in what is referred to as your electronic mailbox, which is analogous to a mailbox to which only you have the key. This is actually a private file or portion of a file area to which only you have access, as it is tied to your online ID or username. Physically, your e-mail is stored on systems operated by the ISP or online service you use.

Replying to an e-mail message involves simple commands, and you can delete messages to and from you if you wish. A system may provide additional e-mail functions, such as the ability to forward an e-mail message to other users, send the same message to multiple users, or attach a file.

REAL-TIME CONFERENCING (CHAT)

Real-time conferencing is probably the most popular (and addictive) of telecomputing activities. In basic terms, real-time conferencing is one-to-one conversation, though on the majority of systems it's not limited to just two people.

Imagine if you will a CB or ham radio conversation in which you type and read rather than speak and listen. This will give you a good picture of what real-time conferencing is all about. In fact, some services call their real-time conversation facilities "CB simulators." (You may find real-time conferencing called chat or other names, depending on which system you're using.)

You'll find real-time conferencing on few BBSs, although nearly all have a provision for the person operating the BBS to break in and chat with you at his discretion, and most allow you to page the system operator. The majority of online services offer a real-time conference feature. Many Web sites also host chat areas.

Finally there are the many pager and chat programs, such as ICQ and AOL's Instant Messenger, that operate on the Internet.

FILE TRANSFER

File transfer is just what the name implies: the process of transferring files between computers. Next to e-mail, it is the most pragmatically useful aspect of telecomputing for business and personal computer users. Files of all types—from manuscripts to database and spreadsheet files to programs—can be transferred between computers.

A major advantage of file transfer is that—with text files, at least—you can transcend the differences in format between computers. So, if you have a Macintosh computer and need to make a lengthy document available to a friend who has an IBM computer, you can use your computer and modem to give him the file in a format his machine can read.

File transfers work in two directions—from your computer and to it. The terms used to describe which way a file is going are relative and easy to remember: If you are sending a file, you are uploading it; if you are receiving a file, you are downloading it. And, in case you're wondering, when a file is sent from one computer to another, it is copied; the file being sent is not deleted from the transmitting computer's disk.

Files can be attached to e-mail messages or stored on an online computer system and accessed via the Internet, an online service, or an ISP.

Files may be transferred using any of several protocols—ASCII for straight text and Xmodem, Ymodem, Zmodem, and other error-checking protocols for transferring program, data, or text files. (You will find more information on the specific protocols named here in Chapter 6.)

By the way, you'll find free software among the major benefits of file transfer. Online services and the Internet offer thousands of public domain or shareware programs for download. Public domain programs are programs that have been made available to the public at no charge by their creators. Shareware programs are programs for which the user is asked to make a monetary contribution if he or she finds them of value.

ONLINE RESEARCH

Talk with many business and professional modem users, and you'll come away convinced that the sum total of human knowledge can be found online.

That's almost true. Sophisticated services like The Dialog Corporation's Dialog Information Service provide access to a wealth of general and specialized information that is nothing short of staggering. Information utilities like Dow Jones offer the latest information in a variety of special-interest areas as well as updates on current and recent events and business news. Business, economic, and general news from AP, Reuters, *USA Today*, and other sources is available online, and many magazines publish online versions. The latter is the case with a number of publications from Ziff-Davis and McGraw-Hill, which publish all articles, columns, and reviews from every one of their issues online. Even cable TV services are online—the Cartoon Network (**http://www.cartoonnetwork.com**), The Weather Channel (**http://www.weather.com**), and the History Channel (**http://www.historychannel.com**), to name a few.

Comprehensive encyclopedias with sophisticated search and cross-referencing capabilities can be found on online services and at Web sites, too.

It should suffice to say that whether you're working on an economic forecast, a technical paper, or a high school homework assignment, you'll find online research beneficial.

Some services do not come free, of course. You pay for the convenience of home access, as well as for the specialized knowledge that you won't find elsewhere.

ONLINE TRANSACTIONS

It is now possible to purchase a surprising variety of goods and services online, as well as to undertake other kinds of financial transactions.

Although banking promised early on to be one of the most-used features offered by online services, it took a nose dive and was used very little until the advent of Web-based banking. Online bill paying is increasingly popular, and credit card companies offer a number of services for cardholders on various online services. You can even apply for a credit card online.

Online shopping is booming. Virtually every major retailer is online, and they are selling more than computers. Still, computer products seem to be the mainstay of online shopping.

In the service category, you'll find psychological counseling, stock and commodity quotes, stock brokerages, and full-service travel agencies online.

Online purchases of all types are normally paid for by credit card, though some shopping services do business on a COD basis where merchandise (as opposed to a service) is involved. Most online merchants offer discounts, periodic specials, or both to attract potential customers. It is this value-added element, plus the convenience of shopping online, that has made the Internet the world's largest shopping mall.

CHANNELS OF TELECOMPUTING

Broadly defined, telecomputing is communication via computer. More specifically, it is the transfer of data between two or more computers. Telecomputing can be as simple as connecting two PCs sitting side by side, or as complex as accessing a mainframe computer several thousand miles away with your laptop computer via a packet-switching-network computer and telephone lines.

Chapter 3, which is a layman's introduction to the technical side of things, provides a close look at the whys and hows of telecomputing, but we'll briefly survey the major channels of telecomputing here.

Local vs. Remote Systems

Note that two computers connected in a telecommunications link are distinguished from one another by the terms *local* and *remote*. These terms are strictly relative, i.e., dependent on the viewpoint of the operator.

From your viewpoint, your personal computer or terminal is the local system, while the computer you dial up is the remote system. To a person who operates a BBS, online service, or ISP, his computer is the local system, while yours is a remote system dialing in. The remote system is often called the *host*, particularly in the case of online services. The term host is also used to refer to any system receiving a call.

Modems

A modem is required for all but direct-connect communications (explained below); any communications via telephone lines require a modem to "translate" computer data into a form that can be transmitted by telephone lines or other means.

Direct-Connect Data Transfer

Data transfer between computers that are within a few feet of each other is most often accomplished without a modem, using what is called a *null-modem cable* (also called a *reversed* or *flipped* cable). This type of connection is known as a hard-wire or direct connection, and is far easier to set up and use than a modem-to-modem connection between two adjacent computers.

A null-modem cable simply reverses the way the wires are connected at the serial port (a.k.a. the RS-232C port) of each computer, so computer A's data-send wire is connected to computer B's data-receive wire and vice versa.

Common applications for direct-connect data transfer include transferring data between two "incompatible" computers (such as the Apple IIe and IBM PC), or between a desktop and a laptop computer. Another application is to connect computers in close proximity that must share data and/or common peripherals in what is known as a local area network (LAN).

Because extremely high data-transfer rates are possible between computers directly connected over a short distance, this is usually the best way to go when you have to transfer large quantities of data between compatible computers. For example, directly connecting two PCs to transfer data between their hard disks is much faster than copying the data from computer A's hard disk to a floppy disk, then recopying the data from the floppy disk to computer B's hard disk. Such transfers are particularly useful for transferring data between a desktop and a portable or laptop computer—an operation that more and more laptop owners are finding vital to their computing activities.

Modem transfers can be conducted using conventional communications software or using special computer-to-computer file-transfer programs.

If your computer-to-computer data-transfer needs are more permanent, you may wish to look into networking computers within a reasonable distance of one another using permanent cable connections and special connection and communication hardware. Such a configuration is often referred to as a LAN (local area network). A LAN typically provides a number of advantages beyond computer-to-computer file transfer—among them being control-level access of one computer by another.

The subject of LANs is at least as involved as computer communications in general, and, although I will refer to LANs elsewhere in this book, I recommend that you search for additional references to LANs.

Dialing Another Computer Direct

If you have a friend who has a modem and a computer, you may be able to dial his or her computer direct or vice versa. Or you may have remote-control software for your laptop computer and use it to dial into your home or office computer. Such communication requires a modem on each end, of course, as does any type of telecommunication via telephone lines.

Dialing a friend's computer is a good way to "get your feet wet" in telecomputing. But be prepared—you may have to experiment with different communications parameter settings before such a link works. One computer's communications software and modem must be set up to answer (this is also called the "host" mode), while the other must be set up to call.

Aside from giving you practice in using your modem and communications software, you may well find business uses for dialing another computer direct. For example, I occasionally call my PR or editing clients' computers direct to transfer documents on a tight deadline. I call my client by voice telephone to let him know I'm ready to send text, and we have one or the other of our computers call the other's number by pre-arrangement.

I also find it convenient to set up my desktop computer to answer the phone so that I can call and view or upload files using a laptop computer when I am away from home. Such activity is made possible by software that enables me to enter my desktop computer's operating system and issue commands after I've properly identified myself to the desktop computer's communications program. I use remote-control software designed especially for this purpose—usually Traveling Software's LaptLink.

Bulletin Board Systems

In the 1980s, most modem users' first experiences with telecomputing were probably with a local BBS. BBSs were (and still are) easily accessible and exist in virtually every region of the world. They usually don't require you to set up a membership or account in advance, nor do they generally charge a fee.

You'll find two main differences between dialing a friend's computer and a bulletin board system:

First, a BBS does not have to be attended.

When you call a BBS you have access to a limited, but extremely useful, range of services. On most systems, you can post and read messages, upload and download files, and, in some cases, delete files. More advanced BBSs also offer online games, and nearly all make some provision for real-time conferences (chats) between the sysop and a user currently online.

Second, as I mentioned a few lines back, very few BBSs charge for access. Those that do normally charge a nominal annual rate for access—perhaps 50 dollars or so—to help the sysop cover the cost of a dedicated telephone line and computer equipment.

The majority of calls to a BBS are from the board's local calling area; for obvious reasons, computer users prefer to find what they want locally rather than spend money on long-distance telephone charges. The more popular BBSs receive calls from all over the world.

GRAPHICS, ANYONE?

Communication with a BBS is primarily a matter of sending and receiving text (file transfers excepted). Quite a few BBSs also offer graphics, with or without color. They do this by sending control and command characters that tell your communications software to display certain colors and certain of your system's graphics characters on your screen. Known generically as ANSI graphics, this kind of graphic communication is dependent on your system's display capabilities, and on whether your communications software can emulate certain kinds of terminals. (More on terminal emulation in a few pages and in Chapter 2.)

In the past couple of years, BBS software developers have been at work on more sophisticated graphic-based systems, which require you to use a front-end program on your end (much like the graphics-based online services you'll learn about in a few pages). This and other developments in BBS software have been spurred on by the advent of the Internet, which has resulted in the decline of BBSs.

Commercial Online Services

Commercial online services may offer some or all of the same features of the average BBS (e-mail, public message areas, and downloadable files), as well as any number of unique services. Examples of commercial online services include America Online (AOL), CompuServe, and the Prodigy service.

Online services differ from BBSs in several ways. First, online services cost money, and in contrast to the vast majority of BBSs, they're in business to make money. Online services operate on expensive mini- or mainframe computers (often more than one), and employ programmers, customer service representatives, and other specialists to keep things running smoothly. They also pay royalties or fees to information and service providers.

In the early days, most online services billed by the minute only, and most still do. However, increasing competition among online services has resulted in some interesting pricing schemes, including flat-rate access for unlimited time—a very popular option. Certain kinds of online services bill by each instance of access—for example, a flat rate for a database search.

Second, online services provide services and features offered by few (or no) BBSs: multiple-user real-time conferencing, personal file areas, and access to fax and Telex service, databases, news services, and other services (some of which were briefly discussed earlier in this chapter). And, last but not least, they provide Internet access—to Internet e-mail, the World Wide Web, and Usenet newsgroups.

Online services are national and international in scope, and are often accessed via *packet-switching networks* (SprintNet, Tymnet, and/or the service's own private network). A packet-switching network is nothing more than a nationwide (or worldwide) network of computers and telephone systems, strategically located in various cities, whose job is to route data between your computer and a host computer (an online service's computer).

TEXT-BASED OR GRAPHICS-BASED?

Online services are often referred to as either text-based or graphics-based. These terms relate to how information is displayed on your computer screen as well as the kind of information delivered. Text-based systems are distinguished by the fact that almost all of the information displayed on your screen in real time is text, looking pretty much like what you see when you use a word processor. Figure 1.1 shows a text-based online service's menu.

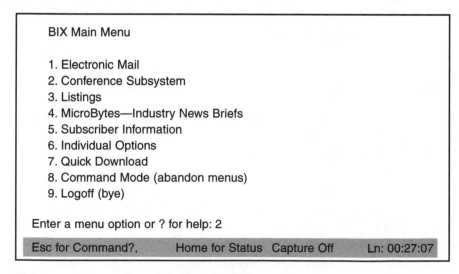

Figure 1.1   A text-based online service

Text-based services can also send graphics (in the form of data files) via file transfer, but you usually don't have access to the data until you're off-line. (Some text-based services make use of "special effects" offered by certain kinds of terminal emulation to provide functions such as screen clearing and even color. But, not all callers use terminal emulation, so this isn't a major element of text-based services.)

Graphics-based online services are distinguished by the fact that almost everything is displayed in graphic form—even text. Menus, messages, illustrations or animated images, and even the "framework" surrounding information are all graphics. Figure 1.2 is a good example of a graphics-based online service.

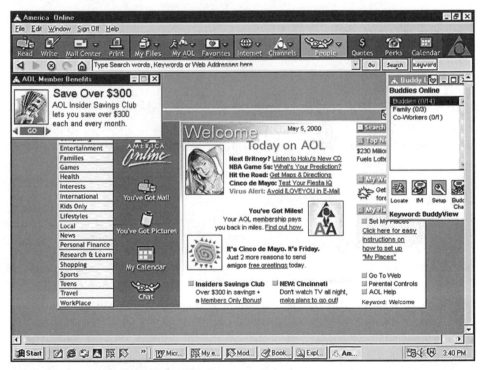

Figure 1.2   A graphics-based online service

Graphics-based services require that you use special software, which is provided by the online service. Rather than framing text in graphics that are static elements generated by the software on your end (which is what text-based "graphic" front ends do), graphics-based systems transmit the graphics. Text is likewise transmitted as graphics, hence the wide variety of text sizes and shapes in Figure 1.2.

Graphics-based services have been around in some form or another (usually primitive) for nearly two decades. It was only in the 1990s that PC technology reached a point where graphics were practical for use by just about anyone with a modem. (The technology in question encompasses operating and connect speed, disk size—since much of what a graphics-based service displays on your screen is stored on your system's hard disk—and display speed and resolution.)

I'll talk about how these systems work in later chapters. For now, I'll note that graphics-based systems are generally as fast as text-based systems, and that most of the older text-based online services were forced to develop graphic front ends to stay competitive—which says a lot for the market appeal of graphics-based online services.

Packet-Switching Networks

Packet-switching networks provide a way for you to call a distant host computer without incurring long-distance charges. In practice, you dial a local telephone number, connect with the packet network computer, tell it which service you wish to be connected to, and the packet network computer connects with the online service via its own system of dedicated phone lines. There is a charge for such access, but it is normally built into an online service's fees.

Public and Open National and International Services: The Internet

A simple description of the Internet might go like this: "The Internet is composed of tens of thousands of computers at locations around the world, each interlinked with the other, providing access to all interlinked computers and their files to anyone who has access to any one of these computers." This description is accurate, but it's too quick and too easy. So, let's take a closer look at the basic structure of the Internet.

First, you need to understand that the Internet is no single entity, nor is it a consumer online service like America Online or CompuServe. For that matter, neither are online services the Internet. However, online services can connect with the Internet. I mention this because sometimes those new to the online world confuse online services and "the Internet," which is easy to do because the Internet holds endless potential for confusion.

The Internet is particularly confusing if you are unfamiliar with the terminology used to discuss it. You won't be among that group by the time you finish reading this chapter; you'll know much more about Internet terminology and the Internet itself.

BASIC INTERNET COMPONENTS: RESOURCES AND LINKS

The Internet has two major components—resources and communications links, which make the resources available to other computers.

There are several varieties of resources, the most important of which are data resources. Data resources consist of millions of data, text, and program files stored on tens of thousands of computers on the Internet worldwide. These resources are the main reason many computer users access the Internet. Data resources make up much of the surface content of the Internet, that is, what many perceive as being the Internet: text in Usenet newsgroups and/or the text and graphics displayed on screen as Web pages.

Not incidentally, Web pages are the result of data and program files being transmitted to your computer. See the following section, "Putting It All Together: Benefits for You," for details.

Data resources may be stored in any of several ways on computers hosting Web sites—on hard drives, in RAM, or by other means. How the data is stored is immaterial; the important thing is that Internet data resources are available to anyone who has access to the Internet.

The storage media, along with the computers on which the data are stored, and associated communications hardware and software represent still more resources—in this case hardware and software resources.

After resources, the other major element of the Internet is its system of communications links. These links interconnect thousands of computers and help modem-equipped computer users access the data resources stored on those computers. Communications links consist of conventional telephone lines, high-speed data lines designed to carry only computer data, satellite and microwave relay links, modems, cable-TV links, and other components—including the computers on which Internet resources are stored.

These communications links provide a means whereby individual computers on the Internet are *networked*, or simultaneously interconnected and sharing data resources—hence, the frequent reference to the Internet as a network of computers, any of which can be accessed at any time by any other computer on the network. In a sense, these communications links are resources, too.

Interestingly, some computers linked to the Internet are themselves a part of networks, in the form of several PCs linked by a LAN. Other computers that make up the Internet include mainframes, minicomputers, and individual PCs.

Cumulatively then, data resources, the computers on which data are stored, and the links that interconnect the Internet's computers with other computers, *are* the Internet. Your perception of the data received from these resources completes the picture.

INTERNET ELEMENTS

The manifestation of the components and data just discussed is called the Internet. However, there are distinct elements by which we perceive the Internet. These are:

- E-mail (private messaging, with mail relayed between computer systems by Internet pathways)

- Usenet newsgroups (public messaging, shared among systems worldwide)

- The World Wide Web, or WWW (a system of publicly available files and Web pages made available on various Internet-linked computers)

These elements are discussed in detail in later chapters.

PUTTING IT ALL TOGETHER: BENEFITS FOR YOU

Now that you have a general idea of what you can do online—and how to do it—you may be wondering, "What does all of this mean for me?" Quite simply, it means you have the power to tap into the most powerful information and communications resources in the history of humanity.

With such resources at hand, you'll realize invaluable benefits, tangible and intangible. Consider just these few benefits of telecomputing:

Telecomputing Saves Time

Online communications of all kinds are instantaneous, as are business and personal transactions. Online libraries, databases, and shopping and travel services are fast, too—a few simple keystrokes can save hours of research time, telephone calls, and running from place to place.

Telecomputing Is Convenient

You can conduct business, do research, shop for computers and supplies, visit with friends, and more—without leaving your home. And you can do it on your schedule; online communications and research services are available 24 hours a day, 365 days a year.

Telecomputing Saves Money

Using an online service's conference facilities during evening and weekend hours often costs less than long-distance voice telephone services. If you have a lengthy—or brief—document to deliver within 24 hours, you may be able to send it online at a cost far below that charged by next-day delivery services. (Also, the cost may be less than sending the document via fax—with the added advantage that the recipient has it on disk.)

If you do a mass mailing to co-workers or members of an association who are online, you will find that e-mailing costs less than a paper mailing (with the advantage of instant delivery). And research services, databases, special interest groups, and other services put information on almost any topic at your fingertips—again at a cost below that of conventional information sources.

Telecomputing Offers Features that Cannot Be Found in Other Media

Because of their very nature, online services and the Internet tend to be faster than other forms of information distribution. Thus, you will often see news and other information available online long before other media present it. And, you may find services and information that exist only online, due in large part to the interactive nature of the online world.

Now, on to Chapter 2, where we examine what you need to get into the game.

CHAPTER 2

Getting Started

This chapter provides a general overview of the hardware, software, and information you'll need to telecompute. I'll illustrate basic elements of telecommunications here to help you understand the roles of various tele-computing elements and how they interact.

WHAT YOU NEED

To dial up another computer, you will need a telephone line, a computer or a communications terminal, a modem, and communications software, as described in the Introduction. You'll also need the number of a local BBS and/or an account with and local access number for an ISP or an online serv-ice. Or, you may have online access from your office.

Telephone Lines and Telephones

You probably won't have to install a separate telephone line to telecom-pute; the line you have now should work just fine. However, if you plan to use a direct-connect modem, make sure the line connecting it to your wall outlet has standard RJ-11 type plugs (shown in Figure 2.1) at each end. This type of plug is used in most modern telephone systems in North America.

Virtually all direct-connect modems are equipped with jacks that accept the RJ-11 plug. RJ-11 jacks and plugs are also known as *modular* jacks and plugs. Figure 2.2 shows a typical RJ-11 jack in a telephone wall outlet.

If your telephone system does not have RJ-11 connectors, converting the existing connectors is a simple matter—and something you should probably do anyway. Conversion kits are sold in any telephone or Radio Shack store, and the procedure is simple. It usually involves nothing more than removing the existing, screw-fastened line and replacing it with a line that has connectors you can fasten with a screw ("spade" or "eye") at one end, and an RJ-11 plug at the other. Figure 2.3 will give you an idea of what's required.

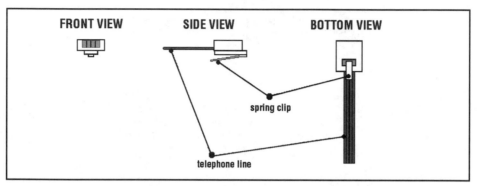

Figure 2.1 RJ-11 telephone line plug

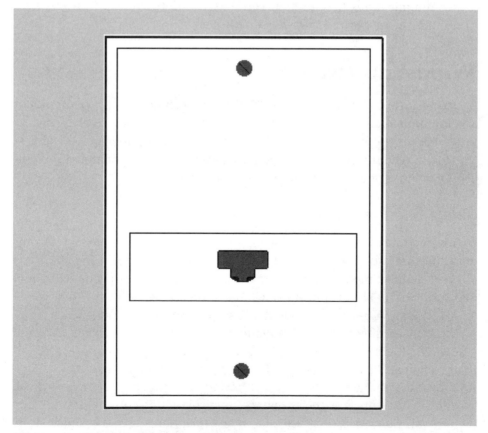

Figure 2.2 RJ-11 jack (receptacle)

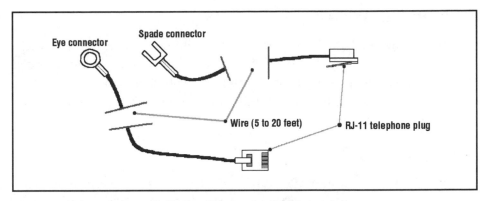

Figure 2.3   Modular telephone line upgrade kit

If for some reason you cannot rewire your phone system, or if you are using a telephone other than at your home (perhaps a pay telephone or a hotel room phone), there are a number of alternatives to making the modem/telephone connection. These include temporarily "hardwiring" the phone set itself or using any of several gadgets designed to connect a modem to a phone that doesn't have modular connectors. Some of these options are discussed later in this chapter.

Additional elements of your telephone system that may affect telecomputing are discussed below.

Call-Waiting

Call-Waiting "announces" incoming calls with a beep-and-click (or, where your phone company has installed newer equipment, a half-second tone). This can interfere with a modem's operation. Sometimes it merely causes random characters (a.k.a. garbage) to appear on your screen, and/or an apparent lockup of your system. (*Note*: You can often "unfreeze" a locked-up system by pressing Ctrl-Q.) More often than not, though, Call-Waiting's signal makes a modem think the telephone carrier has been dropped, or it makes the modem disconnect.

Unless you're doing a file transfer or are using a commercial online service that continues to bill you if you disconnect without signing off, interruption by an incoming call won't necessarily be a disaster. But if you have Call-Waiting, you may have to restrict your online sessions to the times you are least likely to receive calls, take your chances that someone won't call while you're online, or resort to one of the remedies below.

DISABLING CALL-WAITING

You can disable Call-Waiting on many telephone systems. With a touch-tone phone, press *70. With rotary-dial phones, dial 1170. Call-Waiting is disabled for the current call only, and is re-enabled after you hang up.

All telephone companies do not offer this option. Contact your local telephone company for more information.

MODEM SETTINGS

An alternative to temporarily disabling Call-Waiting is to use a certain kind of program to make your modem ignore the beep-and-click and temporary disconnection caused by an incoming call. Basically, such a program sets the modem to "tolerate" carrier disconnection for longer than it normally would. You can do the same thing by putting the appropriate command in your modem's setup string to extend the time the modem ignores a "dropped" carrier. This is usually done by increasing the value of your modem's S10 register. See your modem's manual for specific information.

Such programs are available for various types of computers and modems (usually *Hayes* or *Hayes-compatible* modems). They can be found in databases on local BBSs and online services. I can't vouch for the reliability of these programs—they seem to work with varying efficiency, depending on your hardware and software setup. Overall, the most effective way to deal with Call-Waiting is to either disable it or to install a second line without Call-Waiting for use with your modem.

Telephone Extensions

If you have extension telephones, unplug them or otherwise ensure that no one tries to use one while you're online. When someone picks up a telephone and you're online, whatever is happening on your screen will be interrupted by random characters (as with a Call-Waiting interruption). If you're transferring a file, the transfer may be aborted. Or, you may lose your connection.

Acoustic Couplers and Nonstandard Telephones

An acoustic modem or adapter—also known as an acoustic coupler—can often be used to connect with a telephone that doesn't have RJ-11 connectors. However, you may find it impossible to connect the modem to a decorator-style telephone or other nonstandard telephone set. Acoustic adapter cups are designed to accommodate the handset of a standard desk telephone, as shown in Figure 2.4.

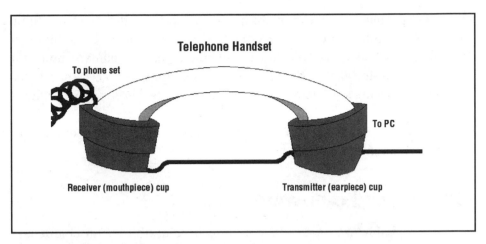

Figure 2.4 One kind of acoustic coupler

Fortunately, there are other kinds of acoustic adapters, designed to fit just about any telephone handset.

(Interestingly enough, acoustic modems were once the only kind of modem that existed. In the days when Bell was *the* name in telephone service, telephone subscribers were not permitted to attach devices not provided by the telephone company to telephone lines. The acoustic coupler was developed to overcome this; it converts modem signals to sounds, and vice versa.)

I'll have more to say about acoustic couplers and means of connecting with nonstandard telephone sets in later chapters.

Cordless Telephones

Routing your modem signals through a cordless phone—even if it has a standard handset—is not a good idea; in doing so you introduce a potential weak link into the communications chain.

Also, a cordless telephone may not use the same frequencies that your modem uses. This can result in data being "dropped."

Cellular Telephones

Cellular telephones present several problems. Since you cannot dial a number with a modem through a cellular telephone, you must set your modem (via a DIP-switch setting or AT command) to make it think it has already dialed a number, after which you can dial the number.

The fact that cellular phones switch over to different transmitter/receivers, or "cells," can present some problems as well, especially where error checking is concerned. A few companies offer rather expensive equipment to cope with these problems, but without the ability to compensate for cell-switching in particular (which sometimes takes place even when the phone is not moving), nontechnical users will find it difficult to use a cellular phone for modem communications. You can sometimes, however, get around this problem by setting a modem to ignore a dropped carrier for a longer-than-normal period.

The best solution for both of these problems is to buy a cellular modem, as discussed later in this book.

COMPUTER HARDWARE

You'll probably use a personal computer to dial up bulletin boards and online services, so we'll confine our discussion of required hardware and software to personal computers. (I'm assuming here that if you can operate a terminal, minicomputer, or mainframe computer, you already know most, if not all, of what you need to know about dialing up another computer.)

Computer Features

At the very least, your personal computer system consists of a keyboard, the computer itself (sometimes built into the keyboard), a monitor, and a mass storage device (a disk drive or cassette player).

To this, you may have to add a *serial port* or card for communicating with a modem. (Actually, most computers come with a serial port nowadays.) A serial port is a must; all but a very few modems communicate with a computer via a serial port. (Internal modems have a serial port built-in, by the way.) Modems that do not use a serial port use a *parallel port*, which is a special card (as in the case of cable modems).

You probably won't have to add a modem, unless your computer is an older one; modems are now standard equipment with computers. With the constantly changing landscape of computer products, I can't recommend a specific brand or type of personal computer over any other for telecomputing. (I use a Pentium-based system, with a fast color SVGA display system for most of my online sessions.) However, these basic features will enhance your online activities:

MONITORS

An 80-column display is pretty much standard for all computer applications, and is certainly desirable when you're online. The graphics-based services (AOL and Prodigy) and the graphics-based front ends for text-based services require them. Most text-based systems can provide 40-column output, but this is a holdover from the days before there were many standards for computers (not that there are all that many now) and online services had to accommodate personal computers with 40-, 65-, and 70-column displays, among other widths. An 80-column display is more efficient and can save time in the long run, as fewer lines have to be sent to display a given quantity of text. Also, many systems offer ASCII graphics or other features that you can take advantage of only if you have an 80-column display.

You'll be looking at a lot of scrolling text online, so you need an easy-to-view monitor. This means a monitor with good resolution, and it's best not to use one with slow decay (i.e., a monitor that retains "ghosts" of previous images). A color monitor is a plus, as many online services and Web sites provide animation and special graphic effects.

(*Tip*: If you have to use a monochrome monitor—as may well be the case if you use a laptop computer to go online—select CGA settings for your communications software.)

OPERATING SYSTEMS

A fast, flexible operating system is an important consideration in any computer application and is doubly important in online activities. In many instances, you may have a limited amount of time online. Or you'll be paying for your time. Either way, you don't want to waste half a minute waiting for your system to open or close a file or respond to a command! Many computers are limited to one kind of operating system, but for some computer brands several operating systems are available.

STORAGE

Here again, time is an important factor. If you plan to do a lot of downloading and uploading, you should have a fast hard disk with quite a bit of available space to speed up read/write access time and thus reduce the amount of time you spend in file transfer and other operations. In addition, you will want to make sure your hard drive is routinely defragmented in order to reduce file search time.

PRINTERS

A printer isn't exactly a required telecomputing peripheral, but it can be useful. You may occasionally want to print out text as it appears on your screen rather than saving it on disk. (I prefer saving text on disk, then reformatting it before I print it out, but maybe that's just a matter of taste.)

SURGE PROTECTORS

A *surge protector* is an excellent investment. The purpose of a surge protector (sometimes called a "spike protector") is to protect an electronic device from voltage surges in a power or telephone line. Such surges are common during thunderstorms and during periods when electrical power consumption is particularly heavy.

Power line surge protectors come in a variety of styles, but all operate in the same manner. Placed in the circuit between your computer and/or modem and the wall outlet, they contain capacitors that absorb and then bleed off excess power, or other special circuits designed to control voltage surges. Figure 2.5 shows a typical surge protector.

Note that power line surge protectors come in configurations other than the one illustrated here. Some are simply small cylinders or cubes and offer only one receptacle. Others are large rectangular boxes that replace a receptacle's cover plate and offer more than one receptacle.

Better surge protectors not only provide protection against power surges, but also filter "line noise" and provide a circuit breaker for protection against electrical current overload.

Telephone line surge protectors operate on the same principle as power line surge protectors. Installed between a modem and its telephone line, a telephone line surge protector absorbs potentially damaging voltage spikes.

Figure 2.5   Power line surge protector

OTHER CONSIDERATIONS

The type of computer you use dictates the types and brands of communications software packages you can run, which in turn partially dictate the features available to you. But, the features available with a particular Windows-based communications software package, for example, can often be found in software for other operating systems' brands of computers. So, you don't necessarily have to buy a certain computer to get specific features; you can probably find all the features you want if you look at enough software packages.

Other elements of your computer system are pretty much a matter of personal preference.

The majority of online services (and BBSs) are "computer friendly," meaning they can communicate with virtually any personal computer. Thus, you should have no trouble accessing another system with your computer, provided you have a compatible modem and appropriate software.

COMMUNICATIONS TERMINALS

Communications terminals (sometimes called *data terminals* or *data communication terminals*) contain some of the same components as a computer: a keyboard for entering data, a monitor or printing device for displaying data, and an interface for modem connection. A terminal usually has a built-in modem that connects directly to a telephone line. It may or may not have disk drives for storage.

The big difference between communications terminals and computers lies in the fact that communications terminals are dedicated computers. They have one function—telecommunicating with another computer, usually a mainframe or minicomputer. You cannot use word processing, database, or other types of software with a basic communications terminal. (A communications terminal runs communications software, of course, and many have "built-in" software, in the form of programming in ROM. Interestingly enough, communications software essentially turns a PC into a communications terminal; that's why communications software is often called "terminal software.")

A communications terminal is, in fact, an extension of the computer to which it is linked. The computers used to make hotel and airline reservations are examples of communications terminals, as are the scanning cash registers used at supermarket and department store checkout counters. The same goes for interactive systems that give you directions or instructions, like those used at malls, amusement parks, and other public places.

Because they have limited capabilities, communications terminals are sometimes called "dumb terminals," a highly appropriate sobriquet in the context of computing capability. On the other hand, like most dedicated computers, terminals usually do their jobs very well. They also provide a number of features that enable you to deal with a remote system as if you were working right there with it (full-screen text editing, for instance), and a number of "bells and whistles" that enhance use of the system.

Some terminals boast special programming or computer-like features, as well as other special features such as graphics display capabilities. These terminals go beyond the realm of being simple extensions of a host computer, and are called "smart terminals." Quite a few offer enough features to be considered PCs. (This is rather ironic, and rather like some dedicated word processors for which manufacturers offer add-ons like database software and communications capabilities. In either case, you would think you would be better off to buy a computer—and you would be correct in your thinking.)

Smart or dumb, terminals are dedicated computers, that is, computers designed for one job. Except in special cases, you're better off using a personal computer for telecomputing. There are a few special cases, including using a portable dedicated terminal in a situations where you have no need for computing applications.

TERMINAL EMULATION FOR YOUR COMPUTER

Many of the features provided by communications terminals are useful enhancements for communication with personal computers. PC communications software designers recognized this early on, so you will find that most PC communications software packages provide what is called terminal emulation—a feature that makes your computer look like a specific terminal to an online service or BBS. If the online service or BBS recognizes the terminal your system is emulating, you can enjoy features such as screen clearing, full-screen editing, and color text. (More on this in later chapters.)

MODEMS

A modem is a device whose primary job is translating data. When a modem sends, it translates computer data into a form suitable for transmission over normal, voice-grade telephone lines. When it receives, it translates incoming data into a form compatible with its computer's internal operating system. This process is described in detail in Chapters 3, 4, and 5.

Most modems you've seen probably look similar to the one shown in Figure 2.6.

A number of companies specialize in manufacturing modems and allied hardware. The quality and capabilities of many modem brands vary little, which makes it difficult to recommend one brand of modem over all others. In general, though, it's best to buy a modem made by a reputable, "name brand" manufacturer—the cost may be higher, but what you save in the long run should more than make up the difference.

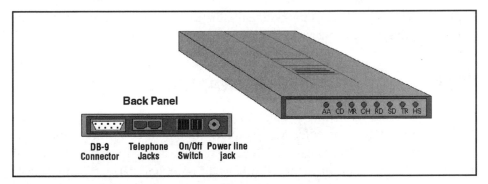

Figure 2.6 An external "desktop" modem

MODEM TYPES

Modems come in two basic types—acoustic and direct connect. These are identified by how they connect with a telephone line. Acoustic modems are connected to a telephone via rubber cups that fit over the telephone handset's earpiece and mouthpiece. Direct-connect modems are connected to the telephone line directly, via a jack that accepts the common RJ-11 phone plug. Direct-connect modems may be internal or external; your computer system should be able to communicate with either type. Each has its advantages and disadvantages, which are discussed in Chapter 4. For most applications, however, a direct-connect modem is superior to an acoustic modem. Whether you use an internal or external modem depends on a number of factors; also in Chapter 4 you'll find a discussion of the relative advantages and disadvantages of internal and external modems.

MODEM OPTIONS

Many features and options are available with modems. These are among the more useful:

- The ability to dial phone numbers
- Tone- or pulse-dialing capability
- A speaker (Actually, I abhor modem speakers, but many people find them useful.)
- Call-status indicators

Modems that offer dialing capability and other advanced features are called "intelligent." The number of features that a modem has isn't necessarily an indication of its quality, but the better-quality modems usually have more features than the bargain-basement variety.

COMMUNICATIONS SOFTWARE

Unless you use a communications terminal or a portable computer that has built-in communications software, you'll have to obtain communications software before your computer can "talk" with a modem. Sometimes called terminal emulation software, or term-soft (another pair of archaic terms), communications software routes data and commands to and from the modem and instructs the modem to use proper protocol in communicating with another system. (Simply put, *protocol* is an agreed-upon procedure for how data is transferred.)

As with computers and modems, I can't recommend a specific type or brand of software; there's just too much out there. And, unlike modems, brand-name recognition isn't always a guarantee of quality. I've seen some real dogs get magazine "best-of" awards. (You can sometimes find a correlation between awards and advertising, by the way.)

(*Note*: I am referring here to communications software that you use to dial up other stand-alone computers, BBSs, and online services. The dialer programs built into Windows systems and/or provided by your ISP are pretty much a plug-and-go proposition, and you won't have to take any of the following into consideration. I am also not referring to online service "front-end" programs.)

COMMUNICATIONS SOFTWARE OPTIONS

At the very least, your communications software should allow you to select the communications speed and set basic communications parameters. It should also provide at least one binary file transfer protocol, such as Xmodem, Kermit, or Ymodem, or its own proprietary protocol.

The better communications software packages offer a variety of features, including, but not limited to these:

- The ability to handle multiple uploads and downloads automatically, with "batch" protocols such as Kermit and Zmodem
- Autodial and redial capability
- Autologon capability (This means a program performs all the steps necessary to sign on to another system, typically via what are called *script files*.)
- Macros, which you can use to send multiple commands to a remote system with one keystroke

As I indicated previously, your software selection is limited (or determined) in large part by the type of computer you own and its configuration, the modem you use, and your budget.

WEB BROWSERS AND OTHER INTERNET PROGRAMS

Accessing the Internet in all its aspects requires a set of specialized programs. There are separate programs for browsing the Web, sending and receiving e-mail, reading newsgroups, and accessing Web sites and online services via telnet (a more direct means of linking two computers using standard terminal emulation software via Internet links).

The programs required are as follows:

- **Web browser.** This is a program that interprets hypertext markup language, or HTML (the special script-like language used to create Web pages). Following HTML commands from a Web page, a browser displays text in various sizes, fonts, and colors; displays graphics; transfers files; and loads additional programs.

- **E-mail program.** Your e-mail program sends and retrieves e-mail, handles file attachments, and stores messages on your PC.

- **Newsreader.** A newsreader program accesses Usenet newsgroups via the Internet. It has some capabilities that are similar to those used by a Web browser to interpret HTML and display graphics.

- **Telnet program.** A telnet program handles connecting and communicating with another computer directly over the Internet. Among the more popular telnet applications is accessing an online service such as AOL or CompuServe via an Internet connection (thus eliminating the need to dial up the service directly).

Some programs combine the features of several of these—for example, Web browsers that provide e-mail and newsreader capabilities. Also, some online services provide all or most of these programs' capabilities. Still, there are many alternatives for each type of program, enabling access to extra features and providing accommodation for a variety of work styles.

We'll take a close look at each of these types of programs in later chapters.

Now that you have an idea of what's out there and what you need to connect with it, move on to Chapters 3, 4, and 5 where we'll look "behind the scenes" to learn how telecommunications software and hardware operate.

CHAPTER 3

How Telecomputing Works

This chapter has a motto: You don't have to understand how something works to use it, but understanding how something works makes dealing with trouble easier. I learned that the hard way with my first car, a 1953 Ford Sunliner convertible. I didn't understand how engines worked when I was 16, and so I didn't know to stop driving when the engine started making a pounding noise. It threw a rod, and I learned a lot about engines from the inside out, the hard way. I haven't lost a car since.

The importance of knowing how something works applies equally to any complex device or system, be it an automobile, the Internet, a VCR, or a library. And it's especially true in using a computer in any application. When you understand even a little of what's happening "behind the scenes," as it were, you'll find that you have a lot more control over what's going on. This idea brings us to my purpose in writing this chapter: I want you to have a solid picture of what's happening when your computer communicates with another system.

We'll first examine the basic elements of telecomputing, followed by data formats. Then we'll segue into how data is transmitted, focusing on hardware and software elements, and wrap up with communications parameters and error-control protocols. (And yes, you can understand all this "technical" stuff; what one human creates, another human can understand, if he or she so desires.) You won't have to pull out engineering texts to keep up with me. I'll explain terms and concepts as necessary, and there's a glossary at the end of this book to supplement my explanations.

If you're relatively new to telecomputing, read this chapter from start to finish. Otherwise, you may skim the headings, if you wish, to find only the information you need to fill the gaps in your telecomputing knowledge.

(*Note*: It isn't absolutely necessary that you read this chapter. If you find things technical to be terminally boring [pun intended], you can go on to the rest of the book and learn what you need to know. But I suggest that you at least try to read this chapter; any information you absorb will be valuable.)

TELECOMPUTING BASICS

As I indicated in Chapter 2, telecomputing is the transfer of data of any type between two or more computers via a transmission link.

Most telecomputing (especially telecomputing involving dial-up systems) goes like this:

1. Computer A transmits binary data (also known as digital data) to a modem in the form of a sequence of bits. The modem converts the bits to an analog signal that mimics the distinction between the binary 1s and 0s. The analog signal is then transmitted over voice-grade telephone lines.

2. At the receiving end, a modem connected to Computer B converts the analog signal back into a binary signal that is basically a copy of what Computer A sent to its modem. The modem then sends the binary signal to Computer B.

3. At this point, Computer B has in its memory a duplicate of the data Computer A originally sent to its modem. (This process works in both directions, of course.) The data can then be displayed, stored, printed, or otherwise manipulated.

This is a greatly simplified description of data transfer from one computer to another via modem, but it should give you a picture of how the basic elements of telecomputing as described below interact. (If any of the terms used in the description caught you off guard, don't worry—they are fully explained in the following pages.)

Basic Elements of Telecomputing

Successful telecomputing involves four major elements:

1. Data
2. Data terminal equipment
3. Data communications equipment
4. A communications link

Various sub-elements are also involved, as described in the text that follows. Figure 3.1 illustrates these elements.

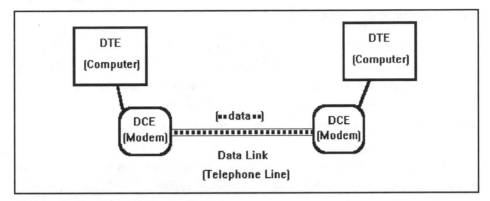

Figure 3.1   Telecomputing elements

DATA

Computer data is defined as machine-readable information of any kind. The information may consist of business or personal messages, other kinds of text files (articles, contracts, jokes, politically incorrect tirades, documentation, reports), spreadsheets, lines of a real-time conference, graphic images, database files, executable programs in binary data format, data files for programs, etc.

Inside a computer, data is handled representationally as binary information (more on this in a bit). It may be entered in real time from a keyboard, retrieved from a mass storage device such as a disk, generated by a program's operation, or received via an interface from an external source, or, in more common terms, typed in, read from a disk file, output from a program, or received from a peripheral like a scanner.

By the way, this chapter focuses more on the format and mode of data transfer—before, during, and after transmission—than on its content. The successful delivery of data with its content intact is of course the primary goal of data communications, but, as you'll learn, data format in large part determines the mode—and success—of transmission.

DATA TERMINAL EQUIPMENT

As imposing as the phrase may sound, *data terminal equipment* (*DTE*) consists of nothing more than the computers or terminals used in telecomputing—the source and destination of data. The use of the word "terminal" in the phrase alludes to the fact that the computers or terminals involved are the beginning and ending points of data transmission, which is just what a terminal is: a place where a journey begins and ends, à la a train or bus terminal.

COMMUNICATIONS LINKS

Computer-to-computer data transfer may take place in a variety of ways. In its most basic form, telecomputing involves linking two computers directly, normally using what is called a null-modem cable to connect their serial ports. In this kind of setup, the computers are only a few feet apart, and data is transferred in true binary format. (A more elaborate kind of direct connection is involved with LANs.)

The majority of telecomputing activities, however, involve telephone lines—using either the public voice telephone system or what are known as dedicated telephone lines as the communications link.

Although it is the least expensive and most readily available channel of data transfer, the voice telephone system cannot handle computer data in its native binary format. A modem is required to translate data from binary (or digital) format into analog format—a format that can be successfully transmitted via ordinary phone lines.

(There is another type of phone system that does accommodate direct binary data transmission. Referred to as a digital network, it is used in applications where extreme speed and accuracy are necessary, but setting up and using such a system is an extremely expensive proposition.)

A telephone link does not consist solely of telephone wires. Electro-mechanical, electronic, and computer-switching equipment is involved, as well as microwave transmitters and satellite up- and downlinks. For the purposes of this chapter, however, such elements will remain transparent.

DATA COMMUNICATIONS EQUIPMENT

Simply put, *data communications equipment* (*DCE*) consists of modems and their associated interfaces, connectors, and cables.

Modems have a number of functions, including but not limited to the following:

- Establishing and maintaining a communications link
- Translating data from digital to analog format, and vice versa
- Transmitting and receiving data

The interface between a modem and its computer is typically a *serial interface* (specifically, an *RS-232C interface*), although a few modems use a *parallel interface*. For the dial-up applications discussed in this book, you'll use a serial interface. The same is true of most other online applications.

DATA FORMATS AND
DATA TRANSFER IN COMPUTERS

As noted above, computer data must be converted from digital to analog format before it can be transmitted via voice telephone lines. Before you can understand how data is converted and transmitted over communications links, however, you need to understand how computers handle data internally.

This section presents important information about digital data organization and handling in both your computer and portions of a communications link. Basically, I'm going to show data to you as your computer sees it.

Computer Data Formats

Continuing improvements in computer hardware and software over the years (as well as competition among various manufacturers) have made for a veritable Tower of Babel when it comes to manipulating, storing, and transferring information. The differences in how data is stored on, say, an IBM AT quad-density disk versus a Macintosh disk are so great that there are few bases for comparison of the two; the same is true of their internal data formats.

Fortunately, all modern computers have one thing in common: They handle data in digital format, which is why they're called digital computers. This means that they "see" data characters as strings of binary digits. Furthermore, almost all computers (some mainframe computers excepted) use the same numeric code to represent each character—numbers from the *American Standard Code for Information Interchange (ASCII)*.

As you'll find in the following pages, computers that share these attributes can easily exchange data.

(*Note*: The terms digital and binary are sometimes used interchangeably. Digital refers to discrete, uniform signals of any type—binary or otherwise—that do not vary in a continuous manner. Rather, such signals are identified by specific levels or values such as "on" or "off." Digital signals change immediately from one state to another, and are the antithesis of analog signals, which vary through the entire range between two states.)

An analogy would be having a radio with only two volume settings, high or low (digital), or a radio with a normal volume control that lets you set the volume anywhere between high and low/maximum and minimum (analog).

Because we are concentrating on binary data and binary signals in this book, the term digital refers to binary data and signals.

BINARY DATA

Even if you're not technically oriented, I'm sure you've at least heard the concept of data being stored and manipulated by digital computers in something called digital, or binary, data format.

If a computer uses binary data format, it means that each character (letter, number, symbol, or control character) a computer handles is operated on and stored as a specific binary number. There are several excellent reasons for this, one of which you'll find below.

BINARY NUMBERS

A binary number is a string of binary digits, such as 1010 or 10011. Only 0s and 1s are used in binary notation (as opposed to the numerals 0 through 9, which are used by the decimal system).

Unlike the decimal system, the values of the numerals themselves (0 and 1) are not used to determine the total value of a binary number; instead, the values of the places marked by a 1 are summed. Each place has a set value. The first place on the right in a binary number has a value of 1, the second place a value of 2, the third place a value of 4, and so on, with the value doubling with each place.

Again, the value of a binary number is determined by adding up the values of the places that contain a 1. If there is a 0 in a place, that place's value is not counted.

Consulting Table 3.1, it is easy to see that the binary number 11 is the same as the decimal number 3 (add the values of the places: 2 + 1 = 3). Similarly, the binary number 1010 is the same as the decimal number 10 (add the value of the places that contain a 1: 8 + 2 = 10). Nothing to it, right? Right!

Table 3.1 Binary Numbering			
0	00000	33	100001
1	00001	34	100010
2	00010	35	100011
3	00011	36	100100
4	00100	37	100101
5	00101	38	100110
6	00110	39	100111
7	00111	40	101000
8	01000	41	101001
9	01001	42	101010
10	01010	43	101011

Table 3.1   Binary Numbering (*continued*)

11	01011	44	101100
12	01100	45	101101
13	01101	46	101110
14	01110	47	101111
15	01111	48	110000
16	10000	49	110001
17	10001	50	110010
18	10010	51	110011
19	10011	52	110100
20	10100	53	110101
21	10101	54	110110
22	10110	55	110111
23	10111	56	111000
24	11000	57	111001
25	11001	58	111010
26	11010	59	111011
27	11011	60	111100
28	11100	61	111101
29	11101	62	111110
30	11110	63	111111
31	11111	64	1000000
32	100000	... 128	10000000
		... 256	100000000
		... 512	1000000000 (etc.)

THE ASCII CHARACTER SET

Now, let's take a look at how the binary numbering system is used by computers to represent specific characters.

In Table 3.2, you will see the decimal value of a number, the binary numeral that represents that number, and how that number in binary form is interpreted by a digital computer.

Table 3.2	The ASCII Character Set			
0	00000	^@	NUL (nothing)
1	00001	^A	SOH (Start Of Heading)
2	00010	^B	STX (Start Of Text)
3	00011	^C	ETX (End Of Text)
4	00100	^D	EOT (End Of Transmission)
5	00101	^E	ENQ (Enquiry)
6	00110	^F	ACK (Acknowledge)
7	00111	^G	BEL (Bell)
8	01000	^H	BS (Backspace)
9	01001	^I	HT (Horizontal Tab)
10	01010	^J	LF (Line Feed)
11	01011	^K	VT (Vertical Tab)
12	01100	^L	FF (Form Feed)
13	01101	^M	CR (Carriage Return)
14	01110	^N	SO (Shift Out)
15	01111	^O	SI (Shift In)
16	10000	^P	DLE (Data Link Escape)
17	10001	^Q	DC1 (Device Control 1)
18	10010	^R	DC1 (Device Control 2)
19	10011	^S	DC1 (Device Control 3)
20	10100	^T	DC1 (Device Control 4)
21	10101	^U	NAK (Negative Acknowledge)
22	10110	^V	SYN (Synchronous Idle)
23	10111	^W	ETB (End of Transmission Block)
24	11000	^X	CAN (Cancel)
25	11001	^Y	EM (End of Medium)
26	11010	^Z	SUB (Substitute)
27	11011	^[	ESC (Escape)
28	11100	^\	FS (File Separator)
29	11101	^]	GS (Group Separator)
30	11110	^^	RS (Record Separator)
31	11111	^_	US (Unit Separator)
32	100000	Space	
33	100001	!	
34	100010	"	
35	100011	#	
36	100100	$	
37	100101	%	

Table 3.2   The ASCII Character Set (*continued*)

38	100110	&	
39	100111	'	
40	101000	(	
41	101001	)	
42	101010	*	
43	101011	+	
44	101100	,	
45	101101	-	
46	101110	.	
47	101111	/	
48	110000	0	
49	110001	1	
50	110010	2	
51	110011	3	
52	110100	4	
53	110101	5	
54	110110	6	
55	110111	7	
56	111000	8	
57	111001	9	
58	111010	:	
59	111011	;	
60	111100	<	
61	111101	=	
62	111110	>	
63	111111	?	
64	1000000	@	
65	1000001	A	
66	1000020	B	
67	1000011	C	
68	1000100	D	
69	1000101	E	
70	1000110	F	
71	1000111	G	
72	1001000	H	
73	1001001	I	
74	1001010	J	
75	1001011	K	

Table 3.2   The ASCII Character Set (*continued*)

76	1001100	L
77	1001101	M
78	1001110	N
79	1001111	O
80	1010000	P
81	1010001	Q
82	1010010	R
83	1010011	S
84	1010100	T
85	1010101	U
86	1010110	V
87	1010111	W
88	1011000	X
89	1011001	Y
90	1011010	Z
91	1011011	[
92	1100000	\
93	1100001	]
94	1100010	^
95	1100011	_
96	1100100	`
97	1100101	a
98	1100110	b
99	1100111	c
100	1101000	d
101	1101001	e
102	1101010	f
103	1101011	g
104	1101100	h
105	1101101	i
106	1101110	j
107	1101111	k
108	1110000	l
109	1110001	m
110	1110010	n
111	1110011	o
112	1110100	p
113	1110101	q

Table 3.2 The ASCII Character Set (*continued*)

114	1110110	r
115	1110111	s
116	1111000	t
117	1111001	u
118	1111010	v
119	1111011	w
120	1111100	x
121	1111101	y
122	1111110	z
123	1111011	{
124	1111100	|
125	1111101	}
126	1111110	~
127	1111111	DELETE character (character delete or time delay)

For example, an ASCII 78 (binary 1001110) represents the upper-case letter N. An ASCII 110 (binary 1101110) represents the lower-case letter n.

Note that only the first 128 ASCII characters—0 through 127—are shown in Table 3.2; certain computers—such as the IBM PC and Apple's Macintosh—use an additional 128 ASCII characters (called *extended character sets*), many of them dedicated to graphics. Not all computers recognize such extended ASCII character sets. Also note, for later reference, that the first 128 ASCII characters—0 through 127—can be represented by a string of seven binary digits, with leading 0s added as necessary.

As you may have inferred from the preceding, a digital computer manipulates characters as the binary counterparts of these ASCII numbers. For instance, the letter A (ASCII 65) is represented within a computer as 1000001, the binary counterpart of 65.

Thus, any computer that uses binary data format and the ASCII character set recognizes the binary digit 1000001 as the letter A when it is received as input via its keyboard or from an external source such as a modem.

Also note that certain characters—in particular the 0 through 31 (binary 00000 through 11111)—have a ^ (caret) before them. This indicates that they are *control characters*, or characters that you can issue from a keyboard by holding the CTRL key and pressing the indicated character. These characters, plus ASCII 127 (1111111), are used by computers to send signals to one another or to peripherals such as printers and modems. The meaning of each such signal is included in Table 3.2, and will be explained in detail in Chapter 6.

BINARY SIGNALS

Within a computer, each string of binary digits representing a character is manipulated as a discreet unit. This unit is called a *byte*. A byte is normally composed of eight *bits*. A bit is the smallest unit of data.

When a computer sends data to a peripheral—printer, modem, etc.— each byte is transmitted as a binary signal. The signal is literally a series of negative and positive voltages, as illustrated in Figure 3.2. The negative state represents a binary 1, while the positive state represents a binary 0.

The particular signal contains the binary number 11000001. And, yes, the order of the binary digits is reversed; that is, the figure does show "10000011," even though the number it represents is "11000001."

The figure is reversed because the binary digits that make up a character are transmitted that way (i.e., the low-order bit—the bit with the lowest-value—is transmitted first). This is done so parity can be calculated as a character is sent (more on that later in the book).

(*Note*: I include this now, so you won't be confused as to why the digits are reversed in the figures in this book that illustrate binary signals, which is pretty much what happened to me the first few times I studied tutorials on data communication. None of the authors explained why the figures showed the data bit order as the reverse of what it was in the text.

(Whether this was out of ignorance or due to a lack of consideration for the reader, I don't know. And I never did find a book that explains this situation; I eventually learned what was going on by asking several engineers who work in the field.

(All of which is not to plug this book as the ultimate resource on data communications for the layman, but to make this point: Books and manuals are not infallible. Writers sometimes assume too much knowledge on the part of the reader, and are occasionally confused themselves. Also, the computer field is notorious for having several terms with the same meaning, or several meanings for one term. So, if something doesn't make sense when you read about it in your modem or software manual, check it out! See if this book provides the information you need. If not, ask someone who knows or should know—contact the modem manufacturer or software publisher whose manual is the source of your confusion.)

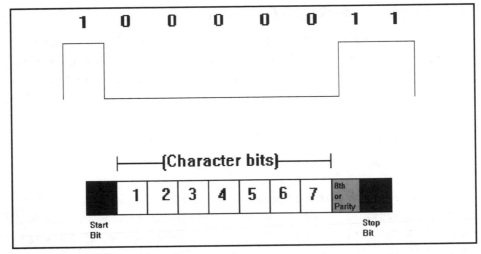

Figure 3.2 A binary signal

Why Binary?

The binary, or two-state, data system is used with modern computers primarily because it is faster and more reliable than analog systems.

A two-state system is extremely simple; one state or another exists—there is no in-between. A signal is either there or not there, positive or negative, etc. In contrast, using analog techniques for information transfer and manipulation requires reading the relative strengths of any of a large number of signals, as well as the calibration and checking of those signals. This slows down data manipulation tremendously.

With a two-state binary data system, there is very little chance of information getting lost or "scrambled." Such information can be received and handled by a computer at extremely high rates. The electronic components used in digital computers (initially transistors and later integrated circuits of various types) exactly mimic the binary system, switching off and on (between two states) at extremely high speeds.

Data Transfer

The astute reader will have realized by now that all that's necessary for the letter A to be transmitted from Computer A to Computer B is for Computer A to send the binary digit 11000001 to Computer B. If you've figured that out, pat yourself on the back—it represents the very essence of telecomputing.

This all looks good on paper, but we still have to move that 11000001 from Computer A to Computer B. This requires a chain of devices and connections, the first link being a computer's port.

SERIAL PORTS AND THE RS-232C STANDARD

Computers aren't telepathic, and they seem immune to magic spells, so they must be connected before they can communicate. Moreover, they must be connected with one another or with their associated modems in a special way.

The hardware medium for such a connection, whether the computers are linked via a null-modem cable or by modems, is known as a *port*.

PORTS

A computer's ports provide the physical (electrical) connections by which its internal workings communicate with peripherals such as printers and modems. A seaport is a valid analogy for a computer's port, as the port is where data is sorted, organized, and shipped.

A port consists of a group of connectors in the form of pins (male) or sockets (female). Note that the word pin is used generically to refer to both male and female connectors, hence terms like pinout diagram and pin assignments. (I realize the male/female terminology isn't "politically correct" in the minds of some, but it is the most common usage. If you are uncomfortable with these terms, feel free to think of the connectors as plugs and jacks, respectively. These are the more formal terms for male and female connectors. I'll be using all three sets of terms in this section interchangeably.)

Not all connectors are used by every computer, but each connector that is used is connected to a specific part of the computer's circuitry where signals are received and/or sent according to instructions from a program or the computer's operating system. (It gets more complicated, but for the sake of keeping with our present topic, I'll leave it at that.)

There are two kinds of ports—*parallel* and *serial*. The name of each describes how it transfers data.

Parallel Ports: A parallel port sends and receives data over at least eight wires at once. This means it transmits all eight data bits that make up a character simultaneously. Parallel ports are rarely used for data communication; they are most frequently used to connect computers with devices such as printers and disk drives, where extremely high data transmission rates are necessary and the short distance involved won't cause problems.

Serial Ports: A serial port is a type of port that sends and receives data over one wire. Figure 3.3 shows a typical serial port configuration.

Serial data transmission is more reliable over long distances than parallel transmission, which is why it is used for modem and direct-connect data transmission.

Figure 3.3   Serial port configurations

Note that Figure 3.3 shows two kinds of serial ports—one with 25 connectors and one with nine connectors. The difference in the number of connectors is a bit confusing, until you learn that not all 25 pins are used. The average microcomputer uses only eight of the pins in data communications applications. (The IBM PC, among others, uses nine pins.)

Serial ports and their associated cables function as an interface between computers and modems, or, if you like technical jargon, as a *DTE/DCE interface.*

THE RS-232C STANDARD

This is where we un-buzz a buzzword, which I think should be done whenever possible. You've undoubtedly heard that this or that port or modem or cable conforms to something called the *RS-232C standard,* and you may have wondered just what that means—and whether there's an RS-232A or B, for that matter. I hope I don't shatter any illusions, but RS-232C isn't as mysterious as it looks in print. Let's examine it.

What It Is: RS-232C (often called simply RS-232) is a reference and recommendation for how a serial port should be set up physically, and how it should communicate. The Electronics Industry Association (EIA) established this recommendation in 1969 to provide a standard for manufacturers of data communications equipment to follow in the design of such equipment. Even though it was never officially adopted as a standard per se, it is accepted as a standard for the design of the interface between a computer and its modem and other serial devices. So, we can refer to it informally as a standard.

Semantically speaking, the designation breaks down like this: RS is an acronym for Recommended Standard, 232 is the ID number for this particular standard, and C is the latest revision of this standard. (The full name of the RS-232C standard, by the way, is "Interface Between Data Terminal Equipment and Data Communication Equipment Employing Serial Binary Data Interchange.")

What It Does: The RS-232C recommendation covers the electrical and mechanical characteristics of the interface, the function of each signal (pin or connector), and, for certain applications, secondary functions of signals.

The reason for designing a serial interface that follows the RS-232C standard is to enable it to exchange data with other serial interfaces in proper form. To this end, the standard dictates how data is to be handled by the port, which indirectly dictates how the port's pins are connected to the computer's or the modem's circuitry. Elements covered by the standard include voltage levels, which pins on the port are used to send and receive data, which pins detect various status signals, and more.

In addition to the above, the RS-232C standard dictates that DCE (modems) uses a female RS-232C connector, and DTE (computers) uses a male connector. The actual shape of a connector (as shown in Figure 3.3) is not covered by the RS-232C standard, however.

What a computer or modem does with a signal received at an RS-232C port is its own business; the important thing is to have the receiving device perceive data it receives in exactly the form it was sent, and at the appropriate location in its circuitry.

How It Works: Serial data ports that are designed in conformance with the RS-232C standard have standardized pin assignments. That is, each pin in the port's connector has a designated purpose, as shown in Figure 3.4.

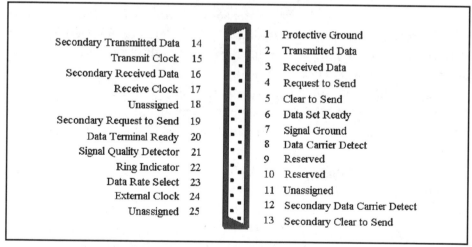

Secondary Transmitted Data	14	1	Protective Ground
Transmit Clock	15	2	Transmitted Data
Secondary Received Data	16	3	Received Data
Receive Clock	17	4	Request to Send
Unassigned	18	5	Clear to Send
Secondary Request to Send	19	6	Data Set Ready
Data Terminal Ready	20	7	Signal Ground
Signal Quality Detector	21	8	Data Carrier Detect
Ring Indicator	22	9	Reserved
Data Rate Select	23	10	Reserved
External Clock	24	11	Unassigned
Unassigned	25	12	Secondary Data Carrier Detect
		13	Secondary Clear to Send

Figure 3.4 RS-232C pin assignments

As you can see, the pin assignments cover just about every job that might come up in transmitting and receiving data. Again, each pin is connected to its device's circuitry as is necessary to route signals to and from the appropriate elements. Thus, a computer with a properly designed RS-232C port should, for example, send data at pin 2 and receive data at pin 3.

In transfers via telephone line, each computer's serial port is connected to a modem via a cable that is wired in conformance with the RS-232C standard. (Presumably, the modem's serial port likewise conforms to the RS-232C standard.) In null-modem transfers, the computers' serial ports are connected via a cable that is wired to match the RS-232C standard for pin connections, but with two connections—the data send and data receive connections—reversed.

Figure 3.4 covers pin assignments for DTE (computer serial ports) only, by the way. A DCE (modem) serial port has slightly different pin assignments, such as using pin 2 to receive data from a computer, and pin 3 to send data.

Other RS-232C Functions: In practice, a serial port is much more than a simple data conduit. In most telecomputing applications, the serial port performs additional tasks, some of which may not be covered by the RS-232C standard. These include organizing the parallel data bits transmitted by a computer into serial form, parity checking, adding and stripping start and stop bits, and, on relatively rare occasions, flow control (more on those in Chapter 6).

Limitations: Because of the low voltages used to transmit a signal via an RS-232C port, the length, or run, of a cable between two serial ports is limited to about 50 feet. If a longer cable is used, there is a good chance that data will be lost.

However, the cable between a computer and modem is generally only two or three feet in length. Thus the RS-232C is ideal for this application. (The same is true of cables between two computers' serial ports.)

The maximum transmission speed of an RS-232C transmitter is far faster than most telecomputing applications.

Connectors and Cables

The cables (and the connectors used with those cables) that connect a computer's serial port with a modem are obviously very important elements in the data communications chain. Like serial ports, connectors and cables used with serial ports must conform to the RS-232C recommendation if they are to function properly.

CONNECTORS

There are two types of RS-232 connectors in common use—*DB-9* and *DB-25*. Remember the diagram in Figure 3.3? It showed a port connector with nine pins and another with 25 pins. Nine- and 25-pin connectors are known as DB-9 and DB-25 connectors, respectively. Each type has numbered connectors (which is very important to know if you intend to make your own cables—it saves a lot of messing around with a continuity tester).

You'll sometimes see the letter P or S appended to DB-9 or DB-25. This letter indicates whether the connector is male (P for plug) or female (S for socket).

DB connectors are essentially mirror images of the serial ports on your computer and modem, and are used at each end of the computer-to-modem connecting cable.

As noted earlier, the physical configuration, or shape, of an RS-232C connector is not defined by the RS-232C standard. DB-style connectors—with the D-shape viewed end-on—have become the de facto standard, however, simply because almost all manufacturers use them.

MIXING CONNECTORS

DB-25 and DB-9 connectors can be used at opposite ends of a cable if necessary (as when a computer's serial port has a DB-9 connector and its modem has a DB-25 connector). Only eight of the pins are used by most systems, and all that's required for the connection to be successful is that the pins on each connector be properly wired (i.e., one connector should be wired as DCE [usually the DB-9], and the other as DTE [usually the DB-25]). Some modem manufacturers, such as U.S. Robotics, provide a DB-25 to DB-9 adapter cable with certain models of their modems.

CABLES

A connecting cable can be a standard bundle of wires in an insulated casing or a ribbon cable, a flat cable with multiple conductors, as shown in Figure 3.5.

There is no real advantage to either in terms of data transmission. A ribbon cable is less likely to become tangled, however.

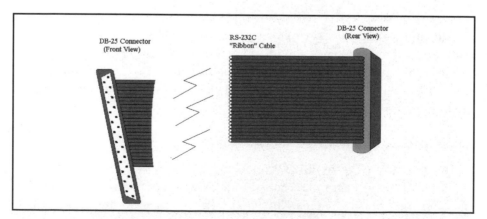

Figure 3.5   Ribbon cable

CONNECTOR AND CABLE "GENDER"

You may recall my saying a few paragraphs back that the RS-232 recommendation specifies that *female* connectors be used on modems, and *male* connectors be used on computers. Thus, a standard RS-232C cable has a male connector on one end (to connect with the modem) and a female connector on the other end (to connect with the computer).

Unfortunately, not all manufacturers follow this standard regarding the gender of their serial ports. So, with certain equipment you may find what is called a "gender problem." (No sex change jokes please—this is serious stuff!) When this is the case, you might want to buy or make a cable with female and/or male connectors at the appropriate ends. Or, you can buy "gender changers," like those shown in Figure 3.6, which are simply plugs that change the gender, or pin/socket configuration, of a cable end by effectively giving you a new connector.

You can also buy adapters that let you connect a nine-pin cable to a 25-pin cable, as shown in Figure 3.6.

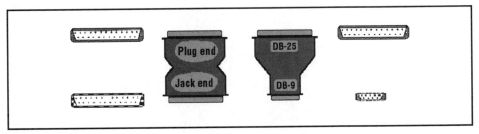

Figure 3.6   Gender changer and DB-9/DB-25 adapter

RS-232 CAVEATS

(*Warning*: Human nature being what it is, a few unscrupulous manufacturers and suppliers are rather more extravagant in their product claims than they should be. The result is that not every cable or device labeled "RS-232C compatible" is set up to operate exactly as an RS-232C device should. Generally, if a reputable manufacturer (or someone you trust) tells you that a cable, modem, or serial port conforms to the RS-232C standard, then it's a fact ... but watch out for Brand XYZ—especially if the company's home office is a post office box.)

You should of course refer to your computer's manual and your modem's manual before making connections of any type. Connecting your computer to a modem may require a cable of modified gender. You may find that, due to the peculiarities of your computer's design, you will need a special cable (as is the case with the old IBM PCjrs and Macs, which don't use a DB connector with their serial ports). Or, it may happen that your computer's RS-232 port is wired slightly different from the standard.

Now that you know how your computer handles data internally, as well as how it communicates with the outside world, let's take a closer look at modems—the workhorses that handle data once it leaves your computer.

CHAPTER 4

Modems

Chapter 2 covered the basics of telecomputing equipment and software, and Chapter 3 explained some of the more technical aspects of personal computer telecommunications. This has prepared you for the in-depth look at modems in this chapter.

The major topics in this chapter are modem types, modem features and options, and important factors to consider when buying a modem. I've included tips on using modems, too—all in the interest of taking the mystery out of them.

MODEM TYPES

Modems come in two basic physical types: *acoustic* and *direct connect*. Most computer systems operate with either type, and each has its advantages and disadvantages, as described below.

Acoustic Modems

The acoustic modem (sometimes called an *acoustic coupler*) is the simplest type of modem. Acoustic modems were originally developed to circumvent now-defunct telephone company regulations that prohibited customers from connecting equipment to telephone lines. No part of an acoustic modem is electrically connected to a telephone or telephone lines. Instead, the modem communicates through telephone mouth- and earpieces via sound waves.

A typical acoustic modem configuration (as shown in Figure 4.1) consists of the modem itself (which may be a stand-alone desktop unit or an internal card) and the "business end," which slips over a telephone handset. There are acoustic modems for both standard and more exotic telephone sets. Many are designed to adapt to any sort of handset.

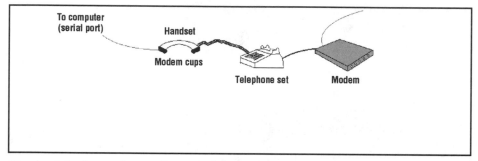

Figure 4.1   Acoustic modem configuration

In operation, an acoustic modem converts a computer's digital signals to audio tones, or analog signals that represent the digital data. These tones are emitted by the modem's speaker cup and are picked up by the microphone in the telephone's mouthpiece. The telephone then sends the signals over the telephone lines. On the receiving end, the modem's microphone cup picks up the tones from the telephone's earpiece. The signals are sent over a connecting line to the modem, which converts them back to digital data.

An acoustic modem is usually less expensive than a direct-connect modem. And, because an acoustic modem requires no special plugs or outlets, it is convenient to use with hardwired hotel or pay telephones. These are the most practical and popular applications for acoustic modems nowadays.

On the negative side, many acoustic modems require manual operation (i.e., you must dial the telephone number and listen for the remote system to answer, hang up the telephone manually, etc.). And, because they are less popular than direct-connect modems, you'll have a difficult time finding acoustic modems with the enhancements offered by direct-connect modems.

Actually, it's difficult now to find acoustic modems at all. This is because the situations that made them necessary in the past have pretty much ceased to exist.

However, acoustic couplers are available for use with direct-connect modems, and are popular with laptop owners. The coupler plugs into the modem's RJ-11 telephone line jack. These are most useful if you use a portable computer and modem. And, fortunately, there are more flexible kinds of acoustic adapters than the one shown in Figure 4.1.

Direct-Connect Modems

A direct-connect modem bypasses the telephone set altogether by connecting directly with a telephone line via a standard RJ-11 jack. As described in Chapter 2, an RJ-11 jack is the receptacle on a telephone into which the telephone line (equipped with an RJ-11 plug) is plugged.

Direct-connect modems are very popular for several reasons. Most feature autodial capability (the ability to dial a phone number without using a telephone set) as well as other features not usually found in acoustic modems. A direct-connect modem may also allow you to connect both the modem and the telephone set to a telephone line simultaneously, which means you don't have to plug and unplug the phone line to switch between modem and voice communications. And because data are not transmitted via sound waves, there is less potential for garbled signals.

There are two classes of direct-connect modems—internal and external.

INTERNAL DIRECT-CONNECT MODEMS

Since almost all new PCs (desktop or laptop) come with internal modems, you are more likely to have an internal modem than an external modem. An internal direct-connect modem consists of a circuit board, or "card," mounted in a computer's expansion slot. A typical internal modem contains the modem plus a serial port and all required connectors, including a modular jack for a telephone line. (Many laptop computers feature built-in internal modems.) Figure 4.2 shows a typical internal direct-connect modem.

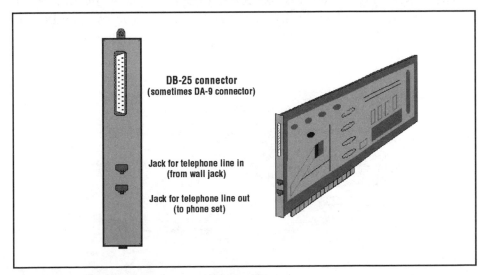

DB-25 connector
(sometimes DA-9 connector)

Jack for telephone line in
(from wall jack)

Jack for telephone line out
(to phone set)

Figure 4.2   Internal direct-connect modem

An internal modem has several advantages over an external modem, not the least of which is reducing desktop clutter. Once an internal modem is installed, there are no cables in the way, and the modem is not susceptible to external physical disturbances. If you have a portable computer, using an internal modem means one less piece of hardware to carry around. And because an internal modem draws power from its host computer's power supply, it doesn't require an extra electrical outlet. Finally, an internal modem leaves a computer's serial port free for other applications, such as a mouse. Most computers come with an internal modem these days.

The major disadvantage of an internal modem is that because it is an integral part of a computer, it is machine specific and can function only with the type of computer for which it is designed. So, if you upgrade to a different kind of computer, you'll have to buy a new modem.

Another disadvantage to using an internal modem is the fact that you cannot monitor a call's status via external indicators. Finally, an internal modem does require a slot, which leaves you with one less slot to devote to another device.

EXTERNAL DIRECT-CONNECT MODEMS

A typical external direct-connect modem (as shown in Figure 4.3) is a thin rectangular box with a power line, one or two modular jacks, and an RS-232C connector. The RS-232C connector accommodates a cable from the computer, and is usually mounted on the back panel. (As explained in Chapter 3, an RS-232C connector can be a five-, nine-, or 25-pin male or female connector. The shape of the connector is either that of an elongated letter D or a circle.)

An external modem usually has a row of LEDs mounted on its front panel. These are the modem's status lights. With status lights, you can monitor the modem's operation and thus the status of a call. An external modem may also have controls of various kinds mounted on its front panel.

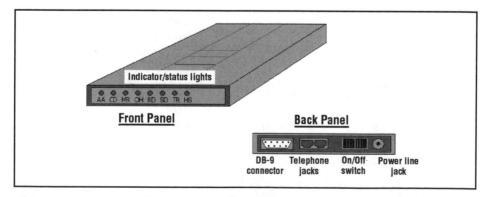

Figure 4.3   External direct-connect modem

The main advantage of external modems over internal modems is the fact that they can be used with more than one kind of computer. But, there are other advantages. If an external modem needs repairs, you can fix it (or take it into the shop) without disassembling the computer. Getting at the modem's DIP switches is easy, too. (That is, you don't have to open your computer; you may have to open the modem, although you can access DIP switches on some modems externally.) If you like being able to monitor the status of a call visually, an external modem's status lights are a welcome feature. (Note that most portable modems have neither DIP switches nor status lights.) Finally, external modems can be used with more than one computer. Unlike internal modems, they are not specially engineered to operate with a certain computer.

On the negative side, an external modem requires a separate power source—more often than not, a transformer that plugs into a wall outlet. There are battery-powered modems and modems that take their power directly from a telephone line, but the former use up batteries rapidly, and the latter are rare. Also, using an external modem means having to find room for one more piece of equipment on your desk or work table.

(*Note*: The comments about external modems apply in general to portable modems as well as desktop modems.)

Several modem manufacturers have experimented with combining a telephone set with a direct-connect modem. This configuration is convenient and saves space, but has not been very popular.

Cable Modems

Cable modems are specially designed modems with proprietary operating systems. These modems translate digital signals from your computer into signals that can be transmitted via the host cable company's media and systems. Cable modems do, however, resemble more conventional modems in one respect: They perform the same operations on data—translation, transmission, and reception. The actual technology is based on that originally developed for "interactive TV," which was conceived in the 1960s and 70s.

Cable modems might be said to "translate" technology as well as data. The majority of cable modems use an Ethernet or LAN-type connection with a PC, which is straightforward use of PC technology. On the other end, the modem communicates with a totally different technology, and thus serves as a translator between the two technologies.

Performance varies by the type of coaxial or hybrid-coaxial medium in use, and the host company's connection and transmission technology. Speeds several hundred times faster than conventional two-wire telephone hookups, and several times faster than digital line hookups are possible—anywhere from 4 to 10 megabits per second (Mbps) and faster.

Not all areas are served by cable companies, of course, and not all cable companies have the technology to provide Internet access via cable. Many are upgrading in order to do so, and a few are offering hybrid cable/phone-line service, by routing incoming data via cable and outgoing customer data through the standard two-wire telephone system.

Additional Classifying Elements

Modems are also classified by whether they communicate in *asynchronous* or *synchronous* mode, and whether they can communicate over common telephone lines to access ISPs, online services, and BBSs, or work over dedicated lines at ultra high speeds (dial-up vs. leased line). These distinctions are described below. (The significance of asynchronous and synchronous is explained in the next chapter.)

Asynchronous/Synchronous Modems

If you use dial-up services such as CompuServe or AOL, a dedicated ISP, or a BBS, you'll never need a synchronous modem. All such systems provide asynchronous service. The same is true of the major packet-switching networks.

Leased-line (see below) and mainframe connections usually require synchronous communications. If your applications are dial-up, make sure the modem you buy is capable of asynchronous operation. If you have applications in both areas, you'll be happy to know there are a number of modems that operate in either asynchronous or synchronous mode.

Dial-Up and Leased-Line Modems

DIAL-UP MODEMS

Simply described, *a dial-up modem* is one that operates within a bps range (0 to 56K) that is effective for data transmission via voice-grade telephone lines. (56 Kbps is the current upper limit for reliable data communications within the frequency bandwidth available on voice telephone lines.) A dial-up modem also uses *communications parameters* (parity, data bits, number of stop bits, etc.) that are compatible with other dial-up modems and packet-switching networks.

Most (but not all) dial-up modems operate in asynchronous mode. Some high-end modems, among them certain Hayes Smartmodem models, are switchable between asynchronous and synchronous modes. Dial-up modems are, in general, less expensive than leased-line modems.

Virtually all modems sold for use with personal computers are asynchronous dial-up modems.

LEASED-LINE MODEMS

Leased-line modems use extremely high bps rates (115,400 and up) over dedicated two- or four-wire telephone lines, or other direct-connect lines shielded against outside interference. (These are also called "conditioned" lines.) Leased-line modems may operate in synchronous or asynchronous mode, or switch between modes, and usually transmit data in full duplex (two-way) mode.

Leased-line modems are useful in LAN and private network applications, such as in commercial applications where large amounts of data pass rapidly over conditioned or four-wire lines. These modems almost always include the more esoteric of the modem options discussed on the following pages, such as data encryption, automatic dialback, and data compression. This is not to say that dial-up modems cannot include these features, though.

Unless you are setting up your own network or intend to use a terminal (or a personal computer as a terminal) to communicate with a mainframe or minicomputer in a nearby location, you won't need a leased-line modem.

Other Types of Modems

Other types of modems are used in specialized applications, as discussed in the following pages. It is unlikely that any of these modem types will be a majority before 2005, even though the technology exists and is in use in many areas. Consumer confusion, price resistance, and the existence of the current infrastructure of serial-port modems make for inertia in favor of conventional, serial-port, and packet-switching-based PC data communications.

ISDN MODEMS

ISDN (*integrated services digital networks*) modems are a special application of technology, as is the case with cable modems. ISDN modems take advantage of specially designed data lines to carry data at nominal speeds of 128 Kbps and speeds up to 1.544 Mbps.

Also as with cable modems, ISDN modems translate technology—from PC technology to the technology used to simultaneously transmit voice, computer and/or fax data, and video on the same digital line. Still, the basic principle behind ISDN modems is the same as that behind conventional PC modems: Data is translated and transmitted in symbolic form.

ATM MODEMS

ATM (*asynchronous transfer mode*) is a multipronged approach to moving data much faster than through a conventional ISDN network. In addition to special data networks (the physical transmission medium), ATM uses an improved packet-switching transmission system and other approaches to data multiplexing as defined by a specific set of standards. The intent is for ATM to supersede ISDN and serve as the basis for *B-ISDN* (*broadband ISDN*).

Data transmission rates of 45 megabits per second and up to 1 gigabit per second are possible with an ATM system. Special modems are of course required to translate data and technology to use the ATM digital data network.

Analog and Digital Modems

The modem applications discussed thus far concern analog modems (that is, modems that transmit and receive data over communications links in analog form).

You'll be interested to know, however, that digital modems can transmit data via special digital networks in true digital form. They don't have to convert data to analog form as analog modems do. Applications for digital modems involve specialized digital telephone networks, such as those discussed in the immediately preceding pages.

SPECIAL NOTE ON PBX DIGITAL TELEPHONE SYSTEMS

Many large offices have their own internal telephone networks. One incoming number handles multiple calls to various extensions, as well as telephone traffic from one office to another. Such a system is called a *private branch exchange*, or *PBX* for short. There is usually no problem with using a modem through a conventional PBX, unless the system has a Call-Waiting-type feature.

However, most modern PBX systems are digital systems. If you wish to telecompute via a digital PBX, you may have to install an analog (standard) telephone line. (This would be a separate line with its own number—one that doesn't go through the PBX.) Try your modem with the PBX system before installing a new line, though; chances are, your modem should operate with the PBX. The way a PBX system handles switching and signals—and thus its effects on analog modem communications—varies by manufacturer and model.

An alternative to having a dedicated phone line installed is to buy a digital-to-analog converter. Also known as analog-to-digital converters, or "A-to-D" or "D-to-A" converters for short, these devices handle changing a modem's analog output to a format compatible with a digital PBX. They also convert incoming data from a digital PBX to the analog format recognized by dial-up modems. Check with your hardware dealer or phone company on the availability of A-to-D converters.

MODEM FEATURES AND OPTIONS

The number of features and options that can be built into modems is rather large and the source of more than a little confusion, especially since communications software packages offer many of the same features. I'll describe the more important features here, to acquaint you with what's available. You'll also find this section handy when looking over a list of specifications for a particular modem, as specification sheets tend to list buzzwords without explaining what those words mean.

Not all software packages can use all the features offered by some modems. Some features may require communications software designed for use with the modem in question. Also, some modem features will not operate unless you're calling a modem with the same features. (Examples of such features are built-in error-checking protocols and proprietary modulation techniques.) You should also be aware that some features are available only with dial-up modems, while others are available only with leased-line modems. Unless otherwise noted, the features discussed in the following pages are available for dial-up modems as well as for leased-line modems. Not every modem offers every feature discussed here. The features are not listed in order of importance; importance is subjective and depends on your application.

Finally, some of the capabilities discussed in the following pages are also available as communications software features. Where appropriate, I've noted when this is the case.

Notes on "Intelligent" Modems and Features

Dial-up modems are frequently advertised as "intelligent." This term usually alludes to their abilities to perform certain functions automatically, such as dialing numbers, answering the telephone, etc. The "intelligence" consists of programming in ROM or hardware features.

Advanced functions offered by intelligent modems are normally performed in response to commands issued from the keyboard or, more typically, by your communications software or in response to signals from the system you have dialed up.

As with people, modem intelligence varies; an "intelligent" modem may offer any number of the functions discussed here. If you see a modem labeled "intelligent" (or "full featured"), don't count on it having everything you want. Be sure to get a complete list of a modem's features before buying it.

Variable Communications Parameters

Unless you plan to use a modem to dial up only one other system, don't buy a modem with fixed communications parameters. Such a modem will not respond to software commands to change parameters. For maximum utility, these parameters should be variable:

- Speed
- Duplex (echo)
- Parity
- Data bits
- Stop bit(s)

All but a very few modems on the market today have variable communications parameters.

AUTOMATIC PARAMETER ADJUSTMENT

Some top-of-the-line modems (both leased-line and dial-up) sense and adjust to the communications parameters in use by a remote system. This capability is often called "automatic feature negotiation."

Autodial/Auto Answer

Autodial and auto answer were considered options on some modems just a few years ago. Now they are standard features, even though some modem ads and packaging still tout them as "extras."

AUTODIAL

Autodial is the ability to dial a number without the use of a telephone set. With autodial, all your communications software has to do is send a command telling the modem to dial a number. The command may come from your keyboard or from a communication program's autologon script file.

Once it receives the dial commands and number, the modem opens the phone line, dials the number, and, if there is an answer on the other end, lets the answering computer know a computer is calling. Most autodial modems can dial using either tones or pulses.

AUTO ANSWER

Auto answer capability means that the modem can detect an incoming ring (via a variation in telephone line voltage), "answer" the phone, keep the line open, and let your software know there is an incoming call. The communications software—assuming it has the capability—takes over from there and sends the appropriate commands to the modem.

Selective Dialing Capability (Tone/Pulse)

Selective dialing capability is the ability to dial by either tone or pulse. While the majority of telephone exchanges in North America handle tone dialing, it is a good idea to have both capabilities.

TONE DIALING

Tone dialing is dialing by sending DTMF signals over the phone line. *DTMF* is an acronym for *dual tone modulated frequency*, which is the type of signal used by a touch tone system. If you have a good ear, you may hear two tones when you press a touch-tone telephone button. The tones are carrier tones, modulated with information that identifies the number pressed. These tones go to a local telephone-switching computer, which uses them to connect you with the number dialed. A modem with tone-dialing capability can generate these tones.

PULSE DIALING

Pulse dialing is used with rotary style phones (the old ones with a true dial rather than push buttons). When a number is dialed with pulses, a series of what sounds like clicks is sent through the telephone line—one click for the number 1, two clicks for the number 2, and so on, all the way up to 10 clicks for 0. This is rather slow, but necessary with old telephone systems in some parts of the country.

You can try pulse dialing manually with your phone, even if it is a touch-tone telephone. Lift the handset, then depress the "hang-up button" rapidly for each number—10 times for 0, once for 1, twice for 2, three times for 3, and so on. You can actually dial a number in this manner, which is the way a pulse dial modem does it.

You may be able to use tone dialing even if there is a rotary phone connected to the line. You'll often find locations that use rotary phones even though tone dialing is supported; it's a matter of economy. So, always try tone dialing before you try pulse dialing. The presence of a rotary phone doesn't mean the phone line doesn't support tone dialing.

If dialing a number using tones has no effect, you can always switch your modem to dial using pulses. Substituting the command "ATDP" for "ATDT" in the dial string normally does this.

TONE DIALERS

If you have a manual-dial modem (particularly a portable), you can upgrade it to autodial capability, even if you have a rotary-dial telephone. All you need is a device known as a *tone dialer*. The basic tone dialer is a hand-held device with a speaker and numbered buttons.

When the buttons are pressed, the tone dialer's speaker emits the standard DTMF signals used by phone systems. These tones are picked up by a telephone's microphone and have the same effect as dialing with a telephone.

Most tone dialers store several numbers for later playback. You can use this kind of tone dialer as an online "phone directory" to speed up manual dialing; all you have to do to dial a number is press a couple of keys. This gives you the convenience of an autodial modem with number storage. It also speeds up dialing and eliminates errors.

Adaptive Dialing

Modems with adaptive dialing sense whether they should use tone or pulse dialing, depending upon whether the local telephone system is equipped to handle tone dialing. This information is present in the dial tone sent by tone-dial telephone systems.

When a modem with adaptive dialing receives a dial command without tone or pulse specification, it will try tone dialing first; if the dial tone is still present, it switches to pulse dialing.

Default Dial Settings

Intelligent modems can be set to dial using tone or pulse only. When so programmed, a dial command sent to the modem doesn't have to include the tone or pulse specification, unless the nondefault setting is to be used.

Pause Capability

The ability to pause during dialing is necessary if a modem is dialing through a PBX, certain long-distance services, or any phone system that pauses before a dial tone comes up.

For example, if a PBX system requires you to dial 9 to get an outside line, you may have to wait one or two seconds after you dial 9 before the dial tone is heard. A communications program can tell a modem with pause capability to wait one second after dialing 9 before dialing the rest of the number. This is normally done by embedding the standard AT pause command (,) in the number, thus: 9,5551969. This sequence sent to a modem as the number to be dialed would tell the modem to dial 9, wait one second, and then dial 5551969.

(*Tip*: I usually use a two-second pause after the outside-line access digit in case there is a longer-than-normal delay in getting the dial tone.)

Speaker

A speaker is useful when you wish to monitor a dial-up. With a speaker, you can hear if there's a busy signal, so you don't have to wonder why you're not getting an answer. And, if you get a voice response ("live," or, in the case of a changed number, a recording), you can respond appropriately. The speaker is mounted inside the modem.

However, I dislike modem speakers; it's rather goofy to have a dial tone, DTMF dialing, the sound of a phone ringing at the other end of the line, and then the whine and hiss of the answering modem blasted into the room. It's so goofy that I can't help laughing when someone uses a modem with the speaker on. So, I always include the command to turn off the speaker (M0) in any dial string.

Not incidentally, a "smart" modem will report to you when a line is busy, if the phone at the other end is ringing, or if a voice answers, provided you make the proper settings in the modem per its manual.

Volume Control

A nice extra that's not available with all speaker-equipped modems is volume control. If you buy a modem that doesn't have volume control, you may wish it did after a few online sessions. Hearing a dial tone and the sound of the modem dialing is reassuring to some, but annoying to others—and, as I said a few lines back, it's goofy in any case.

Most volume controls are external (manual). But many modems let you adjust speaker volume with software commands. Some modems offer both external and software volume controls.

Dual Phone Jacks

External direct-connect modems with autodial capability do not, of course, have to be connected to a telephone set to function. But you may wish to have a telephone set connected to the telephone line along with the modem. This way, you can use either the phone or the modem without switching the telephone line from one to the other.

One way to do this is with a *Y-jack* (sometimes called a *Y-plug* or *Y cable*). This is a short cable with an RJ-11 jack or receptacle at one end, and the other end of the cable splits into two wires, each of which has an RJ-11 plug at its end. The telephone line is plugged into the single RJ-11 jack, and the two RJ-11 plugs are connected to your modem and your telephone set, respectively. You can use a *duplex jack* to do the same thing. A duplex jack is a plastic block with an RJ-11 plug on one end and two RJ-11 jacks on the other, as shown in Figure 4.4.

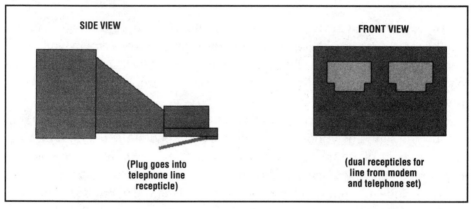

Figure 4.4 Duplex or "Y" jack

A more convenient approach is to buy a modem with two RJ-11 jacks. The incoming telephone line is plugged into one jack, and a short cord with an RJ-11 plug on each end (usually called the "telephone cable" and supplied with the modem) is plugged into the other jack. The free plug on the short cord is then plugged into the telephone set. The net effect is that the modem and telephone are connected to the same phone line in parallel.

Automatic Hang-Up on Carrier Loss

There are a few autodial/auto answer modems that don't have this feature, and it's an important one to have. With automatic hang-up, the modem automatically hangs up the phone (disconnects from the phone line) if the remote system hangs up or is accidentally disconnected. This feature is especially useful if you use a phone line for both voice and data; if it's not present, your phone may stay "off the hook" after a remote system disconnects and prevent calls from coming in.

A few modems with this capability will disconnect only when told to do so by communications software. Because of this, you must check carefully to make sure automatic hang-up means the modem and not the software performs the operation. There's nothing wrong with relying on your software to do this, but the feature should be available if you need it.

Visual Call Status and System Monitoring

Most external desktop modems have status lights (usually LEDs, or light-emitting diodes, rather than lights) on their front panels, as illustrated in Figure 4.5. These indicators provide a way to visually monitor the status of a call and the telecomputing system.

Figure 4.5 A modem with front-panel indicators

Status lights are usually marked with two- or three-letter abbreviations to indicate their purpose. The following are the status indicators provided most frequently:

- **AA or Auto Answer.** This indicator is on when a modem with auto answer capability is set to answer incoming calls.

- **CD or Carrier Detect.** This indicator lights when a modem detects a carrier tone from an answering computer during a call. (At the same time, the modem sends a "carrier detect" signal to its computer.)

- **HS.** When the "HS" indicator is on, it means that the modem is set to 1,200 or 2,400 baud.

- **MR or Modem Ready.** MR lights when a modem is ready to receive or send data (normally on whenever there is power to the modem).

- **OH or Off Hook.** This means that the telephone line connected to a modem is currently in use, as when the modem takes control of the line to make a call.

- **RD or Receiving Data.** This indicator flashes with each bit of data your computer receives.

- **SD or Sending Data.** This indicator flashes with each bit of data your computer sends. (Watch it as you type; it flashes each time you press a key.)

- **TR or Terminal Ready.** This means your terminal is ready to dial out or receive calls.

You may find other, more specialized indicators on some modems. The more elaborate communications software packages (or ancillary programs) provide the same kinds of information onscreen. You'll also find variations on the labels listed here, like "DS" rather than "SD."

MODEM STANDARDS

In an earlier chapter, I promised a more detailed discussion of the various standards, and here it is. This section covers speed standards as well as error-checking and so-called "file-compression" standards. The subject of standards is the single most-confusing element faced by a modem buyer, but it's really not confusing, especially if you remember that a higher number after "V" doesn't necessarily mean a better or faster modem.

The majority of modem standards are set by the ITU (International Telecommunication Union), formerly the CCITT (*Comité Consultatif International Téléphonique et Télégraphique*), headquartered in Geneva, Switzerland. All manufacturers of data and fax modems have adopted the ITU's standards. (The URL for the ITU's Web site is **http://www.itu.int**.)

Speed and Operating Standards

Table 4.1 is a list of the standards that apply to the most popular dial-up modem speeds, as well as the standards used for error checking and pseudo-file compression at each speed.

Use the standards shown in Table 4.1 as your basic reference. Any other standard designates either an extension that adds features, or an alternate transmission technique. For example, 56KFlex (developed by Lucent Technologies and Rockwell), and the USRobotics/3COM X2 standards are proprietary. (Lucent and Rockwell eventually made their 56KFlex standard compatible with V.90.)

Table 4.1 Modem Standards

SPEED	DOMESTIC STANDARD (US)	INTERNATIONAL STANDARD
300 bps	Bell 103	V.21
1,200 bps (600 bps)	Bell 212A	V.22
Error-checking	V.42	V.42
File compression	V.42bis	V.42bis
2,400 bps	V.22bis	V.22bis
Error-checking	V.42	V.42
File compression	V.42bis	V.42bis
4,800 bps (via 4-wire lines only)	V.27 V.27bis for 4,800/2,400 bps 4-wire modems	V.27 V.27bis
9,600 bps (via 4-wire lines only)	V.29 (Also used with Group 3 FAX systems for 7,200 & 9,600 bps in 2-wire systems)	V.29
9,600 & 4,800 bps	V.32	V.32
Error-checking	V.42	V.42
File compression	V.42bis	V.42bis
4,800, 7,200, 9,600, 12,000, and 14,400 bps modems	V.32bis	V.32bis
Error-checking	V.42	V.42
File compression	V.42bis	V.42bis
14,000 & 12,000 bps (via 4-wire lines only)	V.33 Note: Same modulation techniques as V.32.	V.33
Error-checking	V.42	V.42
File compression	V.42bis	V.42bis
14,400 bps	V.32bis	V.32bis
Error-checking	V.42	V.42
File compression	V.42bis	V.42bis
28,800 bps	V.34	V.34
Error-checking	V.42	V.42
File compression	V.42bis	V.42bis
36,600 bps	V.34	V.34
Error-checking	V.42	V.42
File compression	V.42bis	V.42bis
48,000 bps (in 4-wire lines only)	V.36	V.36
56,600 bps (56K) Error-checking File compression FAX compression, transmission speed	V.90 V.42 V.42bis Group 3	V.90 V.42 V.42bis Group 3

Table 4.1   Modem Standards *(continued)*

SPEED	DOMESTIC STANDARD (US)	INTERNATIONAL STANDARD
(9,600 bps), and two resolution levels: 203 by 98 and 203 by 196	Group 3 *(continued)*	Group 3 *(continued)*
FAX transmission via ISDN networks at resolution up to 400 dots per inch	Group 4	Group 4

With that as a basic operating thesis, you should also remember the following points:

- A modem's operating speed is *the number of bits it transmits each second*. A *baud* is a *change in state* of a signal: off/on, high/low, and so forth. The majority of modem transmission modulation techniques transmit more than one bit with each baud, so baud does not equal bit except in instances when only one bit is transmitted per baud, as with 300-bps systems.

- The speed a modem's label or name carries (1,200, 2,400, etc.) is usually its maximum operating speed. The circumstances when the label is misleading include modems whose specs claim "9,600-bps" operation, but which do not use V.32. I'll say more on this later.

- A modem should operate at all speeds less than its maximum operating speed.

- Labels like "V.42" and "*bis*" don't always mean a modem is a 9,600-bps modem. V.42, which specifies LAPM for primary error checking and MNP 4 for "fallback" error checking—and also V.42*bis*, which specifies a CCITT file-compressions protocol and sometimes MNP 5 as a secondary file-compression protocol—can apply to any modem operating at 1,200 bps and up.

Virtually all modems are compatible with the standards for speeds lower than their highest operating speeds; this is implicit in the standards. Modems that comply with these standards automatically adjust to one another's operating parameters. Normally, the answering modem adjusts its speed downward, if necessary, to match the speed and modulation techniques of the calling modem. Adjustment to error-checking and data-compression protocols is negotiated by the modems or based on the calling modem's capabilities. This all takes place in a very short period of time.

Modem Error-Checking Protocols

This section examines the early as well as the more sophisticated and effective modem error-checking protocols in common use today. Basically, modem-implemented error checking looks for errors in data transmitted and requests that the data be re-sent. The data is re-sent until it goes through correctly, or until a "timeout" (a predetermined time period or number of re-sends) is reached. Both modems must support the error-checking protocol in question.

PARITY CHECKING

Parity checking is a rather primitive form of hardware error checking. It works by adding an extra bit to each transmitted byte at the serial port. This bit is called the *parity bit*, and is used to let a receiving system know whether the sum of the high bits in a transmitted byte should be odd (0) or even (1).

This can be a rather inaccurate technique, as it doesn't take into consideration whether several high bits might be missing. Still, serial ports sum the bits in a byte and add a parity bit, which is stripped away by the receiving system's serial port and adds to what is called *bit overhead* (extra bits that are not data).

ARQ

ARQ is an acronym for *automatic request for repeat*. This is a generic name for any error-correction scheme that mimics the way some binary file-transfer protocols work, including MNP and LAPM. Note that USRobotics uses ARQ as an acronym for any error correction technique, so some USR modems may report CONNECT/ARQ for MNP 2 through 4 or LAPM connections (which are to be discussed following). Some Hayes V-series modems do the same.

MNP

MNP, perhaps the best-known error-checking protocol, stands for *Microcom Networking Protocol*, and is a proprietary system of error-checking and file-compression protocols developed by a company called Microcom. There are nine varieties (called "levels" or "classes") in common use. Each successive level provides the features of its predecessors, as well as its own features. MNP 1 through 4 are in the public domain and are part of the CCITT V.42 specification for error control. (MNP serves as a secondary or "fallback" to the primary error-checking protocol for V.42 modems, LAPM, which is described in the next section.)

The nine levels or classes of MNP are described below:

- **MNP 1.** Asynchronous, one-way communication (half duplex). Its main purpose is error checking, which slows down communication approximately 30 percent.

- **MNP 2.** Asynchronous communication, in two directions simultaneously (full duplex). The error checking slows down communication approximately 26 percent.

- **MNP 3.** Synchronous communication, and in both directions at once. In addition to performing error checking, MNP 3 strips out or removes the start and stop bits added to each byte before transmitting data. (You'll recall that start and stop bits are not required during synchronous communication.) Data are then put into packets. (You might think of this as a sort of "physical Xmodem.") Removing start and stop bits means that eight bits, rather than the usual 10, are sent for each byte, resulting in as much as 20 percent increase in data transfer. The time required for the modem to remove start and stop bits before transmission and to add them at the receiving end before sending bytes on to the computer's serial port makes for an effective increase in speed of about 10 percent. (*Note*: While the modems communicate synchronously with one another, they still communicate in asynchronous mode with their host computers. The synchronous operation is transparent to the computers.)

- **MNP 4.** Asynchronous communication, with data placed into packets to reduce errors, which also increases transmission speed. The default packet size is larger than with MNP 3, but this varies as the modem monitors the line conditions. The modem reduces the packet size if there's a lot of line noise, and it increases the packet size if the line is relatively clean. MNP 4 also streamlines some information in packet headers and increases data transmission overall by as much as 22 percent.

- **MNP 5.** This level uses the same kind of error correction and "packetizing" as MNP 4, as well as altering data to reduce its size. This is called "compression," but what is really happening is that the data is encoded so that repeating or redundant data is eliminated and represented by fewer bits. The data is decoded by a receiving modem before it is transmitted to its host's serial port. The effective throughput, or the quantity of useful data that is actually transmitted, can be as much as twice as fast as without MNP 5. However, if a file is already compressed, as with PKZIP, there is less redundant data and it may actually take longer to transmit using MNP 5 than without it. This is because redundant data has already been eliminated.

- **MNP levels 6, 7, and 9** sport improvements in data compression and error checking, and are set up to operate with V.32 modems. (There is no MNP 8.)

- **MNP 10** is used in a cellular modem produced by Microcom.

MNP is usually programmed into a modem's chips. There are some software implementations of MNP, but these are more than a little tricky to get to work and are not popular.

Which MNP?

As a dial-up modem user, you'll deal with MNP levels 4 and 5 most often. Both modems must of course support the same MNP levels. Most packet-switching networks support MNP 4, if not 5—which is rather important, considering the fact that a majority of modems have MNP 4. Both Sprintnet and BT Tymnet support MNP 4, as do various online services and ISPs.

A few modems have problems connecting with another modem using an MNP level higher or lower than they are using, while others ignore the higher level. The former is true of some dealing with certain other modems. If the modem you are dialing handles MNP 4 but not MNP 5, you may find that when you sign on with MNP 5 enabled, binary file transfers are impossible and disconnections are frequent.

LAP/M

LAPM (sometimes written *LAP/M*) is an acronym for *link access procedure for modems*. It is a protocol that provides error control between two modems that implement LAPM. LAPM is part of the V.42 specification. When a V.42 modem connects with another modem, it tries to establish LAPM as the error-checking protocol; if this doesn't work, then it tries MNP 1 through 4 with the remote modem. If the remote modem does not support MNP, a "normal" connection is established. A normal connection is one that allows error correction implemented by software or the computers' serial ports to pass through.

Modem Data-Compression Protocol (bis)

As noted earlier, *bis* appended to a modem standard indicates data-compression capability. The CCITT V.42*bis* standard specifies "V.42*bis*" as the compression scheme. V.42*bis* is used only when the LAPM is in use.

Backing Up and Data Compression

MNP 5 is the backup for V.42*bis* with some, but not all, V.42*bis* modems. MNP 5 is used only when MNP 1, 2, 3, or 4 is the hardware error-checking protocol in use. These data-compression techniques can increase data throughput as much as 400 percent.

However, data-compression protocols do not truly compress data. That's why I frequently allude to these protocols as pseudo data-compression protocols, which brings us to an important issue: the difference between *speed* and *throughput*.

Speed and Throughput

Modem *speed* is a measure of the actual number of *bits* or *characters* transmitted each second (*bps* or *cps*). This is the number of bits transmitted by each baud, or change in signal state, multiplied by the number of bauds per second.

Throughput, on the other hand, is a measure of the amount of useful data bytes transmitted from a file. This is not necessarily the same as the number of bits transmitted per second. Why? Because with the kind of data compression under discussion here, data is encoded in a manner that eliminates repeated or redundant characters (bytes). Depending on the error-checking technique in use, unnecessary bits—start and stop bits—are also removed from each byte.

This is done "on-the-fly." As data is organized into packets to be transmitted by a modem, some data is "tokenized," which means certain (usually redundant) characters are removed and fewer characters are substituted to represent them during transmission. The receiving modem knows how to reconstruct the tokenized data before sending it to its host computer because both modems are using the same file-compression technique.

To look at it another way, assume I tell you the letter "A" represents page 129 of this book, and I transmit "A" to you. How many bits were transmitted in the time it took to transmit that byte? The eight bits that made up the byte, or the several thousand that make up the page in the book? The answer should be obvious. Assuming "A" could represent the chapter, while eight bits were literally transmitted, several thousand bits were effectively transmitted—in terms of modem throughput. All of this is predicated on one byte of a compressed sequence containing more information than just being a single character, which of course is the case when modem data compression is used.

As an example, if a 9,600-bps modem uses a file-compression technique that transmits only 2,048 bytes for a file that is 4,086 bytes in size, the effective useful data-transfer rate, or throughput, is double what would be achieved using a "normal" connection at 9,600 bps. In other words, a throughput of

19,200 bps is achieved. The point is that the 9,600-bps modem is not transmitting characters any faster, but it is transmitting the file faster because it is transmitting fewer characters to represent the data in the file: 50 characters are transmitted for every 100 characters in the file. The process is completely transparent to the computers involved, and to the user.

In theory, throughput up to four times a modem's transmission speed is possible with a V.42*bis* modem. Thus, a 9,600-bps modem can have a throughput of 38,400 bps, but it is still transmitting at 9,600 bps. Similarly, a 2,400-bps modem sending a file that is 400 percent compressed is not a 9,600-bps modem. When it is transmitting data, it is transmitting data at 2,400 bps, period.

If this is confusing, it may help to think of modem data compression as increasing the amount of useful data transmitted in a given period.

UNCONVENTIONAL ACCELERATION

Some modems increase throughput with unconventional compression techniques, but these only work with modems that use the same techniques—modems from the same manufacturer. An example is USRobotics/3COM with its X2 modems.

As noted, some 9,600-bps modems use an extension of the V.32 standard called V.32*bis* to achieve 14,400 bps. Rather than using data compression, however, a different modulation technique is used. The same is true of other modems operating at faster speeds.

Modem Standards in Overview

You'll see a number of claims in high-speed modem ads as to compatibility with and support of various standards. To supplement and synopsize the preceding discussion, here's a quick guide to what does what, and how.

The label "V.32" alone should neither promise nor imply anything other than the modem's ability to transmit and receive data at 4,800 or 9,600 bps, using one or another of the modulation techniques specified by the CCITT. All of which is to say a V.32 modem will communicate with another V.32 modem. A "V.32*bis*" modem uses a different kind of modulation technique to increase throughput to 14,400 bps.

The terms *compliant* and *compatible* can be confusing. The label "V.42 compliant" means a modem supports LAPM and MNP 1–4 for error control (the latter as backups). "V.42 compatible" doesn't always mean a modem uses LAPM; it means the modem uses MNP 1–4 and that it will communicate with another V.42 modem, but not using LAPM. Whether the modem supports LAPM is in the hands of the manufacturer.

"V.42*bis*" indicates data compression, but it doesn't guarantee the modem uses MNP 5. A modem labeled "V.42*bis* compatible" uses the CCITT data compression technique specified in the V.42*bis* standard when communicating with another V.42*bis* modem. The effective throughput is 38,800 bps. Whether it uses MNP 5 is up to the manufacturer. Even with MNP 5 support, a modem uses MNP 5 compression only if MNP 1, 2, 3, or 4 is active, instead of LAPM.

"WARNING, WILL ROBINSON! THAT IS NOT A 9,600-BPS MODEM!"

Remember, for example, that V.42 modems can be low-speed modems. So, just because a modem is labeled V.42 doesn't mean it's a V.32 modem, too. Only 9,600-bps V.42 modems are V.32 compatible. So, when you buy a V.42 modem, make sure it is V.32 compatible, and V.42*bis* compliant or compatible, if you're looking for a 9,600-bps modem.

There are some 2,400-bps modems that are V.42*bis* compliant and that are advertised truthfully as having 9,600-bps throughput. However, this doesn't mean they are 9,600-bps modems capable of 38,400-bps throughput. It just means they can achieve 9,600-bps transmission when connected with another 2,400-bps modem that uses V.42 data compression.

NONSTANDARD MODEMS

There are several reasonably reliable proprietary high-speed modulation techniques, but none are included in the V.32 standard. A modem that uses a proprietary modulation technique may cost much less, but it might not be able to communicate with modems other than those from the same manufacturer.

ADDITIONAL MODEM FEATURES AND OPTIONS

Call-Status Monitoring

If you don't have a speaker (or even if you do), it is nice to have a modem that detects and reports the status of a call by sending messages to your screen similar to these:

- BUSY—busy signal detected
- CONNECT—connection established
- CONNECT 300—connection established at 300 bps
- CONNECT 1200—connection established at 1,200 bps

■ CONNECT 2400—connection established at 2,400 bps

■ NO ANSWER—no response after a specified number of rings

■ NO DIAL TONE—no dial tone present

■ RINGING—the number is ringing

■ UNSUCCESSFUL—the call was aborted or interrupted

■ VOICE—a voice, rather than a modem, answered your call

Advanced communications programs react to such messages by disconnecting and/or redialing as appropriate when, for example, there is no answer or a voice answers the phone. More expensive call-monitoring modems handle these situations without waiting for software commands.

These features are "switchable" in many modems. This means the level of response can be adjusted to brief numeric codes or turned off entirely.

Auto Baud Rate Switching

Auto baud rate switching, which is actually speed switching, is sometimes available whether or not a modem has call status monitoring. A modem with auto baud rate switching senses and matches the speed and modulation technique in use by a remote system when a connection is established.

Auto baud rate is especially convenient when you're dialing a system new to you; you don't have to worry about which speed to use.

Auto Redial

Modems capable of auto redial store the most recently dialed number in RAM, and will redial that number in response to a brief command. This is convenient if you call a system and receive a busy signal, and you wish to try the system again in a short time.

Modems with this feature can often be set to redial a number after a specified time if there's no carrier or if a busy signal is detected. Many communications software packages offer this function, too.

Number Storage

Some modems with autodial capability also store numbers in nonvolatile memory or EEPROM. This means the numbers are "remembered" even when power to the modem is off. Numbers are usually stored in a directory format, accessible by name. Given the proper command, the modem will retrieve a specified number from its memory and call it. Here again, many communications software packages offer this feature, eliminating the need for modem number storage. (I've found that using a communication program's "dialing directory" feature is easier than using that of a modem. This feature is most useful in a modem that you'll be using with different programs.)

Parameter and Configuration Storage

Modems capable of storing and retrieving numbers may also be able to store communications parameters and operating configurations.

PARAMETER STORAGE

Parameter storage is useful if you always use the same communications parameters. With the communications speed, duplex, parity, and number of data bits and stop bits stored in your modem's memory, all you have to do is tell the modem to dial a number. There's no need to set the parameters from your terminal. If you use autologon files with your communications program, however, you probably won't need parameter storage in your modem. Each time an autologon file is run, the communications program resets the modem parameters to those specified in the autologon file.

CONFIGURATION STORAGE

If you change communications software frequently and/or use your modem with more than one computer, you may have to change the modem's operating configuration to accommodate the new software or computer. The elements of a modem's operating configuration include carrier detect override, local echo, result code display, and more. (These elements vary from modem to modem; consult your modem's manual for details.) The operating configuration is normally set via a modem's DIP switches, and resetting it can become a tedious chore if you have to do it frequently. With configuration storage, you can use AT-type commands to reset the modem's operating configuration from your keyboard.

Automatic Fallback

When a poor connection exists as a result of a "noisy" telephone line, it is sometimes necessary for a modem to fall back to a lower transmission speed. Many high-speed modems cannot fall back once a connection is made, but this feature is becoming more common, especially in modems with built-in error correction.

Test Mode

Some higher-priced modems can perform self-checks to confirm the proper operation of all of their elements. Self-testing does not normally require supporting software or hardware. (Many leased-line modems use shared external test equipment, however.)

A self-checking modem may test itself every time it is turned on, continuously while "idle," or it may do a self-check only when commanded to do so. Self-tests may be conducted while online or off-line, depending on the configuration of the testing system.

A few modem manufacturers offer a self-test system that operates with a private BBS. With this kind of system, you dial up the manufacturer's BBS and wait while the dedicated system at the other end tests your modem.

Busy Mode

Busy mode is a useful feature in dial-up and leased-line modems used to answer incoming calls. When a modem is in this mode, the telephone line is effectively off the hook and callers receive a busy signal.

Busy mode is handy when a system operator wants to prohibit incoming calls during system maintenance or for other reasons. The advantage of using a busy mode rather than simply disconnecting the modem from the telephone line is that callers will not assume that the system is out of service, which would be the case if they called repeatedly and received no answer.

Built-In Communications Software

Having communications software built into a modem may seem like a good idea. You don't have to install and load software from a disk, and you know the software will work with the modem.

However, you will probably find it more convenient to use disk-based communications software. Disk- or CD-based software is generally more flexible and easier to use than built-in software. (Interestingly enough, every modem user I've talked with who has a modem with built-in software uses a disk-based program, if possible.)

Automatic Data/Voice Switching

Lower-cost modems may make use of a telephone set's circuitry to generate DTMF signals for dialing, or may require you to dial numbers manually. Such modems must be connected to a telephone set rather than directly to a telephone line, and you have to switch to voice mode to dial out, then to data mode when the system you are calling answers. Switching to data mode allows the modem to route incoming data to your computer.

Similarly, many acoustic modems require that you dial numbers for them, then flip from voice to data mode when the remote system answers.

Manual voice/data switching seems to be the norm for these modems, but it is obviously less desirable than automatic switching, available on some modems that require a telephone set to dial a number. So, look for automatic voice/data switching on any modem that must be connected to a telephone set.

(*Note*: You can avoid the data/voice-switching problem entirely by buying a modem with autodial capability!)

Voice/Data Selection

Voice/data selection is the ability to switch between modem and voice communications without breaking the communications link. Of course, this is only useful if both ends have voice/data selection capability, and if there's a human at the other end of the connection.

The major benefit of this feature is being able to interrupt data communications to discuss transmission problems or other matters with the remote system operator and then return to data communications. This is a common feature with dedicated fax machines, but rather rare among computer modems.

External Controls

Also known as "front panel controls," external controls on both dial-up and leased-line modems let you set various features (such as tone or pulse dialing, or number redial) by pressing a button. This is more convenient than using software commands. It is useful if you have to change certain parameters or features frequently.

Leased-line modems with external controls may also feature a small screen that displays the status of various operating elements, as well as menus to use with the external controls. Leased-line modems have more elaborate external controls than dial-up modems.

External DIP Switches

More and more modems have externally mounted *DIP switches* (switches used to set certain elements of a modem's operating configuration), but most external modems are so constructed that you have to open the modem case to get at the switches. (Fortunately, you probably won't have to get at the DIP switches too often.)

Telephone Line and Battery-Powered Modems

It is possible to buy a modem that draws its power from a telephone line, but this is not an important feature unless you have absolutely no extra electrical outlets available where you use your computer.

The same is true for battery power. Unless you use a portable modem with a laptop computer, battery power is not an important feature. Note, too, that battery life is limited with portable modems. Expect about two hours of use from a new alkaline battery with a portable modem.

Call-Duration Reporting

Modems with a call-duration reporting option can display the duration of calls in hours, minutes, and seconds on your computer screen. This provides an audit record of online activities. This feature also sometimes includes an optional real-time clock.

Inactivity Timer

An inactivity timer is a handy feature that prevents online charges from piling up if you leave your computer and forget to sign off from a commercial online service. Modems with this feature disconnect if there is no activity (data sent or received) after a preset length of time. This feature is sometimes offered by communications software as well.

Built-In Error Correction and Data Compression Revisited

As you know, a popular trend among modem manufacturers is to include built-in error-checking protocol as a feature with dial-up and leased-line modems. Several hardware error-checking protocols are in use, including MNP (Microcom Network Protocol), X.25, LAPM, LAP-B, AFT, and various other proprietary protocols, but the feature is not useful unless both modems involved in a data transfer use the protocol, as noted some pages back.

As of this writing, MNP seems to be the leader among dial-up modems, with LAPM as a backup. Go with MNP 4 at the very least. Modems that follow the V.42*bis* specifications are the leaders in data compression. If you're detail minded, look for a modem whose spec sheet clearly states that it uses MNP 5.

ERROR-CHECKING AND DATA-COMPRESSION SLOWDOWNS

In some instances, using a hardware error-checking protocol slows real-time communications slightly. These protocols typically use a system of sending groups of characters in "packets." Sometimes there is a brief delay before a character is sent because the modem waits to be sure no additional characters are coming before it sends a data packet. (Data packets and related topics are addressed in later chapters.)

(*Note*: This type of protocol should not be confused with software error-checking protocols such as Xmodem, Zmodem, Kermit, etc.)

A similar slowdown hits if you try to transmit already-compressed files (i.e., files archived with PKZIP or a similar program) or files that cannot be compressed by removal of redundant data (like GIF graphics files) using a data-compression protocol. A V.42*bis* may waste quite a bit of time checking a large file for redundant data that isn't there.

Security Features

Security features that limit access to stored telephone numbers, configurations, and other features are included in some dial-up and leased-line modems. Limiting access is normally a matter of requiring the user to enter a password.

For online security, some modems can be set to require a specific "answerback" code from a modem dialing in before they will initiate a connection. This is somewhat different from sending a password, and two modems from the same manufacturer may be required.

Communications software packages may provide similar security features.

NRAM and EEPROM Number, Parameter, and Configuration Storage

If a modem can store numbers, parameter settings, operating configurations, and other information when it is turned off, such information will be stored either in RAM or in what is called an *NRAM chip*. NRAM is an acronym for *non-volatile RAM*. Such information may also be stored in *EEPROM*, an acronym for *erasable electronically programmable read-only memory*.

If the information is stored in RAM, a battery inside the modem supplies a trickle of current to keep the RAM "alive," thus enabling it to retain its memory. However, such a battery wears out after two to five years, and the data in RAM has to be re-entered after the battery is replaced.

With NRAM storage, however, the data is retained whether or not there is power to the chip. This is obviously a superior way to store data, albeit a more expensive one. The same is true of EEPROM storage.

Dial Backup

Dial backup is an extremely important feature for systems with heavy, 24-hour traffic—typically systems that use leased-line modems. A system with dial backup will re-establish a broken data link without being told to do so—something vital for unattended systems and for systems attended by people who are not "system sophisticated." Dial backup is much faster than manually re-establishing a connection.

Dial backup comes into play if a data link is broken by anything other than a normal disconnect (telephone line problems, storms, accidental hang-ups, etc.). When the link is broken, a modem with dial backup immediately dials the system with which it was communicating, and—if so programmed—continues dialing until the connection is re-established. Once the connection is re-established, the modem may alert the system operator.

Line/Frequency Equalization

Modems with a line/frequency equalization feature automatically adapt to line conditions by altering transmission frequencies and other elements of their operations to get the best possible signal quality. Most leased-line and dial-up modems have this feature, also known as "adaptive equalization."

Data Encryption

Data encryption, as the name suggests, is a process that involves "scrambling" and "de-scrambling" data as it is transmitted and received. This prevents persons who may have tapped a communications link from receiving sensitive data in a usable format.

Data encryption normally requires that the same type and brand of modem be in use at each end of a data link. A data-encryption system may also encrypt data for disk storage.

Accessory Hardware

Modem accessory hardware includes racks on which you can mount multiple external or internal (card) modems, diagnostic units, analog converters, and other hardware. You probably won't get into most of this unless you are running a multiple-modem setup (a multiline BBS perhaps).

MOUNTING RACKS

A mounting rack is just what the name implies—a rack on which several external or card modems are mounted. Mounting racks are often used with multiple modems, but they can also serve as an external mount for a single internal modem.

DIAGNOSTIC UNITS

Diagnostic units provide a means whereby modems may be tested manually or automatically and faults reported. They are often set up on a shared-unit basis, which means that several modems can use a diagnostic unit's capabilities.

Diagnostic units are usually designed for use with a modem rack. Some shared diagnostic units also allow you to change parameter settings in all modems to which they are connected simultaneously.

ANALOG CONVERTERS

An analog converter is a device that converts analog signals transmitted by a modem to a telephone line into digital signals. It also converts incoming digital signals (from a phone line) into the kind of analog signals a dial-up modem expects. As described in Chapter 3, an analog converter is also referred to as an "analog-to-digital," "digital-to-analog," "A-to-D," or "D-to-A" converter.

An analog converter is necessary if you wish to access digital network services, such as AT&T's Dataphone Digital Service (DDS), with a conventional dial-up modem. An analog converter is also required in order to use a dial-up modem with ISDN services and with digital PBXs. Your local telephone company is normally a good source for an analog converter.

Modem Hardware Enhancements and Upgrades

Almost every new modem introduced to the marketplace offers desirable enhancements. If you wish to take advantage of such enhancements, you usually have to buy a new modem. However, a few manufacturers make hardware enhancements and upgrades available that allow owners of their older products to add new capabilities to their modems.

One example of this kind of add-on is Hayes V-series Modem Enhancer, an external unit that can be used with certain earlier Smartmodem models to add features available on newer Hayes V-series modems. Another is the programmable EEPROM that Intel includes with some of its modems, which makes it possible to upgrade a modem via a program Intel provides. The program reprograms some of the modem's internal workings to add new features.

Summary

As I stated earlier, many of the options available with dial-up modems are also available as communications software features—redial capability and phone number storage among them. Also, many modem features can be disabled. So, you won't necessarily have to buy a modem with all the features you want as long as you can find a communications software package that offers the features the modem doesn't.

Buying software with all the "bells and whistles" rather than a feature-rich modem is often the least expensive way to go. The ideal modem/software combination is one in which the modem provides the functions necessary to support advanced operations performed by the software, as described in this chapter and the next.

The usefulness of modem features is largely a matter of what you need and what you want. The first several features discussed here are the most important for dial-up modem users. The next few are of interest mainly to those who require optimum system function. The remainder are of interest in more specialized or esoteric applications and may not be a factor in your selection of a modem. Some are, as noted, available only with leased-line modems.

If your application involves a local area network or dedicated two- or four-wire telephone lines, you will use special LAN hardware or a leased-line modem. You'll probably have little difficulty finding a leased-line modem that offers all the features you need, but I advise you to enlist the aid of the modem manufacturer and/or the company or consultant who is setting up your system in selecting your modem.

Selecting a Modem

By now, you should have a fairly good idea of whether you will be better off with an acoustic modem or an internal, external, or portable direct-connect modem. You should also know which features and options you want or need.

Deciding the configuration and features you want is only the first step in selecting a modem, however. You must also consider hardware compatibility, software compatibility, command set, price, and other factors. Features such as autodialing and error checking are pretty much standard among all but the bargain-basement modems.

Hardware Compatibility

A modem must be compatible with your computer system. One way to find out if a modem is compatible with your computer system is to read the modem's specifications, found on the modem package or in advertising material. You might also read magazine reviews, which usually tell you what kinds of equipment you can use a modem with. Or, you can ask the manufacturer. Spending a few bucks on a long-distance telephone call is well worth it; you'll be able to find out immediately whether you can use the modem in question with your system.

If you're lucky, your computer will be compatible with the modem of your dreams. In this case, you only have to make or buy the proper cable to connect the modem to your computer.

The simplest way to ensure that a modem will work with your computer is to buy a "system-ready" modem. A system-ready modem is typically a dial-up modem that operates with a variety of computers, but is packaged with the appropriate cable and documentation for a specific brand/model of computer.

Or, you might look at dial-up modems designed specifically for a computer brand/model, which are commonly internal modems, discussed earlier in this chapter. Both system-ready and brand-specific modems tend to be more expensive than off-the-shelf modems, though.

Some modems are labeled as compatible with any computer. Modems so labeled probably work with just about any computer that has a serial port. Of course, you may have to find or make the proper cable to connect the modem to your computer (see Chapter 3 for more information on cables). To do this, you will have to study "pinout" diagrams for the modem and your computer, and perhaps experiment a bit. (A pinout diagram is a diagram that illustrates a connector's pin assignments.)

Remember, too, that a few modems communicate via a computer's parallel port. So be sure you're getting a modem with the appropriate connection—serial or parallel—for your computer.

If you have any doubt as to whether a particular modem can be used with your computer, contact the manufacturer or a knowledgeable computer salesperson. (Don't count on information from computer salespeople being 100-percent accurate, though. It is an unfortunate fact that all too few computer salespeople are proficient in things technical; after all, most are salespeople first. I'm reminded here of the Cincinnati-area branches of a national computer retail chain that frequently advertise for salespeople, requesting used-car salespeople as prime candidates. This is no exaggeration!)

As a backup to information given to you by salespeople, check out manufacturers' brochures and specification sheets.

You might also check with acquaintances who use your brand of computer. Chances are, you'll find someone who uses the modem(s) you are considering with the computer you use. Or, your friend(s) can advise you as to which modem is best for your computer. If nothing else, you'll learn a lot about other modems that are compatible with your computer.

If you're buying modem accessory hardware or plan to use modem features that require compatibility between two modems, your safest course is to buy all equipment from the same manufacturer.

Software Compatibility

Another important consideration in selecting a modem is software compatibility. That is, the modem you select should work with the communications software you intend to use. This may seem obvious, but not all modems respond to the same set of commands, and unless your software issues commands that the modem will respond to, you'll have trouble using the two together. (I am, of course, speaking of the actual commands the software sends to the modem, not the commands you type at your keyboard.)

Fortunately, most modems use the same base command set (or portions thereof)—a de facto standard called the "AT" or "Hayes" command set, which we'll examine in a few paragraphs.

It also happens that some software packages come with prepared command or setup files that enable them to "talk" with a variety of modems. With this type of software, you merely select the appropriate brand and model of modem from a menu during installation. The program automatically uses the proper command set with the modem. (You will have to change a DIP switch setting or two on some modems, but the software's documentation will tell you how to do this.) Usually only the more popular modems are so accommodated, which is yet another factor to keep in mind when shopping for a modem and software.

The best way to determine modem/software compatibility is to try the software with the modem before you buy either. If you can't do that, consult with someone who already uses the modem/software combination you're considering.

Bundled Software

You'll find communications software included with many modems. This is known as "bundled" software. You don't have to worry about software compatibility when the modem and software come as a package—unless, that is, you find that you don't like the bundled software.

If you don't want to use the software provided with a modem, you'll have to look for a program better suited to your needs and tastes. In this case, you should have a modem that responds to the aforementioned AT Command Set, again because the majority of communications programs use this command set.

Command Set

I can't overemphasize the fact that conflicting standards proliferate throughout the computer industry, and telecomputing is no exception. Fortunately, the standards for modem commands have been pretty well settled. As noted, most communications software publishers have adopted what is known as the AT Command Set, or the Hayes Standard AT Command Set, in recent years. This is partly because, early on, the best-selling modems used this command set, and partly because a standard was needed.

A modem labeled "AT compatible" or "Hayes compatible" uses (or ostensibly uses) the "base" AT Command Set. Not every "Hayes compatible" modem is 100-percent compatible with this command set, but a modem labeled AT or Hayes compatible should be close enough in compatibility that software issuing standard AT commands can communicate with it.

By the way, most modem manufacturers have adopted this command set, too. This way, their products are compatible with popular communications software packages. (This is a selling strategy, of course—the easier a product is to use, the better it sells.)

The AT Command Set is so named because the command used to "wake up" or initiate a modem is "AT," which stands for "attention." Other commands include "D" for "dial," "T" for "use tones when dialing," and "P" for "use pulse dialing." So, the command string "ATDT" tells a modem to wake up and then dial a number using tones. Table 4.2 lists the base standard AT commands used by the majority of modems sold in the United States. With two exceptions, all commands are preceded by AT and followed by a carriage return.

NOTE: Two commands do not have to be preceded by the AT prefix. These are A/ (repeat last command) and +++ (enter command mode). These commands do not have to be followed by a carriage return, either.

Note that the commands listed in Table 4.2 are those commonly used in dialing and answering operations. Your modem may offer additional commands for configuration, setup, and self-diagnostics, particularly if it is a Hayes modem. (Also, your modem may vary some of the commands slightly.)

Most modem manufacturers use what is called an "extended" AT Command Set. This is a set of specialized commands—based on the AT Command Set—used to access their modems' special features. These are typically prefaced by the characters "&" or "%," as in "AT&M0" used by Intel modems to turn off MNP. The base AT commands shown in Table 4.2 also operate with such modems, of course.

Table 4.2 Standard AT Command Set

COMMAND	FUNCTION
AT	"Wakes up" modem, clears the command buffer. Precedes almost all commands, such as: ATA, ATCO, ATDT, and so forth
A	Set to answer mode; manually answer an incoming call
C	Enable/disable carrier signal
C0	Disables carrier transmitter
C1	Enable automatic carrier off switching by modem
Dx	Dial the number following (where x is the number to be dialed, as in ATD5551212), and switch out of command mode to communications mode. Can also be used with the modifiers following.
DP	Dial the number following, using pulse dialing
DT	Dial the number following, using tone dialing
DT6	Tests DTMF dialer (ATDT6)
DTR	Instructs modem to switch to answer mode and issue carrier frequency when connection is established (used to call originate-only modems)
DTW	Wait for dial tone before dialing
DT,	Pause before dialing (comma can be placed anywhere in dial string—after dial command, between numbers, etc.); length of pause is determined by S-register setting
DT/	Pause 0.125 second before continuing dial command
DT;	Dial, then remain in command mode
DT!	"Hookflash," hang up for 1/2 second, then reconnect
DT@	Wait for silence before dialing (time to wait is determined by S-register setting)
E	Enable/disable character echo (toggle when used alone, as ATE)
E0	Disable character echo
E1	Enable character echo
F	Set duplex (toggle)
F0	Half duplex
F1	Full duplex
H0	Hang up
I	Query for information about modem
I0	Product code
I1	ROM check (checksum)
I2	ROM memory test

Table 4.2   Standard AT Command Set *(continued)*

COMMAND		FUNCTION
L		Speaker volume control
	L1	Low volume
	L2	Medium volume (usually the default)
	L3	High volume
M		Speaker on/off toggle
	M0	Speaker off
	M1	Turn speaker off after modem dials and detects a carrier from answering modem
	M2	Speaker on
O		Return to connect/online mode (used after entering command mode while connected: ATO)
Q		Enable/disable result code display when dialing (toggle)
	Q0	Enables result code display (default)
	Q1	Disables result code display
Sxn		Sets register x to value n
		S-registers are used to change timing for delays and other functions, as well as setting features such as the number of rings before a modem answers, special characters, etc.
Sx?		Displays the value of S-register x
		Functions of a given register vary by modem manufacturer
V		Specify the type of result codes displayed (Verbose or numeric)
	V0	Numeric result codes (1, 2, 3, and so on)
	V1	Verbose; result codes are displayed as words (OK, RING, NO CARRIER, etc.)
Xx		Enables call-monitoring and -detection features (features implemented depend on the modem, but may include dial tone, busy signal, voice, and transmission speed detection)
Z		Restores all default ("factory") settings and clears command buffer
[Enter]		Implements commands entered
AT&x		AT& is a prefix for advanced commands (not available with all modems)

The chances are good that any modem you are considering uses the AT Command Set. But, again, make sure about this before you buy it. Otherwise, you could find yourself stuck with a limited range of choices in communications software, unless you want to write your own!

Special Considerations in Selecting a Modem

CONFORMANCE TO STANDARDS

As I've mentioned several times, hardware conformance to recommended standards is very important. Any modem you buy should meet the standards that exist for modem configuration and operation, including the use of an RS-232C interface for connection to a computer, standard connectors (typically, DB-25 or DB-9 for the serial port and RJ-11 jacks for telephone line connection), and conformance to the appropriate Bell and/or CCITT standards.

REPUTATION

Check with modem-using friends and acquaintances on the reputation of the modem you wish to buy, as well as the reputation of its manufacturer. Is the product reliable? Does it deliver what its advertising claims? Does the manufacturer back up its warranty?

DOCUMENTATION

Does the modem include a manual, or just an instruction sheet? Is the manual well organized and easy to understand? Does it include illustrations where necessary and (very important) an index? Is a quick-reference card provided? (*Note*: Some modems, such as USRobotics' Courier series, include a command and operation reference "card" printed on the bottom panel of the modem.)

I mention this because I frequently get questions about two specific brands of modems by users who bought them new but didn't get a manual. I can't understand this, as the manuals exist. (Other users who did get manuals usually answer the questions.) Software without a manual I can understand— that's simply a matter of someone having pirated software. But make sure you get your manual.

EASE OF USE

Is the modem ready to use, or do you have to change DIP switch settings to get it to function properly? If you have to change DIP switch settings, does the manual explain what's required, and clearly? Ideally, the modem's manual should provide not only an explanation of what each switch does, but also a chart that shows the DIP switch settings to use with various popular communications software packages.

Service and Support

Can you get service and advice through your dealer? Does the manufacturer provide telephone support? These factors may be very important.

Selecting a modem deserves at least as much thought and consideration as selecting a computer. Some bargain-priced modems can be costly in terms of living with your mistakes. So, take your time and choose carefully!

Notes on Modem Use

As with any electronic device, it is important that you connect your modem properly and use it under practical operating conditions. Study the manual or instruction sheet that comes with your modem to assure proper connection, and observe the following during modem setup and use:

Telephone Company Regulations

Local telephone company regulations may vary, but in general these regulations are in effect:

- Some telephone companies must be notified that you are connecting an FCC-registered device to your telephone line before you connect it, and that you are disconnecting the modem when you disconnect it permanently.

- You cannot connect a direct-connect modem to a pay telephone, nor to a party line.

Plug/Jack Types

Before you plug a modular plug into a modem, determine the plug's type. As mentioned in Chapter 2, most modems have RJ-11 jacks, but modular (RJ) jacks and plugs come in more than one variety. Some are cross compatible, and some aren't.

Generally, a home or single-line business telephone system uses RJ-11 plugs, and these present no problem, even if the plugs are set up for use with a "Trimline" phone or other lighted dial telephone set. There is one important exception: Do not use an RJ-11 plug that provides power for a lighted dial with a modem that uses an RJ-12 or RJ-14 plug. RJ-12 and RJ-14 jacks may route damaging voltage from such a plug into the wrong parts of a modem's circuitry.

RJ-41 and RJ-45S plugs are also safe to use with most modems; the exceptions may be modems that have RJ-12 or RJ-14 plugs. See your modem's documentation for details. If your in-house telephone system is a multiple-line or "key" telephone system, you must use a modem that can interface with RJ-12 or RJ-14 plugs, such as a Hayes Smartmodem 2400. The modem you use must also be software-switchable to RJ-12/RJ-14 operation.

Ventilation

Don't use a modem as a bookshelf or repository for other materials. While an external modem may serve as a resting place for a telephone set, it's not designed to be smothered by papers, disks, etc. A modem's electronic components generate heat, and the heat must be able to dissipate; too much heat buildup interferes with proper operation of the modem. Therefore, heat vents—as well as most of the top of the modem—should be uncovered.

Weather Conditions

Never use your modem during a severe thunderstorm, nor any time you observe lightning. Lightning is a guaranteed source of power surges in both telephone lines and AC power lines. Unless you've installed a surge protector on your modem's telephone line and on the power lines to your computer and modem, there's an excellent chance that your modem and/or computer will be zapped by a current surge. Even with surge protectors you're taking a chance.

Power

If your modem has a power switch, use it to turn the modem off and on. Leaving the switch in the ON position and plugging and unplugging the modem's power supply is not a good idea. This can cause power surges, electrical current overload, or rapid on/off switching as you fumble with a hard-to-reach plug. When changing the battery in a battery-powered modem, the power switch should be in the OFF position, for the same reasons.

Don't plug your modem into an overloaded or faulty circuit. Aside from the fire hazard this creates, overloaded circuits often have low voltage, and low voltage causes excess heat and poor performance in electronic equipment.

CHAPTER 5

Fax

This chapter presents the following:

- Basic facsimile (fax) terminology
- Applications for facsimile transmission
- How fax machines see graphic images
- Equipment associated with facsimile transmission
- Fax communications channels
- Capabilities and limitations of facsimile transmission
- Technical background on facsimile technology
- Fax features and options

GETTING THE WORDS RIGHT

Before proceeding, let's examine some terms you'll see frequently in this book and in other literature about fax.

Text and Graphics

The terms text and graphics describe two entirely different types of visual material, but are sometimes confused. And, even though a dedicated fax machine does not distinguish between the two, it is often important to speak of each as discreet elements.

TEXT

When discussing facsimile transmission, "text" means letters, words, numbers, and spaces (also referred to as characters) that are combined to form words or numeric data. Text characters are those characters found on a standard typewriter keyboard.

In general, text consists of machine-produced or -generated characters, i.e., typewriter or computer printer output, or characters generated by a computer and stored in the computer's memory or on disk. Handwritten text is generally regarded as graphics. These distinctions are important, particularly where using PC fax boards or online services are concerned.

GRAPHICS

Graphic material is any visual image that does not consist exclusively of machine-produced text characters. Graphics can include lines, curves, angles, lettering, dots, varying tones or color intensity, halftones, cursive, designs, logos, etc. Graphics to be scanned and transmitted by fax can be produced or generated by any of several methods, individually or combined:

- Human drawing or writing (freehand, or with drafting equipment or other aids)
- Computer printers (dot-matrix, ink-jet, and laser)
- Photography
- Photocopying existing graphics

Pages, Documents, Messages, and Images

The terms page, document, message, and image appear to be used interchangeably—and often are. The explanations below demonstrate how the terms are distinguished from one another, and how they are used in this book and in other venues. (*Note*: Fax refers to both machines and documents.)

PAGE

"Page" generally refers to a sheet of physical paper scanned or printed out by a fax machine. The word is also to describe a unit of information transmitted via fax—i.e., the information content of a sheet of paper, which can be text, graphics, or both.

DOCUMENT

A document is a page or group of pages transmitted by fax, which can also be described as the sum total of information transmitted during a single fax transmission.

MESSAGE

The term message is also used frequently to refer to a page or group of pages transmitted by fax, but is usually used with reference to a document of one or two pages. As with "document," "message" does not exclusively refer to a text-only message.

IMAGE

The word image alludes to the contents of a page, or, more often, to the electronic form of a scanned page, i.e., the binary or analog data in which a page is stored and transmitted.

Group "X" Fax Machines

You will see many references to "Group 3 fax" in product literature and advertisements, and some references to Groups 1, 2, and 4 fax machines. Simply explained, the number in the phrase "Group x fax" refers to the generation or sequence in the evolution of fax technology in which the machine in question belongs. The numbers match the age of the technology—Group 1 being the oldest and Group 4 being the newest.

The technology itself is defined by the graphic resolution (the detail of the image), the speed at which data is transmitted, how data is scanned and stored preparatory to transmission, and other elements.

With rare exception, the technology used in fax machines (the means whereby images are scanned, encoded, transmitted, and decoded for printing) follow a set of recommendations. The majority of modem standards are set by the ITU (International Telecommunication Union), formerly the CCITT (*Comité Consultatif International Téléphonique et Télégraphique*), headquartered in Geneva, Switzerland. All manufacturers of data and fax modems have adopted the ITU's standards. (The URL for the ITU's Web site is **http://www.itu.int**.) This means that modern fax machines the world over are compatible, or are able to communicate, with one another.

Group 3 is the most common type of fax machine currently in use. (Industry estimates indicate that 90 percent of the fax machines in use in the world are Group 3.) Group 3 fax machines are distinguished by the fact that they scan and store images as digital data; earlier fax machines used strictly analog scanning techniques. Group 3 fax machines boast a finer resolution than that of Group 1 or Group 2 fax machines, as well as higher speeds in scanning and transmitting images.

(*Note*: While Group 3 machines use digital scanning and storage techniques, they must still transmit image data as analog signals, due to the nature of the voice telephone network. This, as you will learn, is why fax machines have built-in modems.)

Group 3 fax machines are 100-percent compatible only with other Group 3 fax machines. This means they may not be able to communicate with Group 1 or 2 machines. Some Group 3 machines can recognize transmissions from Group 2 machines, and can thus receive documents from the older machines. Some Group 3 machines can also send documents in a format recognized by Group 2 machines. (Very few Group 3 fax machines can communicate with Group 1 machines.)

If you expect to be communicating with Group 2 fax machines (it is not likely you will be dealing with installations using Group 1 machines), make sure your fax machine can communicate with Group 2 fax machines. Group 2 capability is not available on all Group 3 machines.

In general, incompatibility between older fax machines and Group 3 machines is not an issue. As previously indicated, the majority of fax machines in use today are Group 3 machines, so you have little need to be concerned about the compatibility of a recently purchased dedicated fax machine.

PC fax boards and modem fax services are set up to communicate with Group 3 fax machines, and some may communicate with Group 2 machines, as well.

Group 4 fax machines are extremely expensive and specialized communications tools. When they transmit data many times faster and with less chance of error than Group 3 machines, they communicate in digital rather than analog fashion. Group 4 fax machines are not generally compatible with Group 3 machines and require special digital telephone networks, referred to as ISDN (for Integrated Services Digital Network).

Due to the fact that Group 4 fax machines require such digital links and cannot use the existing voice-telephone network, it will be several years before they become a significant force in the marketplace. Specifically, when larger-scale ISDNs now planned and under construction are in place, Group 4 fax will be widely available, affordable, and of interest to the general fax user.

FAX APPLICATIONS

Specific applications for fax transmission are virtually endless. Due to the fact that the initial cost of fax machines was relatively high until recently, most fax transmissions are business oriented. However, as with computers, consumer demand and manufacturer competition is resulting in price reductions, which in turn is making fax more accessible to the public. Thus personal and hobby fax applications are becoming prevalent.

Business Applications

Typical business applications for fax include transmitting drawings, photographs, signed contracts, memos, letters, and lengthy documents (with or without graphics).

There are several advantages to being able to send graphic images and documents by fax:

- Fax delivery is nearly instantaneous; even next-day delivery services cannot compete with fax in delivery time.

- You can send and receive fax messages at your convenience; you're not dependent on the schedules of next-day delivery services.

- Fax delivery is, in general, less costly than other forms of rapid delivery of hard copy.

(*Note*: With reference to signatures on faxed contracts, while they are accepted as binding by the parties to such a contract, the question of their legality is still a gray area as far as the courts and most attorneys are concerned. In general, faxed signatures have been regarded by the law as being in the same category as photocopied signatures.

(While there is some precedent for signatures on faxed contracts being accepted as valid by individuals, attorneys, and courts, it is best to back up a faxed contract with the original, when possible.)

Fax Abuse

As with the telephone and e-mail, many enterprising (and some desperate) individuals and organizations devised ways to use fax communications for commercial enterprise—much to the annoyance of millions of fax users. Specifically, advertisements and useless information is being broadcast to known fax telephone numbers. Fortunately, the U.S. Congress passed a law against such practices.

Personal Applications

Personal applications for fax are somewhat limited. Because fax machines are not as prevalent as telephones, and because it is easier to use a telephone for local and long-distance personal communications, individuals have been largely without real incentives to buy fax machines. However, some individuals find personal applications in using fax machines in the workplace and at home for sending advance lunch orders to local restaurants, requests to radio stations, and the like. Fax is also becoming a popular substitute for ordering and paying for goods and services by telephone or mail where credit cards are involved, because with fax one can include an authenticating signature.

Hobby Applications

The major hobby applications for fax seem to be the novelty of using fax, finding new applications for fax, and modifying fax machines and/or interfacing them with other electronic devices.

IT's ALL IN HOW YOU LOOK AT IT: TEXT VS. GRAPHICS AND FAX

As you are aware, both text and graphics can be transmitted via fax. However, you may not be aware of an important fact: Both text and graphics are the same where fax is involved, because a fax sees both text and graphics as graphics. That is, when a fax machine scans and records a character (a letter or number), it is not treating it as a letter; instead, it treats the character as an element in a picture, just as it would treat a small sketch or hand-written character. Further, the graphics are perceived and printed as patterns of dots.

The software behind PC fax boards and modem fax services perceives characters as characters, but when the characters are translated to fax format, the same graphic-view effect is created.

FAX EQUIPMENT

There are three categories of equipment used to originate and receive fax messages: dedicated fax machines, computers equipped with PC fax boards, and computers equipped with modems that make use of online services to transmit fax messages.

Dedicated Fax Machines

A dedicated fax machine is exactly what the name implies: a piece of equipment designed and used primarily or solely for facsimile transmission.

Figure 5.1   A dedicated fax machine

Dedicated fax machines are similar to a business telephone set or photo-copier in appearance. (A typical fax machine is shown in Figure 5.1) The primary elements of a fax machine are a scanner, which reads words and images from a sheet of paper and converts them to electronic signals; a modem, which, as described in Chapter 1, converts the electronic signals to a format that can be transmitted by telephone line (and, in the case of received fax messages, converts the signals back to the electronic format used by the scanner); a printer, which converts the electronic signals supplied by the modem into words and images on paper; and the telephone interface, which handles dialing.

Optional dedicated fax machine elements may include a memory for storing telephone numbers and/or fax messages, a programming element to set up delayed message transfers, automatic paper feeders, a display to provide call-status information, and other support hardware.

The vast majority of fax messages are transmitted via dedicated fax machines. This is primarily because it requires less knowledge to operate a dedicated fax machine than to operate a computer, and because a dedicated fax machine costs less than a PC.

PC Fax Boards

A PC fax board translates computer text and graphics contained in a computer's memory or stored on a computer disk into the kinds of binary signals used by fax machines. Special software that works with the PC fax board reads the text or graphics, and a built-in fax-type modem translates these signals into the analog form used by fax machines for telephone-line transmission, then transmits the text and/or graphics that comprise the pages of the fax message. When the receiving fax machine receives these signals, it sees them in the same all-graphics format used by fax, whether text or graphics are involved.

PC fax boards receive fax messages in a manner similar to that of dedicated fax machines. The big difference, of course, is that received text and/or graphics are stored in the computer's memory or on disk.

Once a message is stored, it can be accessed with any of a variety of computer programs, printed out, or retransmitted.

A useful feature of PC fax boards is their ability to translate and transmit (or receive) graphic image files created by popular personal computer graphics programs. PC fax board-equipped computers are not limited to transmitting only computer-generated text and graphics. If you have a scanner, you can scan paper documents and drawings, which are stored on computer disk. The PC fax board's software can access the files just like any other disk file. As shown in Figure 5.2, PC fax boards are similar in appearance to other add-on boards. The electronic components are mounted on a printed-circuit board, and an edge connector on one side of the board is used to connect it with the computer.

Figure 5.2   A PC fax board

Most PC fax boards also incorporate a conventional dial-up modem (or vice versa). PC fax boards are popular among computer users for several reasons:

- A PC fax board provides fax access at a cost equivalent to or less than that of a dedicated fax machine, without cluttering the computer user's desk top with another piece of equipment.

- Using a PC fax board saves time and trouble by eliminating the need to print out text or graphics, then scan the printed pages with a dedicated fax machine.

- Most PC fax board/software combinations can be directed to send or receive fax transmissions automatically, without supervision.

- Graphics that might otherwise be inaccessible due to a lack of the appropriate printer type can be delivered via fax.

- Veteran computer users find PC fax boards easier to learn to use than stand-alone fax machines, and being able to do fax-related work from their computers is more efficient than switching gears to another machine.

Fax Without Fax via the Internet and Online Services

If you don't have a fax machine or PC fax board, you can still send faxes. A variety of Internet sites and online services offer fax service.

Two kinds of online services handle fax traffic: online services for modem-equipped computers and online services that can communicate with fax machines. Both kinds of online services are based on and controlled by computers.

COMPUTER FAX ONLINE

If you have a computer, a word processing program, a communications program, and a modem, you can send text fax messages via the Internet or almost any online service to any fax machine in the world. This kind of fax communication is also referred to as modem/fax service. Figure 5.3 shows a Web site that offers this service.

Logistically, sending a message to a fax machine via the Internet or an online service is simple: You transmit a message from your computer, enter the telephone number of the fax machine that is to receive the message, and the host computer calls the designated number and transmits the message.

Depending on the word processor you use, you may need to make changes in documents produced with it before you can send the documents as a fax message in this manner. This usually involves saving a document as plain text or in pure ASCII format.

The major differences between transmitting a fax message via dial-up modem and via a fax machine or PC fax board are as follows:

Figure 5.3   Online fax service site

- You can only send text on most services.
- You cannot receive fax messages on most services.
- The text you send must be in a file on your computer's disk.
- Messages are not transmitted directly from your computer; instead, they are stored for a short period, then forwarded to the designated recipient.

(*Note*: Some services can transfer graphic images created with popular PC graphics software, and a few allow you to receive text messages sent from dedicated fax machines or PC fax boards. You can also transfer files from popular word processors without preparation to several Web sites and online services, which translate the files and send them to a specified fax number.)

When you transmit a message online and specify fax delivery, the message is stored on a host computer, which calls and makes a connection with the fax machine designated as the receiver. How often and for how long a time period the online service's computer will attempt to deliver your fax message can vary, depending on which service you use; some services allow you to specify the duration and interval of retries.

You can, by the way, specify more than one fax telephone number on almost all the services when you send a message by fax.

When a connection is made with the receiving fax machine—which may be minutes or hours after you transmit it to the service depending on whether or not the receiving fax machine is online and not busy—the host computer sends your stored message to the receiving fax in the special format required by fax machines. The conversion is handled automatically.

When a receiving fax machine receives a message from the service's computer, it sees it in the all-graphics format used by fax, whether text or graphics are involved, and reproduces the message just as it would a message from a dedicated fax machine—which is to say that the receiving fax machine doesn't make distinctions as to the origins of a message. Thus, when printed by the receiving fax machine, a message sent in this manner looks like any other text-only fax message.

Sending a fax message via an online service has several advantages:

- You do not have to worry about whether or not the receiving fax machine is connected, nor do you have to wait until the fax machine isn't busy.

- For those who create documents via computer, using a fax/modem service to deliver a message or document to a fax machine can save a lot of time and trouble; you don't have to print or scan the document.

- You can easily send the same message to multiple fax machines, in a fraction of the time it takes to manually send the same message.

Fax via fax/modem service is ideal for those modem-equipped computer users who primarily need to send (not receive) fax messages, and/or whose fax traffic is perhaps too small to justify investing in a dedicated fax machine.

Wireless Fax: Cellular Phone and Radio Fax Transmission

There are some products available that transmit fax via radio; however, until recent years these were intended mainly for licensed amateur radio hobbyists. Various manufacturers have marketed consumer versions of radio-fax devices, which operate in much the same manner as cellular.

(*Note*: Fax transmission via telephone lines sometimes involves transmission via radio during some stages of the transmission, especially over very long distances. Some elements of the telephone line link may involve sending the signals via microwave radio transmission rather than telephone wires [telephone company microwave relays]. Also, if one end of a fax link involves a cellular telephone, radio transmission is used. However, these elements are transparent to you, the fax user; as far as you're concerned, there is one wire connection between your machine and the fax machine with which it is communicating.)

Still another type of radio fax system comes with some personal organizers. These are generally very functional, but tend to be more costly to buy and use than cellular phones.

TELEPHONE LINES: THE FAX COMMUNICATION CHANNEL

As implied in the preceding section, there is really only one fax communications channel: the worldwide voice telephone network. (Even Group 4 fax uses a telephone network, though the ISDN required to support Group 4 technology is not yet widespread enough to make Group 4 fax competitive with Group 3 technology.)

Accessibility: The Secret of Fax's Success

No matter what you use to send or receive fax messages, the messages are carried over ordinary telephone lines (radio fax transmission excepted, of course). This is the main reason fax has become so popular; anyone who has access to telephone service has access to fax service. (Again, for the purposes of this book, microwave and other non-wire links in the telephone network are considered to be one with telephone lines.)

FAX DIMENSIONS AND LIMITATIONS

While fax is a marvelous tool, its capabilities are not unlimited. We'll take a look at just how far fax goes in the next few pages.

How Much Can You Send?

There is no limit to the quantity of information that can be sent via fax; transmission speeds may vary, based on the equipment being used and the quality of the telephone connection, but you can transfer as many pages of text and/or graphics as you wish during a fax session.

Can You Send and Receive During the Same Call?

With a few exceptions, most fax machines will only transmit or receive during a call. The current standard protocol is that the calling machine sends data, while the answering machine receives data. Some machines can be polled, which means that another fax machine can call them and request that a document be sent. Even so, once a fax link is established, the sending and receiving machines remain in their respective modes.

Certain advanced fax machines have the capability to change transmission direction during a call, thus saving the time, trouble, and potential long-distance expense involved in making a second call.

How Fast Is Fax?

The speed at which fax messages are sent is determined by the fax's modem speed. For Group 3 fax machines, this is a maximum of 9,600 data bits per second (data bits are explained in detail in Chapter 3), also referred to as bps. Group 3 fax machines can send a page in 15 to 20 seconds, depending on the page's content. If the connection between the sending and receiving fax machines is poor, the time can double or quadruple, because the fax modem will fall back to slower transmission speeds—7,200, 4,800, or 2,400 bps. (*Note*: To be considered Group 3 fax, a fax machine must be able to transmit data at a *minimum* rate of 2,400 bps.)

PC fax board modems and online services transmit translated fax messages at the same speed as dedicated fax modems.

What Kinds of Information Can Be Sent?

Anything that you write, print, paint, or photocopy on a sheet of paper of standard thickness (standard being defined as 16- or 20-pound bond paper, or standard typing paper) can be faxed.

The images created by fax machines are not unlike those of standard photocopiers (and, in fact, many fax machines use photocopier technology and double as photocopiers). Thus, you cannot transmit color images via standard fax; only black-and-white images or images with varying shades of gray can be transmitted and printed by fax printers. If you scan a color image, the colors will be transmitted and printed out in black and white or in shades of gray.

If you have to fax material from paper that is too thick or too thin for your machine's scanner, use a photocopier to copy it on to paper of an appropriate thickness.

How Much Per Page?

The physical dimensions of the paper that a fax machine can scan and print vary from one machine to another, and depend in part on the physical makeup of the fax's scanner.

PAPER SIZE LIMITATIONS

Scanners that require you to insert the paper between a platen (roller) and a scanner or between two platens will typically take paper that is 8-1/2 inches wide—the width of a standard sheet of typewriter or copier paper. Not all such machines will accommodate the full 11-inch length of standard sheet of typewriter paper, however. (Refer to your fax machine's operation manual for information on the paper size you can scan.) The maximum size of a page may vary (one popular machine will accept sheets 8.7 inches wide by 39-1/2 inches long), but machines that use sheet feeders typically accept standard 8-1/2 x 11-inch paper.

Scanners that are configured like photocopiers—i.e., you place the page to be scanned on a flat, clear glass or plastic surface under a cover—can usually scan any size paper up to the size of the surface on which you must place the paper to be scanned. However, there may be limitations on the area of a page scanned, so you should leave wide margins on the paper. Machines with either type of scanner may have minimum limits as well. If you are in doubt as to whether a fax machine's scanner can capture everything on a page, use a reducing photocopier to create a smaller version of the page.

PRINTED PAGE SIZE

The size of a printed page varies from one fax machine to another. Some dedicated fax machines can print on standard-size bond paper, but the majority use thermal paper on rolls or in sheets. The printing process is the same as with thermal calculators. No matter what the physical size of the page from which a fax message was scanned, a receiving machine will reduce it as necessary to fit its printer's paper.

Very large documents or drawings may have to be sent in several pieces. If, for example, you want to fax a certificate or drawing that is 24 inches on a side, you can copy sections of it to standard paper using a photocopier. Such documents can be reassembled by cutting and taping together the pages printed out by the receiving fax machine, as appropriate.

How Good Will It Look?

The quality of graphic images (be they letters or drawings) sent by fax — referred to as the resolution—is another element that varies from one machine to another. The resolution is in large part determined by three elements:

1. The resolution mode in use (standard or fine)
2. The quality of the sending fax machine's scanner

3. The type and quality of the receiving fax machine's printer

Fax printers of all types create an image by placing dots on paper, the locations of which are based on information generated by the sending machine's scanner. Each dot is called a *pixel* (short for "picture element"), which is the smallest possible unit of a picture.

RESOLUTION

In fax, machine resolution refers to the detail of scanned and printed images, that is, both to how closely a fax machine scans a page and to the relative density of dots in its printouts.

Resolution is measured by the number of lines printed per square inch—referred to as lines-per-inch, or *lpi*. You will also see lines-per-inch referred to as *pels* and as dots-per-inch, or *dpi*. Dots-per-inch is probably more appropriate, since this is the actual basis for measurement.

In terms of scanning, higher resolution means more points, or pixels, are seen on a page (in other words, the pixels are smaller). In terms of printing, higher resolution means that more dots are printed per square inch.

Most modern fax machines have a Standard resolution of 98 x 203 lpi and a Fine resolution of 196 x 203 lpi. You will find a few more-advanced fax machines capable of what is called Super-Fine mode, which produces a resolution of 391 x 203 lpi. In each instance the first number is horizontal and the second number is vertical. The horizontal measurement is actually the maximum number of dots in a horizontal line an inch wide (left to right). The vertical measurement can be interpreted as the number of lines or dots per vertical inch (top to bottom). Standard resolution is of a higher quality than either standard dot-matrix printers or computer monitors, but even Fine resolution does not produce as good a quality an image as a laser printer, which can produce an image of 300 x 400 dots per inch or higher. (Interestingly enough, some high-end faxes use laser printers that can not only reproduce Super-Fine resolution scans, but can also enhance the appearance of Standard and Fine resolution scans.) In contrast, the density of a standard typeset page is approximately 1,000 x 1,200 dots per inch.

When communicating with Group 2 fax machines, resolution will drop to 98 x 98 lpi. Documents and graphics sent via PC fax boards or modem/fax services are normally Fine resolution.

It's worth noting here that a low-quality or standard-resolution printer will not reproduce the resolution of an image scanned by a fine-resolution scanner; similarly, a fine-resolution printer cannot make a page scanned with a poor-quality or standard-resolution scanner look as good as the original. In other words, the quality of a printed fax message can be no better than what the fax machine's printer is capable of, and no better than the scanned image that is sent to it.

You now have a basic understanding of the methods and equipment used in facsimile communication, and the capabilities and limitations of fax. Let's examine in detail just how fax works and what's available in terms of fax features and options.

CONVENTIONAL FAX AND HOW IT WORKS

As you know, conventional facsimile transmission is accomplished in four stages:

- A document (text, graphics, photograph, etc.) is translated into binary signals by a fax machine's scanner.

- The fax machine's modem converts the binary signals to analog signals that can be transmitted via telephone line.

- The modem transmits the analog signals over a pre-established telephone connection to another fax machine, whose modem converts the signals back to binary form.

- The receiving fax machine's printer reproduces the original document and/or graphics, in effect reversing the scanning process of the sending fax machine.

Let's examine each of those steps in detail.

Scanning

A scanner is a device that converts the characters, lines, etc. on a sheet of paper or photograph into electronic signals, which are sent to the fax's modem (or temporarily stored) for transmission. When a dedicated fax machine is used, a sheet of paper containing the material to be transmitted (as previously noted, text and/or graphics) is moved past a scanning device (or vice versa).

The scanning device uses photoelectric elements (typically, photodiodes) that allow current to flow or not flow depending on whether a high or low intensity of light reaches their surface. A simple scanner sees a page as thousands of tiny points, each of which is perceived and recorded as either white or black, based on the amount of light reflected from or passed through the page at the point being scanned.

This simple two-state scanning system is used in the transmission and reproduction of faxed material, as well. (As you'll learn in a few paragraphs, more sophisticated scanning techniques are used by fax machines that can distinguish various shades of gray in addition to black and white.)

The points on a page that are scanned by the photoelectric elements are referred to as pixels and are the smallest elements of a picture. You may be familiar with the term and concept as applied to television or computer monitors.

The size of pixels—and the distance between them—is determined by the resolution capability and setting of the scanner. A Group 3 fax scanner can perceive 98 or 203 pixels in a horizontal inch, and 98, 196, or 391 pixels in a vertical inch. The number of pixels per inch is dictated by the increments in which the paper is moved past the scanner (or vice versa) and the sensitivity of the photoelectric elements in use.

The state of a pixel—either black or white—is converted to a representational electrical state in the fax machine's circuitry. As with dial-up modems, the electrical state is a binary digit, or bit. At the same time, the location of the pixel is recorded, using additional bits, creating the strings or groups of binary digits called bytes. This process of *encoding* such information about a picture element is called *digitizing*.

HOW SCANNING WORKS

Here's what happens when a page is scanned:

When the scanner moves over a dark point on the page, no current flows through the photoelectric element; this registers as a black pixel and is recorded as such in the binary data format used by the fax machine. When the scanner moves over a light point on a page, current flows through the photoelectric element and the pixel is recorded as white. Figure 5.4 is a simplified representation of the scanning process.

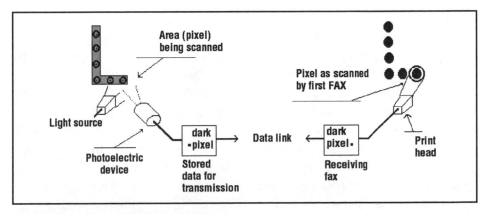

Figure 5.4 Fax scanning process

CONVENTIONAL TWO-STATE (BLACK-AND-WHITE) SCANNING

Note that, in the scanning process just discussed, only two states are perceived: white and black. Because of this, most light gray pixels register as white when scanned, and most dark gray pixels register as black. (In binary terms, a pixel is either "on" or "off.")

Just how dark a pixel must be before it registers as black can vary greatly, depending on the sensitivity of the scanner. The sensitivity of some scanners is adjustable; if you increase a scanner's sensitivity, it will perceive almost all gray areas as black—the higher the sensitivity, the lighter the pixels perceived as black can be. It's like selecting a Light Original or Darker setting on a photocopier; make the scanner more sensitive, and you get more black pixels in the scanned and transmitted image. This is also known as *contrast control*.

HALFTONE AND GRAY SCALE

More sophisticated scanning techniques are used to perceive more than two states in scanning and recording pixels by distinguishing the relative lightness or darkness of a pixel. Fax machines that can perceive varying levels of gray are said to have *halftone* or *gray-scale* capability, and their scanners can distinguish eight, 16, 32, or even 64 or more different shades (scales) of gray. Such scanners are most useful in transmitting black-and-white or color photographs, or any graphic image whose details depend on varying shades and contrast. Without halftone capability, most of the detail in such an image is lost, relegated to plain black and white.

The varying shades are perceived through the use of analog sensing by photoelectric elements. The analog sensing process makes use of photodiodes that are able to sense the relative shades and record them using the same binary data format used to record pixels as straight black or white.

Fax machines that offer halftone capability are normally switchable between standard black-and-white scanning and halftone scanning to accommodate transmissions to machines of lesser capability.

The quality of a halftone scan when it is printed out is, of course, entirely dependent on the capability of the printer on the other end, which may or may not be able to reflect varying shades of gray by using different sizes of dots in printing, or by increasing or decreasing the density of the dots. When you are sending a document and time is more important than document quality (as is often the case with text-only documents), set your fax machine to use the lowest resolution it offers. This reduces the time required to scan and transmit the document.

Data Transmission and Reception

Once the data from a scanned page has been converted from digital to analog signals, it is transmitted over a telephone line—either the public voice telephone network, or, in the case of many Group 4 fax machines and some Group 3 machines, dedicated telephone lines, or even ISDN lines.

(*Note*: Digital networks accommodate direct transfer of binary information for Group 4 fax, but these are at present extremely expensive and used only in applications where high speed and accuracy are necessary.)

A telephone link does not, by the way, consist solely of telephone wires. Electro-mechanical, electronic, and computer-switching equipment are involved, as well as microwave radio relays, transmitters, and satellite links. For the purposes of this book, however, such elements are transparent.

A modulated analog signal is carried by voice-grade telephone lines as a series of tones. The tones vary as the modulation varies. The frequency of the tones is limited to the range used by the voice telephone data network, which in turn limits the speed at which fax modems can transmit data to 9,600 bits per second.

At the receiving end of a fax transmission, incoming tones are converted to binary data in a process that is basically the reverse of the process used to modulate the carrier wave. This process is called demodulation, and it recreates the binary data that the sending fax's modem converted to analog data.

(*Note*: The majority of dedicated fax machines can either transmit or receive only during a call; they can't do both. If you dial up another fax machine and send a document, you have to disconnect and make a new connection to receive a document. However, an increasingly popular feature on more advanced fax machines called turnaround polling enables you to both send and receive documents during the same call.)

At this point, the receiving fax has in its circuitry a copy of the binary data the sending fax's scanner generated, and can either store the data or output the data to its printer.

Physical Connections

As previously indicated, a fax machine is directly connected to a telephone line. Modern fax machines have a jack (receptacle) designed to accommodate the standard telephone line connector—the RJ-11 plug. An RJ-11 jack is the plastic connector found at either end of a telephone line; one end is plugged into the telephone wall outlet, and the other end is plugged into the telephone or, in this case, the fax machine.

Because virtually all fax machines are equipped with an RJ-11 jack, your telephone line should terminate in an RJ-11 or similar plug. If the line does not have an RJ-11 plug, ask your telephone company to upgrade the telephone line. You can do this yourself, if you wish; the conversion is quite simple. Most telephone companies, as well as electronics stores such as Radio Shack and telephone specialty stores, sell kits with which you can convert any telephone line or outlet to use RJ-11 plugs and jacks. Either way, you will have to have a telephone line that terminates in an RJ-11 plug to connect a fax machine to your telephone line.

Other Modem Functions

In addition to data conversion and transmission, fax modems handle these tasks:

- Establishing and maintaining the telephone link between fax machines
- Checking data for errors

These tasks are examined in the following pages.

ESTABLISHING AND MAINTAINING A TELEPHONE LINK

Just as a fax's modem communicates data via tonal signals, it also uses tones to establish and maintain communication with another fax machine's modem. In fact, if you are using a speaker-equipped fax machine (or if you dial up a fax machine with a telephone and listen) the first thing you hear will be a high-pitched squeal. This is an identifying tone, to which a calling fax's modem must respond with a similar tone before a communications link is established. Carrier tones are a bit quieter.

Fax modems perform the housekeeping chores of transmitting a tone that turns off transponders (special kinds of signal boosters) used on telephone circuits to eliminate data alteration, and of keeping the communications link open by generating an empty carrier wave when data is not being sent. If no carrier wave is present, a modem will quickly drop a connection (or disconnect).

More intelligent fax machines not only handle initiating and maintaining the communications link, but also dial phone numbers. This feature, called autodialing, is becoming more and more common, even on low-end fax machines. Some will even dial numbers and send documents at preset times, unattended. This feature works best if the fax machine has a memory in which a document can be stored beforehand.

ERROR CHECKING

A relatively recent innovation in fax is error checking. Dubbed Error Correction Mode, or ECM, this is an optional feature whose operation has been standardized by the CCITT so that fax machines made by different manufacturers can use it. With ECM, each page is automatically checked for errors. The receiving fax machine communicates information about the data it has received to the sending machine, which checks the information against its own information. If an error is corrected, the page is sent again.

Printing Faxed Documents

After a signal is received and converted from analog back to digital format, it is sent to the fax's printer (or, with some machines, stored in memory for later printout). The printer reproduces the pattern of dots recorded by the sending fax's scanner as closely as possible by printing arrays of dots on paper. This is to say that the pattern and density of dots printed reflects the pattern and density of the dots as seen by the sending machine's scanner.

The resolution and detail of the printout is, of course, entirely dependent on the capability of the receiving fax's printer. If, as mentioned earlier, a halftone scan is transmitted to a fax whose printer cannot reproduce the varying shades of gray in a halftone, the quality will be about the same as a standard scan. If a 196 x 203 lpi scan is transmitted to a fax whose printer is capable of 98 x 203 lpi output, then the image will be printed in 98 x 203 lpi resolution.

How the dots are placed on the paper varies, depending on the type of printer used. There are four types of printers used by fax machines; these will be discussed in the following section.

CONVENTIONAL FAX: HARDWARE FEATURES AND OPTIONS

The range and variety of features available on dedicated fax machines are almost endless (and some are useless). However, there are a number of basic and advanced features with which you should be familiar. Whether the features discussed in the following pages are standard or optional (or even available) with a specific fax machine is entirely up to the specific machine's manufacturer.

Telephone-Related Features

How a dedicated fax makes use of and interacts with the telephone system is important. Certain telephone-related features can make using fax easier and less time-consuming, and some are vital for frequent fax users.

AUTO ANSWER

The ability to answer an incoming call is vital and almost omnipresent with modern fax machines. An auto-answer fax machine typically answers the phone on the first or second ring, then emits the characteristic high-pitched identifying tone, after which a communication link is established if it is another fax machine that is calling. You should be able to disable this feature.

AUTODIAL

As explained earlier, autodial is the ability of a fax machine to dial telephone numbers on its own, without the aid of a telephone set. This feature is an invaluable convenience; without it, you have to connect a telephone set to the fax machine. Fax machines with autodial capability have a numeric keyboard used to dial numbers, similar in appearance to the layout of buttons on a push-button telephone.

DIALING FEATURES

In addition to autodialing capability, more sophisticated fax machines offer many of the same features as advanced office telephones, such as tone/pulse dialing, memory dialing, and additional features described below.

AUTOMATIC CALLBACK

Single-key automatic callback is usually included with faxes that offer memory dialing. This feature redials the most recently dialed number, whether it is dialed direct or from memory.

REPEAT DIALING

This is another feature that may accompany memory dialing and is a sub-feature of automatic callback. If a number is dialed and is busy, a fax machine with this feature will wait a specified amount of time, then try the number again. It will repeat this process a specified number of times or until a connection is made.

Back-Up Number Dialing

This feature is one for high-volume fax usage. If a number is dialed and is busy, a fax machine with back-up number dialing will dial a designated back-up number. This feature is useful when you need to send a document to someone who has two or more fax machines that are frequently in use.

Other Dialing Features

Some nice extras that may or may not be included on a fax machine equipped with memory dialing include an LED or liquid-crystal display that shows the number being dialed and/or a name associated with it, and the ability to search for and dial numbers based on the entry of a letter or two (or a number that represents a letter).

If you intend to use a fax machine in an office with a PBX system, you'll want to be sure it has pause capability, that is, the ability to pause between digits when dialing a number. Most PBX systems require that you dial a number (such as 9) before you can call out, and you usually have to wait a second or two before you get a dial tone. Thus, you must be able to direct an autodial machine to pause as necessary.

Out Telephone Jacks

A telephone jack (a receptacle into which you can plug an outgoing telephone line to connect to a telephone set) enables you to use a single telephone line for either fax or voice telephone communications without having to disconnect the fax machine. Even if you have a dedicated fax line, you should still have this option; sooner or later you'll want to use it. You should, of course, be able to disable the fax machine's auto-answer feature, or toggle a switch from "fax" to "telephone" to accommodate the use of a voice telephone.

This feature can also be used to share a phone line with a modem—a not-uncommon situation when you already have either a modem or a fax machine on a dedicated line and want to add the other communications device.

Voice/Data Switching

If your auto-answer fax machine shares a line with a voice telephone (whether the phone is plugged into a phone jack on the fax or on an extension), voice callers will be rudely greeted by the fax's answering squeal—and will probably hang up before you can disable the fax and answer the phone—unless you disable the fax machine. This can be done by turning the fax off, or by manual or automatic voice/data switching.

Manual voice/data switching is accomplished via a toggle switch or setting on the fax machine. Set it to "fax," and the fax's modem will answer when someone calls; set it to "voice," and the phone will ring until you answer it or until the calling party hangs up.

Many upper-end fax machines handle voice/data switching automatically.

Voice Telephone Function

Many fax machines combine a telephone set with a fax machine. Having this combination is advantageous when you must share a telephone line between a fax and a voice telephone, because it combines both into one compact unit, and you don't have to worry with extra connections.

Some machines limit this feature to using the fax machine as a telephone or a fax; on more advanced machines, you can interrupt a fax transmission to talk with the party on the other end of the connection, then resume fax communication. (The other fax machine must, of course, have the same capability.)

Scanner Features

The most important feature on a scanner is its maximum level of resolution. Transmitting graphic-rich or even text-only documents will sometimes require as much detailing as possible. In addition to resolution, halftone capability, contrast control, how the scanner physically handles pages, and page reduction and enlargement are important features to consider in a scanner.

Halftone Capability

As explained earlier, a scanner with halftone (or gray scale) capability can distinguish more than two image states. That is, instead of just perceiving black and white pixels, a scanner with halftone capability perceives and records up to 64 shades of gray.

If you intend to fax copies of black-and-white photos, color artwork or photos, and/or shaded line art of any type, you should buy a fax machine with halftone capability. Remember, however, that halftone transmissions to fax machines that do not have halftone capability will not be of the best quality. (*Note*: Fax machines that have scanners with halftone capability also have printers with halftone capability.)

Contrast Control

As with photocopies, faxed images are often reproduced darker than the original, which destroys some of the detail. Contrast control lets you decrease or increase the sensitivity of a scanner's photoelectric sensing elements. This means you can remove some darkened areas from a dark image to increase its clarity (select greater contrast) or darken the lines in a light image (select lesser contrast).

PAGE HANDLING

How a fax machine handles pages to be scanned is very important because the physical configuration of a scanner can both limit and enhance the usefulness of your fax machine, depending on your applications. There are two common physical configurations for scanners: *sheet* and *flatbed*.

SHEET SCANNERS

The sheet scanner configuration is the most common among low- and medium-priced fax machines. This configuration uses a roller or rollers (platens) to move pages to be scanned past the scanner. Sheet scanners usually require you to manually insert the pages of a document, although some have automatic document feeders that will accept several standard (8-1/2 x 11-inch) pages stacked in a tray and move them through the scanner themselves.

The maximum size page that a sheet scanner accepts is usually standard or legal size. However, some will accept standard-width pages that are up to 39 inches in length. (Sheets of this size require manual insertion).

FLATBED SCANNERS

Flatbed scanners are used almost exclusively with higher-priced fax machines. The flatbed consists of a flat sheet of glass on which pages to be scanned are placed. This configuration is the same as that of most photocopiers and may also include an automatic sheet feeder of the type used by many photocopiers.

The maximum size page that a flatbed scanner can scan is limited by the size of the glass; in addition, most flatbed scanners will not scan the entire width and length of the glass area. So, in addition to making the usual allowances for the possibility of unscanned margins (i.e., allow for a half inch of unscanned space all the way around), you will have to follow the manufacturer's instructions as to the maximum size page that can be scanned. Document feeders are an option with most flatbed scanners and are standard for some. If your fax traffic volume is high, it's best to have a document feeder in any case.

PAGE REDUCTION

As noted earlier, all fax machines reduce the size of a received image, if necessary, to fit the size of paper they use. However, there are some situations in which it may be useful to reduce the size of a page before it is transmitted, for instance, when you want to fax a large spreadsheet. Some flatbed scanners have an option that enables them to scan a larger area than they normally would, and proportionally reduce the size of the material on the page.

PAGE ENLARGEMENT

Some documents can benefit from being enlarged, in particular, extremely detailed line art. Some scanners (both flatbed and sheet) can enlarge a drawing by a set or a specified percentage in much the same manner as an enlarging photocopier enlarges copies.

Modem Features

Group 3 fax modems offer four options: speed, the absence or presence of error checking, automatic fallback, and compatibility with Group 1 or Group 2 fax machines.

Printers

Until the 1980s, most fax machines used thermal printers. This was primarily because this was the only truly cost-effective means of printing graphics. (Other kinds of output—including video—might have been used, but the cost of fax machines was already as much as the market would bear.) Thanks to the development of relatively low-cost, high-quality printing technologies for personal computers, however, there are several options available to the fax buyer in terms of printed output.

PRINTER TYPES

There are five basic types of printers available with fax machines: thermal, electrostatic, dot-matrix, ink-jet, and laser.

THERMAL PRINTERS

You are probably familiar with thermal printers from using inkless printing calculators or early computer printers. Thermal printers print characters and images on heat-sensitive paper. The paper is called, appropriately enough, thermal paper.

An array of electrically charged wires (or, sometimes, one wire) is used to place miniscule dots on the thermal paper in locations corresponding to pixel locations in a transmitted image. When a dark pixel occurs, the print head is charged at the appropriate location on the paper. This generates heat and darkens the area of the paper adjacent to the wire.

Thermal printers offer several advantages. Thermal printing is a fast and virtually soundless process. You don't have to worry about running out of ink, toner fluid, or ribbon because thermal printers use none of these. Some thermal printers use single sheets, but many use paper that comes on a roll and feeds through the machine on its own, which means you don't have to keep a constant watch on an incoming document. There are few moving parts to break down or wear out, and, finally, a thermal printer is the least-expensive kind of printer to have.

On the negative side, thermal paper is somewhat more expensive than normal paper, and it tends to deteriorate after a time. If exposed to direct or indirect heat—even sunlight on a hot day—thermal paper darkens, which means you can lose a valuable document (or lose your stock of blank thermal paper) if you don't handle it with care. Many thermal printers use a narrow roll paper that, combined with relatively low resolution, makes for a nonprofessional appearance. You have to cut continuous roll thermal paper (or add a paper cutter to your fax machine) if you prefer to have the pages of your documents in individual sheets. Single-sheet thermal paper doesn't have to be cut, but it must be fed into the machine manually unless you add a sheet feeder.

ELECTROSTATIC PRINTERS

The electrostatic printing process is the same used by photocopiers to place images on specially coated or regular bond paper. A black pigment (toner fluid or powder) is attracted and bonded to the paper whenever an electrical charge is generated by the printer's print head. The print head is so activated wherever a pixel occurs, attracting the fluid or powder to the paper at that point, printing a dot on the paper. (The image is later fixed by fusing the pigment to the paper with a small amount of heat.)

DOT-MATRIX PRINTERS

Dot-matrix printers used with fax machines operate in the same manner as the once-ubiquitous dot-matrix computer printers. The tips of fine wires in the print head are driven against a ribbon, on the other side of which is a sheet of paper. Each time a wire impacts the ribbon, a dot is placed on the paper. Each wire is, in effect, an electromagnet's core and is activated when electrical current is passed through the wire surrounding it. A wire is activated whenever it is in a location where a pixel occurs. (Because the wire actually strikes the ribbon, this kind of printer is more properly known as an impact printer.)

Ink-Jet Printers

A variation on impact dot-matrix printers is the ink-jet printer. Ink-jet printers place dots on paper using jets of ink activated by current flow, a process that is quieter and faster than impact printing. Like impact dot-matrix printers, ink-jet printers can use almost any kind of paper, but the ink supply must be replenished periodically. The output is far superior to dot matrix, near the quality of laser printers.

Laser Printers

The laser printing process, originally developed for use with computers, has been adapted for use with photocopiers and fax machines. Laser printing uses a process similar to that used by electrostatic printers, but augmented by the use of a tiny laser beam to create the necessary electrostatic charge. The laser beam speeds up the printing process and, more importantly, creates more sharply focused images for higher resolution.

Laser printers provide the best of all possible worlds where printing is concerned. They use standard paper, they are fast, they use inexpensive pigments, and they are silent. And, best of all, they produce the highest resolution of any fax printing process.

Printer-Related Features

The major printer enhancements and options available for fax machines are paper cutters, sheet feeders, and document feeders. Fax machines that can store documents in memory typically store them automatically if paper runs out.

Copier Function

Many fax machines can be used as photocopiers. It's a simple enough option to implement—merely a matter of sending a scanned document directly to the fax's printer rather than to the modem. Depending on the kind of printer used by the fax, the quality of the copy may not be the best.

Document Storage (Memory)

One of the most pragmatically useful fax options is the ability to store incoming or outgoing documents in memory. This feature, used alone or in conjunction with other features, enhances a fax machine's ability to operate unattended.

Being able to store scanned documents in memory (rather than transmitting them as the pages are scanned) means you can scan a document now and send it later. Finally, being able to store a document in memory makes it very easy to broadcast the document to more than one fax machine.

Scheduled Transmission and Other Programmable Features

Fax machines that feature document storage in memory may also offer options that make use of memory—specifically, memory that you can program to send documents when and where you wish, unattended.

SCHEDULED/DELAYED TRANSMISSIONS

The most useful (and used) programmable fax feature is scheduling document transmissions. Scan a document into a memory-equipped machine, program it to dial up and transmit the document at a specific time (or after a certain period of time has passed), and you can enjoy the ultimate in unattended fax operation.

BROADCAST FAX

A silly, pretentious, and confusing misnomer, broadcast fax is nothing more than calling and delivering the same message to one fax machine after another. (In the true sense of the word, "broadcast" implies simultaneous delivery.) To broadcast, a fax must have enough memory to store all the numbers to be dialed and the ability to be programmed to dial them in sequence, then automatically transmit the document in its memory.

POLLING

Polling is the ability of one fax machine to dial up another machine and request that a document stored in the called fax's memory be sent to it. (This is the reverse of conventional fax communication in which the calling machine always sends.) In most cases, the machine to be called must be set up to send a document when called.

TURNAROUND POLLING

As has already been established, each machine in a conventional fax communication is assigned a role: The calling machine sends a document, while the machine being called receives the document. However, a fax machine with turnaround polling capability can reverse roles during a call and receive a document after sending one.

STORE-AND-FORWARD

Store-and-forward is a sophisticated feature that "turns around" a received document and transmits it to another fax machine. Store-and-forward requires document memory storage capability, of course, and may be used in conjunction with scheduled transmissions, automatic redialing, back-up number dialing, and broadcast.

Support and Miscellaneous Functions

More sophisticated fax machines, typically those with memory and programming functions, offer a variety of functions that support fax management and record keeping, and/or provide other convenient information.

TRANSACTION JOURNAL/ACTIVITY REPORT

An important support feature for high-volume fax operations is the ability to generate records of transactions, or fax calls and other activities. A typical transaction report (shown in Figure 5.5) is generated by pressing a button on the fax machine and consists of detailed information on recent incoming and outgoing calls.

```
*  COMMUNICATIONS REPORT  *     AS OF  AUG 23 '00  16:42  PAGE 01
                                       PRODUCT MANAGEMENT

      TOTAL PAGES                      TOTAL TIME

      SEND      : 0001                 SEND      :  00:00:22
      RECEIVE   : 0002                 RECEIVE   :  00:00:42

         DATE   TIME  TO/FROM          MODE  MIN/SEC PGS CMD# STATUS
      01 8/23   16:29 PITNEY BOWES     UP--R 00:42   02           OK
      02 8/23   16:39 EQUIP CONTROL    UP--S 00:22   01           OK
```

Figure 5.5   Fax transaction report

SECURITY FEATURES

With fax technology handling an ever-increasing percentage of business, government, professional, and personal communications, the security of fax messages both incoming and outgoing has become a subject of concern. Thus, many medium- and higher-priced fax machines offer security features such as these:

■ Requiring certain recognition codes before sending a document to a fax that calls and polls for document transmission

■ Encrypting data during transmission

■ Requiring password entry via a numeric keyboard before stored documents can be printed (or, before the fax machine can be used at all)

The first two features normally require that the two machines involved use the same code-exchange or encryption protocols, which usually means that they must be made by the same manufacturer.

Automatic Cover Sheets and Document Headers

Many high-end fax machines can transmit information about a document along with the document in the form of a cover sheet (separate from and preceding the document itself), which contains information pertaining to the source and intended recipient of the document. Some also generate document headers that contain the date and time the document was received, a running title, and a page number, as well as internal reference numbers.

Self-Testing

The ability to perform a self-test is a handy feature because it provides a quick way to determine whether a transmission or printing problem is the result of a problem with your machine, the fault of the machine with which you are communicating, or a poor connection. Self-testing can eliminate downtime and money wasted on needless service calls.

Information Display

A frequently seen feature on high-end fax machines is a digital display, which is used to display information such as the date and time. Such displays may provide several lines of information, and in addition to the date and time, may provide information on the operating status of the fax machine, including the telephone number being dialed, whether the machine is sending or receiving, programming and memory data, and other information.

Serial Port

A relatively rare feature on fax machines is a serial port. This is a standard RS-232C connection that can be used to connect a fax machine to other devices capable of serial communication, including dial-up modems and computers. A fax machine that is equipped with a serial port can be used to communicate with dial-up modem services or as a printer for a computer.

PC Fax Boards

A PC fax board is a computer communications device designed to send and receive fax documents. A PC fax board works in conjunction with special software to convert computer-generated text and graphics into the format used by dedicated fax, and to convert fax transmissions it receives into the format its host computer uses.

PC fax boards are internal devices, which means they are installed inside a personal computer's housing. In appearance, a PC fax board is similar to other internal devices (disk drive controllers, internal modems, etc.). A typical PC fax board consists of a printed circuit board that is stuffed with microprocessors and other components required to do its task.

To communicate with dedicated fax machines, a PC fax board must use a fax-type modem, which is built into the PC fax board. The PC fax board's main external connection (i.e., connection with a device other than the host computer itself) is a telephone line jack—an RJ-11 jack into which you can plug a telephone line. Other external connections may or may not be present, but the telephone line jack is present on every PC fax board, since fax communication is via telephone lines.

How a PC Fax Board Works

A PC fax board's primary jobs are as follows:

■ Converting data stored in its host computer's memory or in a disk file to the format used by fax machines

■ Converting incoming fax transmissions to the format used by its host computer

■ Establishing communications links with fax machines, or with other PC fax board-equipped computers

■ Sending and receiving documents in fax format

■ Printing and/or storing faxed documents

Data Sources and Conversion

The source of a document to be sent via a PC fax board can be a disk file, an area of the computer's memory in which text or graphics are being created, or, with PC fax boards that will transmit the contents of the computer's screen, the computer's screen memory. If an optical scanner is being used to scan a paper document, some PC fax boards use the scanner's data directly.

(Scanner data is usually handled by storing it in a file, then reading and sending the file contents.)

No matter what the source of the document, PC fax boards accomplish data conversion in a manner that is different from conventional fax machines. (Data conversion when an optical scanner is used is another matter and will be discussed later.) Rather than scanning a physical page and converting the pixels perceived into electronic signals that represent the pixels' locations and states, a PC fax board and its software must read and interpret binary computer data. It must then convert the data into a reasonable facsimile of what the same data would look like if it were printed out and scanned by a dedicated fax scanner.

How PC Fax Converts Data

Obviously, the task faced by a PC fax board when sending a file is to convert the bytes that represent computer characters into groups of binary digits (1s and 0s) that represent these characters—and their relative locations—in a dot-by-dot, or pixel, format.

The conversion and encoding is accomplished in the computer's memory and/or in temporary disk files, with the PC fax board's circuitry and its attendant software working together to perform the conversion. Such a conversion involves a process that is, in effect, scanning the textual and graphic elements of the file, and arbitrarily assigning pixels to create the equivalent of the image as it would appear when printed. The pixel types and locations are stored in a reasonable facsimile of the binary format created by fax scanners.

Special Note on Converting Fax Text Images to ASCII Characters

Almost without exception, PC fax boards use a timesaving shortcut and automatically store an incoming document as a graphic image—even if it contains only text. This is fine if all you need to do is view or print out the document. However, if you want to access the text with a word processor or other text-based program, you'll have to use special software to scan the graphic image of the text and convert it to a true text file using the proper ASCII equivalents of the characters in the file.

The software you'll need is called optical character recognition (OCR) software. OCR programs scan the graphic image of the characters in a fax document and convert them into standard ASCII characters. Some PC fax boards include OCR software, and some don't. Either way, you should have OCR software if you're using a PC fax board because you'll have a use for it sooner or later.

This software is built into or included with some PC fax boards, providing optional or automatic conversion of text in fax documents.

Note that OCR software is far from perfect in its ability to translate, and a file created by OCR software generally requires extensive manual editing.

ESTABLISHING AND MAINTAINING COMMUNICATIONS LINKS

PC fax board modems handle communications in the same manner as dedicated fax machine modems. The only difference is that all PC fax boards have autodial and auto-answer capabilities, in addition to any other dialing/telephone options they may sport.

DATA TRANSMISSION AND RECEPTION

PC fax board modems basically operate in the same manner as dedicated fax modems (explained in detail earlier in this chapter). When sending a document, the modem varies a carrier wave on a telephone line in a pattern that imitates the pattern of the binary data composing a stored document. When receiving a document, the modem recreates binary data based on the analog patterns it receives via the telephone line.

PRINTING AND STORING INCOMING FAX DOCUMENTS

When a PC fax board receives a fax document, it can be handled in any of several ways:

- The document may be routed directly to the printer, as a graphics image, or as text (provided the board has performed the necessary OCR conversion first).
- The document may be displayed on-screen.
- A file may be created to store the document for later printing and/or OCR or graphics conversion.

PC Fax Boards and Scanners

As implied earlier, documents that you wish to fax via PC fax board and computer don't have to be computer generated; with the addition of an optical scanner, you can input text and graphics into your computer for storage in memory or on disk. Then the document can be handled just like computer-generated text and graphics.

With some PC fax boards you can route scanner input directly through a modem to a receiving fax. With others, scanning is a separate operation, and scanned images are stored in a file, which can then be transmitted like any other file.

Note that most optical scanners offer a maximum resolution (300 to 400 dpi) that is far beyond the capabilities of current Group 3 fax machines, so some of the detail of scanned documents that may be visible on a computer screen or when printed out will be lost.

(Interestingly enough, it is possible to use a dedicated fax machine that is equipped with an RS-232C port as a scanner for a computer. All you have to do is connect the fax machine to the computer's serial port, direct the fax machine's output to the RS-232C port, and scan a document. Appropriate scanner and/or OCR software is required.)

DIRECT TRANSMISSION OF SCANNER INPUT

If you have no reason to retain a computer file version of a document scanned with a computer scanner, having to store it on disk before you can transmit it is a somewhat useless step. You can eliminate this step and save time with a PC fax board that will transmit a document as you scan it.

PC Fax Board Features and Options

PC fax boards offer many of the same features and options as dedicated fax machines, as well as a few that are unique. PC fax board features that are counterparts of dedicated fax features include modem and dialing/calling options, speed, error checking, automatic speed fallback, polling, number storage, phone lists, distribution lists, broadcast transmission, scheduled transmission, store-and-forward, automatic cover sheets, document headers, transaction/activity reports, and additional phone-related features.

Scanner and transmission features and options, as well as those for printing, are of course wider in range because you can attach any of dozens of scanners and printers to a PC. Resolution of documents and how halftone (gray-scale) documents are created are likewise of greater potential.

SOFTWARE

A few PC fax boards are not accompanied by the software necessary to operate them. The software is in some cases supplied by the PC fax board manufacturer, sold as a separate item, or (rarely) offered by a third party.

GRAPHIC FORMAT CONVERSION

If you use graphics programs to create fax images to send, or if you wish to incorporate fax images in graphics created with such programs, you'll find graphics conversion an important option. Graphics conversion is necessary because, in the MS-DOS world in particular, PC fax boards usually use their own proprietary methods to store fax documents on disk.

SCREEN PRINT SEND

If you want to send a number of brief messages by fax, or send specific screen displays, being able to transmit the contents of the computer screen is an extremely useful option. This is faster than creating a document, saving it to disk, then transmitting it from disk because you eliminate the save-to-disk operation, and because scanning and converting on-screen text is much faster than scanning and converting a disk file.

PRINTER OUTPUT TO FAX

This option is similar to a screen print, except that it intercepts text and/or graphics that a program is sending to the printer, then sends the file as a fax document.

BACKGROUND OPERATION

Some PC fax boards and their software offer a background operation option. This is extremely useful when you have to fax a large file or a large number of files to one or more faxes. Set up transmission parameters—file(s) to be transferred and the number(s) to call—exit the PC fax program, and you're free to use your computer for other things.

TEXT EDITOR

Among the more useful options offered by PC fax boards is a text editor. A PC fax board text editor is a simplified word processor that you can use to create text-only documents for immediate fax transmission. This is especially useful for those users whose fax applications require a lot of communication via short memos. With this option, you can create a message and send it right away, without having to go through the process of storing and reading it.

ON-SCREEN DOCUMENT DISPLAY

PC fax boards will display a document on-screen in lieu of printing it, which is useful for previewing purposes. Various enhancements to on-screen display include scrolling, color changing, rotating, zooming (focusing on and enlarging one element of a drawing), and extracting a portion of a document to a separate file. An interesting option that's not always included among a PC fax board's features is the ability to display incoming fax documents on-screen in real time (i.e., as it's received).

DIAL-UP TELECOM MODEM

A few PC fax boards combine the best of both worlds in telecommunications by including a standard dial-up modem. This offers some cost advantage over buying both a PC fax board and a modem, although you won't normally be able to use both at once unless you have a separate telephone line for each device.

CUSTOM FONTS

Because text in fax documents is really graphics, a PC fax board can be set up to display and print text in almost any form.

ON-SCREEN HELP

Following the lead of high-end modems, some PC fax boards offer "online" help—abbreviated explanations of specific operations that are called up when a certain key combination is issued, or via menu selection.

SECURITY FEATURES

PC fax boards offer varying levels and kinds of security. Some PC fax board software programs can be set up to require a password before allowing access to their functions. Data encryption may also be offered.

PC FAX BOARD OR DEDICATED FAX MACHINE?

If you have a computer, you may be wondering, even after reading the preceding, whether a PC fax board is for you. The answer to that question depends on your applications and on the options included with the PC fax board and software you select.

In general, if you have a lot of computer-generated documents to fax, you can benefit from using a PC fax board. However, there are some obvious and not-too-obvious limitations and advantages to using a PC fax board.

PC Fax Board Limitations

In case you missed the stated and implied (and potential) limitations of PC fax boards earlier, here's a roundup:

■ Like dedicated fax machines, not all PC fax boards can communicate at the maximum Group 3 transmission speed. Many lower-priced PC fax boards cannot.

■ Some PC fax boards have an upper limit on the number of pages that can be transmitted as one document. This may be anywhere between 300 and 999 pages.

■ Unless you have an optical scanner (a separate item), you cannot scan and send hard-copy documents via a PC fax board. Alone, PC fax boards are capable of sending only the contents of a computer's memory (working RAM or screen memory) or disk files.

■ Since PC fax boards commonly receive, recognize, and store all elements of an incoming fax document as graphics, you may need to add an OCR software package to your system to convert the text in fax messages into ASCII characters.

■ You will need quite a bit of hard-disk capacity to accommodate incoming and outgoing documents. Even short documents can be several megabytes in size.

■ Your computer may be tied up whenever you want to send or receive fax messages.

■ PC fax boards and their software are not compatible with all software.

PC Fax Board Advantages

PC fax boards offer several potential advantages over dedicated fax machines:

■ With a PC fax board, you can transmit computer-generated text and graphics without having to print them out first, and at the best possible resolution.

■ PC fax board-equipped computers provide automatic document storage in memory.

■ You can merge text and/or graphics from faxed documents into word processing, desktop publishing, or graphics files for later printout or transfer. To do the same thing with fax documents received via a dedicated fax machine, you would have to scan a printed-out document, perhaps losing some data or resolution in the process.

■ A PC fax board that can operate in background gives you the best of both worlds: fully automated two-way fax communication and the use of your computer for other tasks.

CHAPTER 6

File Transfers

The idea of sending a file over telephone lines may be a bit intimidating at first. What, you may ask yourself, if something goes wrong? What do I need to know? Does file transfer involve complex procedures? In partial answer to those questions, consider this: Modem file transfers are today as common as long-distance voice telephone calls. Millions of executable programs, database and spreadsheet files, and documents of all types flow over telephone lines 24 hours a day, seven days a week. The vast majority of these transfers goes through without a hitch, and many of them are conducted by people who have less technical knowledge than you do.

This is not to say that file transfer is strictly a "plug-and-go" proposition. Knowledge of certain terms and concepts is helpful and often necessary. And, as with other elements of telecomputing, it helps to have behind-the-scenes knowledge, which brings us to the purpose of this chapter: to show you what file transfer is all about. Here, you will learn the terminology, techniques, and technical ins and outs of modem file transfer.

(*Note*: Chapter 3 contains important background information having to do with topics discussed in this chapter. So, to better understand file transfers and file-transfer protocols, read Chapter 3 now if you haven't already.)

WHAT'S IN IT FOR YOU?

File transfers offer many benefits. Sending a file via telephone lines is, for instance, faster than any same-day delivery service could ever hope to be. Where text files are involved, computer-to-computer transfer eliminates computer incompatibility problems. And in particular, file transfer offers these features:

- Convenience—Send and receive files when it fits your schedule.

- Independence from having to use a specific word-processing or other data-creation program. File transfer capability means you can create documents off-line with the word processor of your choice. You can then transfer the document in the word processor's format if you wish, without converting it to seven-bit ASCII.

- Access—Literally thousands of programs and information files that might otherwise be difficult or impossible to obtain are available on the Internet.

FILE TRANSFER BASICS

Simply defined, file transfer is the process of sending a file (text, binary data, or program) from one computer to another. The computers may be mainframe or minicomputers and/or personal computers.

Regardless of the file or computers involved, the basic steps are fairly simple. The sending computer's hardware and software read a file's contents. As it reads the file, the computer sends what it reads to its modem, which converts the data to analog form and transmits it to the receiving system via telephone lines. (Null-modem transfers, covered later, do not use a modem.)

The receiving modem converts the data back to digital form and sends it to its computer. The receiving computer reads the data and stores it in a buffer or file. Note that what is actually sent is a copy of a file; the file on the sending end remains intact.

Depending on the transfer method, the sending and receiving systems may check for transmission errors and may or may not alter file content before sending so as to reduce the number of bits transmitted.

From the hardware viewpoint, the transmission takes place in pretty much the same way as keyboard input is transmitted. Serial ports and modems may handle flow control and error checking differently, however.

On the software end, both the sending and the receiving system require commands to initiate transfer. Online systems often use special software file-transfer protocols to handle data flow and error checking during transfer.

Uploads and Downloads

In case you missed it earlier, a file transfer can take place in either of two directions—to your computer or from it. The terms that describe file transfers refer to the direction in which data is moving and are relative. When sending data to another computer, you are *uploading*. When receiving data, you are *downloading*.

FILE TRANSFER METHODS

ASCII Transfer and Error-Checking Protocols

The two basic file-transfer categories are *ASCII transfer* and what are called *binary* or *error-checking protocol transfers*. ASCII transfer is the transfer of seven-bit ASCII files. Error-checking protocols transfer files in groups of bytes, can transfer data containing eight-bit or binary characters, and use sophisticated error-checking routines to verify the integrity of each group sent.

Batch File Transfers

Only one file can be transferred at a time between asynchronous dial-up systems. If you want to transfer more than one file, you have to issue new commands for each. However, some binary file-transfer protocols, such as Kermit and Zmodem, as well as proprietary file transfers used by online service front ends and various browsers, let you specify a group (or batch) of files for transfer. Afterward the program takes over and handles the commands, transfer, and storage operations for each file. (This includes providing the file names for the receiving system.)

This kind of operation is known as *batch processing*, or *batch-file transfer*. Batch-file transfers are especially convenient when you have to upload or download several files, but can't be at your computer to direct and supervise the transfers.

File Transfer Channels

There are two possible channels for file transfer. The first is *direct* (or sender-to-receiver) file transfer. In direct transfer, the individuals who wish to transfer a file or files connect their computers. The second channel is *store-and-forward*, or what I call *third-party transfer*. Here, an online system serves as an intermediary mover and storage place for files transferred between two other computers. This third party may be a server tied into the Internet, an online service, or even a BBS. We'll take a closer look at these channels in the final segment of this chapter.

ASCII File Transfer

For most computer users, the simplest file transfer is an ASCII transfer. Limited in a practical sense to files that contain only seven-bit ASCII characters, it is commonly used to transfer small- and medium-sized straight text files. (The term "seven-bit ASCII characters" here refers to the letters, numbers, space, punctuation, and other symbols found on most keyboards.)

You can sometimes use ASCII transfer with binary files if they are output as text in the form of hexadecimal numbers, or, as is the case with some BASIC programs, in straight ASCII text. However, this method is accommodated by few systems and is very tricky. Whether you can do this depends in part on the kind of computer you use. (Binary files of some types can be converted to seven-bit ASCII for transmission, too. They must be reconverted—off-line—before use at the receiving end, however.)

Eight-bit ASCII transfer is possible, too, provided both systems are set up for eight-bit communication, but the applications for eight-bit transfer are limited. Many communications programs offer the option of stripping, or removing, the eighth bit from bytes in eight-bit files, thus enabling you to transfer eight-bit text files in seven-bit (and human-readable) form.

MIME and Other Seven-Bit Transfer Methods for ASCII Files

MIME is a technique of tokenizing eight-bit characters with seven-bit characters so that it is possible to transmit a file that has eight-bit characters as a file of all seven-bit characters. One or more seven-bit characters are substituted for each eight-bit character in a file (i.e., each character on the ASCII table from 128 through 256). Substitutions are made in a specific pattern, which enables such a file to be reconstituted as an eight-bit file by a program with this capability.

Most browsers and some utility programs recognize MIME and similar file formats, and can convert seven-bit MIME files back to eight-bit or binary files.

How ASCII File Transfer Works

When a file is transmitted using ASCII protocol, it is read from a computer's disk or memory and is sent character by character. This is the same way it would be sent if you were typing it at your keyboard. The transmission rate is much faster than you can type, though (unless you are a very fast typist and comparing yourself to 300 bps transmission!). When received, the file is handled just like any other input destined for storage. It is sent to the computer's buffer, then written to the disk.

Data Buffering and Flow Control

Almost all computer systems use data buffering, which means that incoming or outgoing data is temporarily stored in what is called a buffer. Data buffering speeds up file transfer by reducing the number of disk accesses.

At the sending end of a file transfer, enough data is read from the disk to fill a RAM buffer, and is then sent to the serial port. When the send buffer is empty, the disk is read again. Because the buffer holds enough data for several seconds of transmission, there are fewer pauses for disk access. The sending computer doesn't have to stop to read its disk each time it sends a line.

The reverse occurs at the receiving end. Data is written to disk only when the buffer is filled. The flow of incoming data is paused when this occurs, usually controlled by XON/XOFF (^Q/^S) protocol. Under this protocol, a system pauses its transmission when it receives a CTRL-S (ASCII), and resumes transmission when it receives a CTRL-Q (ASCII).

Additional *flow control* may consist of *turnaround characters* or *time delays*, or hardware (modem or serial port) control.

Flow Control

Although any system you connect with will communicate at the same speed as your system, data flow control is still necessary. Data must be paused and restarted periodically so the receiving computer can store it on disk or in memory, or output it to a peripheral like a printer. In any event, the receiving computer may need to move data from its incoming buffer as the buffer fills. (Without flow control, the buffer would overflow and lose data.) The sending system also requires starts and pauses to accommodate disk access. The receiving and sending system can be either your computer or the remote system; for the purposes of this discussion, it is your system.

Buffering and flow control are necessary because the data transfer rate between computer and printer or computer and disk differs from the bps rate between computers.

Flow control is handled by serial ports or by software. Software flow control uses what is called XON/XOFF. This involves sending a ^S (ASCII character 19 or DC3) to pause the data flow and a ^Q (ASCII character 17, or DC1) to restart it.

In practice, a program sends ^S to pause data whenever its capture buffer is full and waits to send a ^Q until data in the buffer has been written to disk or sent to the printer. Once the capture buffer is clear, the program sends ^Q to tell the sending computer to restart data transmission.

Being able to turn off software flow control can be a useful feature. For instance, if you are downloading a binary file using Xmodem at 2,400 bps using a modem equipped with MNP protocol, software flow control can cause the transfer to lock up. This is because ^S characters may be included in the data.

It is also useful to be able to specify characters other than ^S and ^Q for flow control, something the better software packages will allow you to do. Nearly all online systems recognize XON/XOFF (^Q/^S) signals, but you may encounter a system that uses different characters for flow control.

Upload Control

Although some systems will take anything you throw at them in the way of an ASCII upload, most require some control, either flow control via ^S/^Q, or, depending on the nature of the system, a turnaround character or a time delay.

UPLOAD CONTROL VIA A TURNAROUND CHARACTER. A turnaround character (also called a prompt character) is the prompt that a communications program waits for before it sends a line during an ASCII text-file upload. Turnaround characters are typically used in message entry functioning as prompts during manual text entry. Some systems also use them during uploads to file areas. (In either instance, you may be asked if you want to use a turnaround character, or you may be asked if you want a prompted upload. They are the same things.)

A turnaround character provides a kind of flow control without using ^S/^Q. The receiving system pauses after each line of text before sending the turnaround character to allow each line to be stored in its text buffer. Thus, the sending system (your computer) does not send a line of text until the receiving system signals it is ready by displaying (sending) the turnaround character.

Turnaround characters vary from system to system. Common turnaround characters are ">" and "?". If you are going to be uploading text to several different systems (especially BBSs), you'll need to be able to change the turnaround character. And sometimes you will want to turn the turnaround character feature off.

UPLOAD CONTROL VIA TIME DELAY. Some systems provide neither ^S/^Q flow control nor a turnaround character. Instead, your system must wait a certain length of time before sending a line. (This is to allow the receiving system to store the line in its buffer.) Many BBSs require this kind of delay.

A good communications software package lets you vary the time delay, or the length of time usually entered in response to a prompt after the time delay command is given.

CHARACTER FILTER. Being able to filter out specific characters is often a more-than-welcome feature. A BBS or online service may send characters that your computer cannot use (codes used in terminal emulation, for example) or extra characters you just don't want to see. A character filter stops these characters before they reach your display or capture buffer.

This feature is also useful in filtering out control characters that may send orders to your software or printer, not to mention the annoying Control-G. Control-G is the bell signal that makes your computer's speaker beep. As you might infer from my earlier diatribe on modem speakers in Chapter 4, I dislike having my computer beep at me.

Some character filters allow you to filter only selected characters, while others let you specify the characters or strings of characters to be filtered.

The overall process is pretty much the same as exchanging text between computers in real time. As you've seen, the same systems of buffering and flow control are used. Aside from the speed, the main difference between real-time data entry and text-file transfer is that when a file is transferred, text is created and stored at each end without human involvement.

Advantages of ASCII File Transfer

The main advantage of using ASCII file transfer is ease of use. All you have to do is tell the remote system that you want to send or receive a file, switch to your communications software's command mode, and type something like SEND <filename> to transmit a file or RECEIVE or CAPTURE <filename> to receive a file.

ASCII transfer is simple to implement in a program, too. The only requirements are a capture buffer to temporarily store incoming data, a series of commands to read and write to a disk file, and a flow-control technique. With the exception of disk access commands, communications programs and online systems have everything they need for ASCII file transfer built in.

Because it is easy to use and implement, almost all online systems provide ASCII file transfer. (This is not true of all error-checking protocols.) And, even if an online system doesn't provide an ASCII download command, turning on your communications program's capture-to-disk function while a text file is displayed is the same thing as doing an ASCII file download. Also, uploading a text file into an open message you're creating is usually the same as typing in the message, only much faster.

Disadvantages of ASCII File Transfer

Data may be lost or garbled during an ASCII transfer where large files or noisy telephone connections are involved. This is because parity checking (the only type of error-checking protocol used in ASCII transfers) is sometimes not used, as when communications parameters are 8N1. Even when it is used, parity checking rarely provides for retransmission of garbled data. (Other error-checking protocols do retransmit garbled data.) The chance of losing data increases with communications speed.

Another major drawback of ASCII file transfer in the modern world of tele-computing is its inability to handle binary data files, programs, and most other eight-bit files, for reasons discussed in the paragraphs immediately following.

Error-Checking (Binary) File-Transfer Protocols: What They Are, and How and Why They Are Used

In the early days of telecomputing, all file transfers consisted of simple seven-bit ASCII text files—messages, program source code, reports, and the like. As telecomputing evolved, there emerged a need to transfer other kinds of files. A reliable method of error checking was also needed. Error-checking file-transfer protocols (sometimes called binary protocols or simply proto-cols) were developed to meet these needs.

As noted earlier, error-checking protocols operate by sending data in discrete groups. The integrity of these groups is tested at the receiving end to ensure error-free transmission. Error-checking protocols can be used to transfer any type of file, from binary data files and machine-language pro-grams to seven-bit text files.

Transferring Binary Data and Programs with Error-Checking Protocols

Programs, binary data files, and certain other types of files cannot be trans-ferred via conventional ASCII-transfer methods for two reasons. First, they may contain certain seven-bit control characters that the receiving system will perceive as commands. Second, they may contain eight-bit characters from a computer's extended ASCII character set. Eight-bit characters may be ignored or converted to seven-bit characters; either way, data is corrupted.

In other words, seven-bit ASCII-transfer methods deal only with seven-bit, alphanumeric characters. Control characters may be ignored or perceived by software or hardware as commands, and eight-bit characters are truncated.

When you attempt to transfer anything other than seven-bit alphanumeric characters via modem, all sorts of problems can pop up. Here are a few examples:

1. The receiving system may interpret some characters (like ^S) as a flow-control or other command character and then lock up.

2. The data file may contain what the receiving system uses as an end-of-file marker (typically a ^Z) and stop accepting data. The result is an incomplete transfer.

3. Eight-bit characters will be truncated (i.e., the final bit in each byte ignored), which will result in the wrong characters being received.

4. The receiving computer or either of the modems may, depending on their internal makeup and configuration, interpret seven-bit control-characters or eight-bit characters in unpredictable ways. The results can be lost data, system lockup, disconnection, etc.

Error-checking protocol transfer eliminates these problems. Control characters are transmitted in such a way that they are not perceived as such by the receiving system.

Also, protocol transfers usually take place using eight data bits, so eight-bit characters when sent individually are handled without truncation. (The serial ports do not remove the eighth bit.) If the transfer takes place at seven bits, as is the case when the Kermit protocol is used, eight-bit characters are translated into passable seven-bit characters for transmission.

On top of all this, error-checking protocols provide the bonus of reliable error checking. When you're transferring a large file of any type, error checking is a very welcome bonus because the odds are high that some sort of telephone-line noise or other garbage will be introduced into the file. When binary data or program files are involved, error checking is a necessity because it's almost impossible to find garbled data in such files after downloading.

Transferring ASCII Text Files with Error-Checking Protocols

Error-checking protocols work with seven-bit text files as well as with other types of files. In fact, you should use an error-checking protocol to transfer large text files for two reasons. First, as I've pointed out before, the simple parity checks performed during an ASCII file transfer are all but worthless. By comparison, some error-checking protocols can transfer files with a reliability of more than 99 percent. Second, depending on the method used, error-checking protocol transfer is often faster than ASCII transfer.

Add to these advantages the byte-by-byte reports and other extras provided by some communications programs during file transfer, and it is easy to see that error-checking protocols are by far the better way to transfer files. I've found error-checking protocols to be so useful that I routinely use the Xmodem or Kermit error-checking protocol for even the smallest text-file transfers. I reserve

ASCII transfer for use with systems that don't accommodate error-checking protocols and for inserting small files into messages I'm composing online.

How Error-Checking Protocol File Transfer Works

When a file is transferred using an error-checking protocol, data is transmitted in groups of characters called blocks (sometimes referred to as packets or frames) rather than one byte or one line at a time. The blocks are usually of a fixed size, such as 128 bytes or 1,024 bytes.

A simplified description of the process goes like this:

1. The sending computer transmits no data until it has read enough from a file to make up a block.

2. The data is combined into a block, and information about the data itself may be added to it.

3. The computer then transmits the block.

4. At the receiving end, the computer unpacks the block and adds the data to the file in which it is storing the incoming data. It also reads and acts on any information about the data included in the block.

During a protocol transfer, the computer systems involved usually exchange information about the transmission between blocks. They use a mutually recognized set of control signals to signal data receipt or error, mark the end of a transmission, and perform other chores related to file transfer and error checking. These control signals sometimes vary from one protocol to another, and consist of certain device and communications control characters from the ASCII character set designated by the American National Standards Institute (ANSI). Table 7.1 lists these codes and their applications in device and communication control.

The following assignments and definitions were developed by the American National Standards Institute (ANSI) for special communications control characters, and are used by most online systems.

ANSI Character Functions

The following list of ANSI character functions applies in some instances to peripherals other than modems—most often to printers, as data is communicated to printers in much the same manner as data is communicated by modems.

Some characters are used in both asynchronous and bisynchronous applications, while others apply to only one type of data transmission.

Table 7.1 ANSI Character Designations

Character Mnemonic	ASCII Value		Character
	Decimal	Binary	
NUL	0	00000	^@
SOH	1	00001	^A
STX	2	00010	^B
ETX	3	00011	^C
EOT	4	00100	^D
ENQ	5	00101	^E
ACK	6	00110	^F
BEL	7	00111	^G
BS	8	01000	^H
HT	9	01001	^I
LF	10	01010	^J
VT	11	01011	^K
FF	12	01100	^L
CR	13	01101	^M
SO	14	01110	^N
SI	15	01111	^O
DLE	16	10000	^P
DC1	17	10001	^Q
DC2	18	10010	^R
DC3	19	10011	^S
DC4	20	10100	^T
NAK	21	10101	^U
SYN	22	10110	^V
ETB	23	10111	^W
CAN	24	11000	^X
EM	25	11001	^Y
SUB	26	11010	^Z
ESC	27	11011	^[
FS	28	11100	^\
GS	29	11101	^]
RS	30	11110	^^
US	31	11111	^_
DEL	127	1111111	

- **ACK (Acknowledge).** Sent by a receiving system to verify accurate receipt of transmitted data following error checking—used during Xmodem transfer

- **BEL (Bell).** Transmits a Control-G, which, on most personal computers, causes the speaker to "beep"

- **BS (Backspace).** Moves the cursor one character to the left, overwriting the character in that location

- **CAN (Cancel).** Normally used as an error signal, to tell a receiving system to ignore data just received

- **CR (Carriage Return).** Moves the cursor to the first column of the current line; this may not be the same as pressing ENTER, as a line feed (see LF) is not always transmitted with each CR

- **DC1 (Device Control 1).** Typically used to restart flow of text that has been paused with Control-S (DC3)—also known as XON

- **DC2 (Device Control 2).** Provides specialized command functions for some online systems (such as Redisplay on DELPHI)—also used to toggle features or states on certain computer peripherals (Applications vary from system to system.)

- **DC3 (Device Control 3).** Typically used to pause the flow of text—also known as XOFF

- **DC4 (Device Control 4).** Provides specialized command functions for some online systems—also used to toggle features or states on certain computer peripherals (Applications vary from system to system.)

- **DELETE (Character delete or null).** Deletes a character under or to the left of the cursor—occasionally used as a null character to provide a time delay or filler during data transmission

- **DLE (Data Link Escape).** A special character used to modify the meaning of a certain number of characters following it during bisynchronous transmission

- **EM (End of Medium).** A special control character used to indicate the end of a storage or transmission block or area

- **ENQ (Enquiry).** A character used by a receiving system to query the sending system in specialized applications

- **EOT (End Of Transmission).** Indicates the end of a transmission, especially during a transmission initiated by SOH (Xmodem uses this character to mark the end of a file.)

- **ESC (Escape).** Used to signal the transmission of control characters to printers, and in other peripheral control applications

- **ETB (End of Transmission Block).** Marks the end of a block during data transfer—frequently used in bisynchronous data transmission

- **ETX (End of Text).** Bisynchronous data transmission signal that signals the end of the data content of a block, preceding checksum characters (Compare with STX.)

- **FF (Form Feed).** A printer command that advances a printer's print head (normally via a tractor feed device) to the top of the next page or to a specified position on the next page

- **FS (File Separator).** Marks the boundary between files during multiple-file transfer

- **GS (Group Separator).** Marks the boundary between groups of data

- **HT (Horizontal Tab).** A printer command that moves a printer's print head to the next tab position as set by controlling software or the printer's ROM programming; on some online systems, moves the cursor a preset number of spaces to the right (usually five to seven)

- **LF (Line Feed).** A printer command that advances the print head (normally via a tractor feed device) one line; on most online systems, also moves the cursor down one line and typically accompanies a CR

- **NAK (Negative Acknowledge).** A character sent by the receiving system to the sending system during file transfer to signal an error in data (based on the receiving system's error checking), which usually results in the sending system retransmitting the most recent block of data—also used by the receiving system to signal ready during Xmodem transfer

- **NUL (NULL/nothing).** A nonprinting character that is used as a time delay or to fill up a partially filled block of data during error-checking protocol transfer

- **RS (Record Separator).** Marks the boundary between records during data transmission

- **SI (Shift In).** Used to reset a peripheral, such as a printer, with which data is exchanged

- **SO (Shift Out).** Extends the character set used by some printers

- **SOH (Start Of Heading).** In bisynchronous data transmission, indicates the start of a message/block header

- **STX (Start of Text).** Signals the end of header data and the beginning of content data during bisynchronous data transmission (Compare with ETX.)

- **SUB (Substitute).** A command character that causes a character sent in error—specifically a character that the receiving device can't handle—to be replaced

- **SYN (Synchronous Idle).** Used during bisynchronous data transmission to synchronize sending and receiving systems, and to signal the transmission header or other data

- **US (Unit Separator).** Marks the boundary between data units

- **VT (Vertical Tab).** Advances a printer or onscreen display a set number of lines while keeping the print head or cursor in the same column location

Error Checking

Accurate error checking is accomplished by any of several methods, which may be implemented in modem firmware programming, but is usually handled by software working with a computer's serial port. Information about the number and type of bytes or bits in each block may be included with the block in what is called a block header, or transmitted before or after the block. Additional bits may be added to each block for the receiving system to use in determining (by calculations based on the sum of the binary ones in a block) whether a block has been properly received. Or the sending and receiving systems may exchange information about the content of blocks after a block or group of blocks is transferred.

It is sufficient to say that the integrity of each block is checked. If the block is "good," the receiving system sends an acknowledgment signal (usually an ACK) to tell the sending system to transmit the next block. If a block is "bad" (i.e., the information about the block doesn't agree with the block contents as received), the receiving system asks the sending system to resend the block by sending a negative acknowledgment signal (usually a NAK).

Retries

As indicated above, bad data blocks are automatically retransmitted by protocol transfer systems. However, a transfer is terminated if a block is retransmitted a set number of times (usually nine) without success. This provides extra insurance against bad data getting through and also eliminates the possibility of computers being tied up for hours while a bad block is transmitted over and over again. The number of retries can usually be set within a communications program, and some online systems will allow you to do the same in an online profile or configuration area.

Timeouts

During protocol transfers, both systems allow a preset period of time for each data block transfer. The sending system waits for an acknowledgment that the data were properly received. The receiving system waits for the next block. If either side's time limit (for acknowledgment or for the beginning of a new block) is exceeded, the transfer is terminated. This is called a timeout. As with the number of retries, protocol transfer timeout can usually be set within a communications program and on some online systems. You can set the time limit along with the number of timeouts permitted (the number of retries) before termination.

Buffers

Most error-checking protocols take advantage of data buffering, in which incoming data is temporarily stored in RAM. Data buffering speeds up file transfer because it reduces the number of disk accesses during transmission.

A buffer holds several blocks of data so the sending computer doesn't have to stop to read data from its disk each time it sends a block. (As many blocks as possible are read into RAM from disk when the buffer is empty.) At the receiving end, the system doesn't have to stop to read each incoming block to disk. Data is written to disk only when the receiving buffer is filled.

Bit Overhead and Speed

You may have wondered whether adding extra bits for error-checking purposes adds enough overhead to a file to slow down a transfer. It might, if not compensated for. Most error-checking protocols, however, eliminate start, stop, and parity bits. The net result is that the total number of bits transferred is less than it would be if the bytes were sent via ASCII transfer.

Some protocols compress data before transmitting it, too. (The data is decompressed at the receiving end, of course.)

Reports

As you know, error-checking protocols exchange information on the status of a transfer. The information exchanged consists of a few bits or bytes that mean something only to the software involved. However, most implementations of error-checking protocol in communications programs provide some sort of ongoing report on the status of protocol file transfers. Information such as the number of blocks and/or bytes transferred, the percentage of the transmission completed, and more is available at any point during the transmission.

Online systems often report on the final status of error-checking protocol transfers with a quick summary that scrolls onto the screen at the conclusion of each transfer.

This is a general description of the way error-checking protocols work; there are some more esoteric approaches, but this is the most common. The descriptions of specific error-checking protocols that follow contain additional details on particular protocols.

A NOTE ABOUT BLOCK PADDING AND DATA AND PROGRAM FILES

When a binary file-transfer protocol transmits data as blocks, all blocks are the same size. This is both an advantage and a disadvantage. It is an advantage because it provides uniform data packets, which are basic elements of any binary file-transfer protocol. It is a disadvantage because the final data block (or another block) is padded with null characters if there are not enough characters in the file to make all blocks sent equal, that is if the original file is not a multiple of the block size used by the protocol.

The padding is in the form of digital zeros (0). This has no effect on text files, but can result in disorganized or corrupted binary data or program files. When transferred using binary file-transfer protocols discussed in the following pages, a data or program file will usually be of a different size than the original. The transferred files will be inaccessible or will not run.

To eliminate this problem, you can use an archiving or packing program like those discussed in Chapter 11. File-transfer protocol "padding" doesn't affect the integrity of an archive, and you'll benefit from the reduced file-transfer time. So, don't transfer a program or data file—even via a null-modem hookup—without archiving the file first.

An alternative solution is to alter the size of the blocks to a number that can be divided into the file size. However, this requires some experimentation, and only a few file-transfer protocols (like Kermit) let you alter the block size.

COMMON FILE-TRANSFER PROTOCOLS AND HOW THEY WORK

Discussing every public domain, commercial, proprietary, and machine-specific error-checking protocol in existence is beyond the scope of this book.

However, we'll take a brief look at the most popular protocols here, along with machine- and system-specific protocols and proprietary protocols.

Xmodem, MODEM7, and WXmodem

Xmodem file-transfer protocol (sometimes called MODEM7 or Xmodem/Checksum) is an error-checking protocol you'll encounter very frequently. Created in 1978 by Ward Christensen and placed in the public domain, Xmodem has become a de facto standard for binary file transfers.

Virtually all BBSs and online services use Xmodem. And if a communications program offers any error-checking protocols at all—even just one—Xmodem will be among them. (Systems and programs that use strictly proprietary protocols, like America Online, are excepted, of course.)

How Xmodem Works

Xmodem transfers files in blocks of 128 bytes each. It adds an extra bit—called a checksum—to each block, which the receiving system uses to calculate whether or not the block was accurately transmitted. (A complex algorithm, based on the contents of the block, is used for this calculation.) If the checksums don't agree, the receiving computer requests the sending computer to retransmit the packet by sending a NAK. Otherwise, the receiver sends an ACK, and the sending system transmits the next block. This process is repeated for each block until the entire file is transferred, or until the transfer is aborted by the user, by too many retries, or by a timeout.

Although it is a superb error-checking protocol, Xmodem has a couple of drawbacks. It cannot be used to communicate at seven data bits, as it transmits files in eight-bit format only. (If you try to use Xmodem with a seven-bit system, not all the bits transmitted will be received or the system may lock up.) If a hardware error-checking protocol or flow control is in effect, some Xmodem characters can be perceived as control characters, with unpredictable effects.

You may encounter some versions of Xmodem that offer batch-file processing. Such implementations are generally difficult to use, however.

Overall, Xmodem is a superior approach to error-checking protocol design. It is relatively easy to use, and offers as high as 96 percent reliability, which is extremely high where file transfers are concerned, and far better reliability than can be achieved with ASCII transfers.

Xmodem/CRC

CRC (cyclic redundancy check) is an Xmodem option that modifies how Xmodem checks for errors. CRC adds a second checksum bit to each block to enhance error checking. The fact that an extra bit must be transmitted with each block makes for a noticeable difference in transmission times only for extremely large files, and the gain in efficiency is worth it. Using the CRC option with Xmodem increases its reliability to as much as 99.6 percent!

Xmodem/CRC programs on online services can usually detect whether or not another system is using CRC, and then use CRC or not as appropriate. GEnie is one example of a system that can detect and adjust to the presence or absence of the CRC option.

Don't count on every system being able to sense CRC, though. If you plan to use CRC for file transfers with a particular online system, look for a terminal settings option on the system where you can specify Xmodem/CRC as a default, or always select Xmodem/CRC specifically at a download menu. If there is no such selection available, your software or the other system may adjust for CRC automatically. If nothing happens when you try to send or receive a file using Xmodem/CRC, you'll have to cancel the file transfer and redo it with straight Xmodem.

WXMODEM

WXmodem stands for "windowed Xmodem." Like Xmodem, WXmodem transmits 128-byte blocks; unlike Xmodem, it does not wait between blocks for an ACK or NAK. It monitors for those signals, but it assumes each block has been transmitted successfully and immediately sends the next block.

In transmitting blocks in this nonstop manner, the sending computer is always one to four blocks ahead of the receiving computer's ACKs or NAKs. (The receiving computer's buffer must be large enough to accommodate this slightly faster influx of data, or WXmodem will not work.) The difference between the block being sent and the most currently received ACK or NAK is called the window, hence the name "windowed Xmodem." Under ideal situations, WXmodem keeps track of this difference, and so knows which block is referred to and must be retransmitted if a NAK is received.

Kermit

Kermit (yes, it's named after Kermit the Frog) is equal in popularity to Xmodem in some quarters, as finicky as it is to use. Created at Columbia University in 1981, it was designed to be more flexible and more convenient to use than Xmodem. It is not yet implemented on as many online systems and programs as Xmodem is, but this is changing as computer users discover the program's usefulness.

How Kermit Works

Kermit is similar to Xmodem in that it transfers files in blocks—or packets, as they are referred to in Kermit. It also resembles Xmodem in its use of a checksum technique for error checking. A checksum bit—based on packet contents—is included with each packet.

Special Features

Kermit differs from Xmodem in several ways, not the least of which is the fact that it can transfer files using seven data bits. Where necessary, Kermit converts eight-bit characters in a file to seven-bit characters by stripping the eighth bit and sending it as a separate bit. Kermit also converts control characters into other ASCII characters that can be safely transmitted.

Another interesting feature of Kermit is that its packet sizes can be changed to accommodate fixed packet sizes on remote systems or varying transmission conditions. This is another approach to eliminating the problems caused by padding data blocks, discussed earlier.

Finally, Kermit programs can resynchronize their transmissions if interrupted by line noise—something else that isn't true of Xmodem.

Wild Card Transfers

If these advantages aren't enough, Kermit also allows *wild card file transfers*, which means you can use an asterisk in place of a file name or extension to transfer all files of a certain type. For examples, typing "MIKE.*" would transfer all files named MIKE, no matter what their extensions. Typing "*.TXT" would transfer all files with the extension TXT.

File Compression

Kermit saves time by using a clever transmission technique in which repeating characters in certain kinds of files are sent only once; this can result in a significant time savings. Naturally, both the sending and receiving computers must use the same Kermit protocol, as quite a bit of decoding is required at the receiving end.

The Kermit Server Mode

Most versions of Kermit also offer what is called a server mode, a mode in which your software will take over and issue all commands necessary for transferring singly or in batches.

Ymodem and YAM

Ymodem is similar to Xmodem. The major difference between the two is that Ymodem transmits data in 1,024-byte (1 KB) blocks, rather than in 128-byte blocks. Its major application is transmitting very large files.

You may encounter a UNIX or MS-DOS version of Ymodem called YAM. YAM in UNIX format is the protocol from which Ymodem is derived.

YMODEM ADVANTAGES

Ymodem's large block size increases transfer speed significantly when few or no errors are encountered. Also, some implementations of Ymodem, like Batch-YAM, offer batch processing.

YMODEM DISADVANTAGES

At first glance, Ymodem may seem imminently superior to Xmodem, due to its larger block size. It is—sometimes. The checksum error-correcting scheme used by Ymodem is similar to that of Xmodem/CRC in that it uses two checksum bits at the end of each block. However, if there is a lot of line noise, Ymodem's automatic block retransmission slows down transfer significantly.

Zmodem

Zmodem has become the file-transfer protocol of choice among those who do a lot of uploading and downloading. It is faster than Xmodem, it uses larger blocks, and it is nowhere near as difficult to get working as Kermit is.

Zmodem operates like Xmodem, but it does not wait for ACKs; instead it watches only for NAKs at the sending end. Zmodem blocks are 512 bytes in size. The protocol is fast, even though it uses no buffering in some implementations. (This means a pause for disk access each time it sends or receives a block.)

Zmodem is pretty much an automated protocol. Like Ymodem, Zmodem lets you do wild card transfers. And, you don't have to enter names for files you're receiving; Zmodem does that for you. It also retains the time/date stamps of files.

As with Xmodem, everyone offers Zmodem. When you have a large file to transfer, and you have a choice, I recommend using Zmodem.

Which Protocol?

As just implied, Zmodem is the most popular binary file-transfer protocol among those who seek high speed and quality data transfer. Ymodem is a close second. However, Xmodem is the most prevalent; you'll find it on just about every online service and BBS. This is why I suggest that a stand-alone communications program offer Xmodem if no other file-transfer protocols. But, if you're interested in high-speed file transfer, be sure your program can handle Zmodem or Ymodem, as well.

The protocols used by your Web browser and by online service front ends, as well as by Telnet programs, are built in, and may be any of the above or proprietary.

Machine-Specific Protocols

There are a number of machine-specific protocol transfer programs, among them Telink for the IBM PC and others for other types of PCs. You'll also find protocols specific to operating systems like UNIX. Such protocols aren't generally used, but can be found on BBSs and a few online services that cater to specific computers.

System-Specific Protocols

Certain online services offer special file-transfer protocols designed to make optimum use of their software. CompuServe, for example, offers B Protocol, which was quite popular among users. It was supplied with all CompuServe VIDTEX software and front ends, as well as with many public domain, shareware, and commercial programs.

Other systems with specific protocols are AOL and the PRODIGY Service, and they, likewise, include the protocols in their front-end software.

Proprietary Protocols

Various modem and software manufacturers have developed what are called proprietary error-checking protocols. These are protocols that use special file-transfer and error-checking techniques developed by the manufacturer and not released to the public.

As with other error-checking protocols, successful use of a proprietary protocol requires that the same protocol be used at each end of a file transfer. Because some of these protocols are available only with a specific modem or software package, the product in question must be used at both ends. This means, in turn, that the manufacturer or publisher sells more modem units or copies of software.

This may sound mercenary, but the tactic is not all bad. Proprietary protocols often offer advantages that make restriction to a particular modem and/or software package worthwhile. Some of those advantages are discussed in the following paragraphs.

SOFTWARE PROTOCOLS

Proprietary error-checking protocols implemented in software vary in design and features, but generally use the block- or packet-based file-transfer approach discussed earlier.

Sometimes a proprietary protocol is the only protocol provided with a communications program. Because such a program focuses on one job—transferring files via a specific protocol—it may include features such as file compression and adaptive parameter block size in addition to what its designers feel is the best file transfer technique available. If you use this kind of program, however, you can transfer files only with programs that use the same protocol.

Ideally, a program with a proprietary protocol should provide some of the more common protocols, such as Xmodem and Kermit, as well. Exceptions to this are programs designed for null-modem transfers, such as LapLink and Hotwire. These use their own file-transfer protocols, but you really don't need other protocols because you won't be using these programs with systems that use other programs. (You use the same program at both ends of the link.)

Some proprietary software protocols are available with more than one program. The Hayes protocol, for instance, is offered by many programs other than Hayes' designated software, Smartcom. The same is true of Crosstalk's protocol.

No matter if a proprietary protocol is available with only one program or with several, as using one may result in improved transfer efficiency and ease of use. This is because the implementations of proprietary protocols do not vary and use the same set of commands and signals. Also, you can usually use the default communications parameters provided with the program, which greatly streamlines operation. This is the case when using any of the ProComm programs—ProComm, ProComm Plus, or ProComm Plus for Windows.

HARDWARE PROTOCOLS

Modem manufacturers implement several error-checking protocols (among them MNP) in hardware. When these protocols are used, data is collected into blocks (packets or frames) before transmission. Virtually all such hardware protocols use an approach similar to the checksum/CRC method to check for errors.

Hardware protocols are particularly effective in eliminating the telephone line noise problems and may offer data compression and other enhancements.

On the negative side, using a hardware protocol can cause minor delays during real-time operations. When the protocol is active, the modem may not send typed-in characters until enough have been entered to fill a packet. Or it may wait until a certain number of milliseconds have passed before sending characters—to make certain that no more are immediately forthcoming. Such delays are sometimes perceptible in real time, sometimes not, but it is best to disable hardware protocols during direct, real-time communication with another system. Save the error-checking protocol for transferring files or if a connection is bad.

Hardware error-checking protocols sometimes interfere with software error-checking protocol transfer, too. This kind of problem can be overcome, but you'll probably have to consult with the modem's manufacturer.

Finally, some hardware error-checking protocols are not recognized by some online systems, and this can create problems.

Modem manufacturers are particularly competitive in this area, and proprietary protocols are jealously guarded. However, a number use licensed file-transfer protocols like MNP, so it is possible to use some hardware protocols with modems from different manufacturers. (MNP is almost universally accepted by BBS, online service, and packet-switching network hardware, by the way.)

FILE TRANSFER CHANNELS AND CATEGORIES

Now that you're familiar with file transfer methods, let's take a closer look at the file-transfer channels available to you. These channels consist of modem links between your computer and any of the following:

- Other personal computers
- Public and private BBSs
- Online services
- Private minicomputers and mainframe computers
- The Internet

Private minicomputers and mainframe computers are typically encountered in work situations. From the viewpoint of the person dialing in, these operate either like BBSs or online services, depending on their software. Therefore, information on BBSs and online services in the discussion that follows applies to private minicomputers and mainframe computer systems, too.

File Transfer Categories

File transfers can be categorized by the kinds of files involved, but the categories overlap. A clearer distinction is whether a file transfer is private or public. No matter what you're transferring or why, the transfer is either public or private. For convenience of discussion and to better present the information that follows, I'll use these categories as defined below.

PRIVATE FILE TRANSFERS

A file transfer is private when it is directed to an individual computer user or to a limited group of users. A common private file-transfer situation is when two personal computers are linked directly by a single-user line, as might occur if you dial up a friend or business associate's computer. Private file transfers also take place on BBSs and, more frequently, on the Internet and through online services. (The host system must provide the appropriate utilities or services to enable private file transfer.)

PUBLIC FILE TRANSFERS

Public file transfers make files available to a large number of users (typically anyone who has access to a system) or draw on publicly available files, such as those available at **http://www.download.com** or **http://www.shareware.com**. Such transfers include uploading programs or other files for inclusion in public database areas on the Internet, BBSs, and online services, and downloading files from those same databases.

PRIVATE FILE TRANSFERS

A list of all the applications for private file transfer would probably take up most of this chapter, but here are a few examples:

- Collecting and distributing business sales and marketing data
- Delivering reports and other data to clients
- Delivering/receiving software or information products
- Expediting collaborative efforts of all types, from science fiction novels to software
- On the hobbyist level, doing a direct upload or download just for fun

The logistics of private file transfer depend on the channel used, and, as you'll learn, vary quite a bit.

One on One:
Transfers Between Personal Computers

Direct transfer between personal computers can be conducted with both computers attended, or with one or both computers unattended.

ATTENDED TRANSFERS

For small, infrequent file transfers, simply dialing up the computer of the person with whom you are exchanging files is the best route. Once the link is established, you can use your respective software to send and receive files by whatever method you prefer. When you're not actually transferring a file, you can chat by typing back and forth. (This is, of course, how you let each other know when a file transfer is to take place.)

Be advised, however, that establishing a link and successfully transferring a file usually require some experimentation. Unless the same communications program is being used at both ends, don't be surprised if you experience several failed connections and aborted transmissions.

To ensure a good connection and to avoid the more common problems of a direct link, follow these steps:

- Establish via a preliminary voice telephone call the communications parameters you'll be using: bps rate, data bits, parity, and stop bits.

- Make sure one computer's software is set to half duplex and the other to full duplex. If you don't, you may not see what you type onto your screen, or you may see double characters.

- Disable any error-checking, flow-control, data-encryption, or data-compression protocols that your respective modems may use. These may interfere with certain file-transfer protocols.

- Don't jump in and try to transmit a file right away. Type a few lines back and forth first to establish that the communications link is stable.

- If possible, transmit a small file as a preliminary test of your communications link.

Transferring files in this way has its drawbacks. Someone must be at each end of the computer link to direct and supervise file transfers. This is time-consuming and, at times, boring. Also, when the transfer takes place depends on your respective schedules.

UNATTENDED TRANSFERS

If you frequently exchange files with another personal computer user, you should consider automating the process. You'll need communications software you can program (usually via script files) to dial up or receive calls from another computer and exchange specified files at a specified time. This frees you from having to coordinate your schedule with the other party. All that's necessary is that you agree on whose computer does the dialing and that you make sure each computer is set up before that time.

Such an arrangement can involve quite a bit of planning and effort, however. An even better approach is to use a software package that is specifically designed for computer-to-computer transfer. This kind of software, which requires that the same package be used with both computers, replaces programming with relatively simple command and data entry. Or use the same general communications program with each computer—but make sure it is a program that allows command access by a calling system. (Some such programs let you set up passwords for access.)

Before you put your file transfers in the hands of an automated system, make several dry runs transferring small files with someone watching on each end. Check to make sure the software does everything on time, that it can find the files to be transferred, and that the files are transferred intact.

Alternately, you can go the full route and set up a BBS with BBS software. However, this can be a complicated, expensive proposition. The best solution is to use the same software at each end, with or without password protection as necessary.

PRIVATE FILE TRANSFERS ON BBSS

If direct communication between your computer and another is impractical (or, in some cases, impossible), a BBS may present a solution to your private file-transfer needs.

Because of software and hardware limitations, many BBSs can't handle the private transfer of nontext files. Those BBSs that can handle private transfer of both text and nontext files handle each in a different way. (Some BBSs cannot handle private transfer at all.)

E-MAIL

If you want to transfer a text file privately, the obvious way to do it on a BBS is by private e-mail, assuming the BBS has a private e-mail system. However, you may run into problems on systems that place a limit on the size of e-mail messages. If you have a large document to transfer, you'll have to either break it up into several smaller documents and send it as several messages or upload it to a file-transfer area (see the section "Transferring Nontext Files" below).

With very few exceptions, you'll be limited to ASCII file transfer in a BBS's e-mail system. Depending on the system, you may have to use prompting and/or time delays when you upload a text file. To download a message file, you simply open your capture buffer and display the message.

TRANSFERRING NONTEXT FILES: FILE TRANSFER AREAS

Trying to transfer a nontext file as a straight e-mail message on any online system is not a good idea. For openers, if you try an ASCII upload of an eight-bit file, you're likely to lock up either system.

If a file is successfully uploaded and sent by e-mail, you'll still encounter difficulties. Most systems are set up to properly display e-mail messages in seven-bit ASCII format only. If you try to display an eight-bit file in normal e-mail, the results will be unpredictable. Some characters may not be displayed. Your system or the remote system may lock up or disconnect. And even if you can display and capture the entire file, you probably won't be able to use it.

Even if you can download and save a binary or program file, the file may be corrupted by header strings and display control characters. And there's always the problem of mail message size limits.

More sophisticated BBSs offer private file transfer areas where you can upload and address a file to a specific individual. These areas are usually set up so that only the individual to whom the file is addressed can see the names of files addressed to him or her and download them. Others either won't see the file name in the directory or, if they can, will not be able to download it.

A few systems are set up with no directory for the file transfer area; only those who know the name of a file in the area can download it. (Presumably, the intended recipient will be advised of the file name by the uploader.)

In general, private file transfer on BBSs is practical only if you transfer small- and medium-sized messages and programs on an occasional basis. Aside from limitations on file size and transfer protocol, BBSs are normally single-user systems and you may not be able to access a BBS when you wish. There's also the fact that most BBSs are operated as a hobby and can vanish overnight.

On the whole, if you need a reliable third-party transfer system, an online service is the way to go. The only advantage a BBS has over an online system is that a BBS costs little or nothing to use. Otherwise, the average online system presents none of the limitations of a BBS and offers quite a few advantages.

Private File Transfers on Online Services and the Internet

As in other areas, online services and ISP-provided e-mail systems have far more to offer than BBSs when it comes to handling, storing, and transferring files. They also offer some unique features, as you'll see in a few lines.

PERSONAL FILE AREAS

The majority of online services offer personal file areas. These are special areas or menu selections that accommodate a variety of file-transfer protocols and provide private online file storage. Such an area can be used to transfer files to other users on the service, if any of certain utilities are available in the file area. These utilities are:

- The ability to file e-mail messages in a personal file area
- The ability to send files as e-mail messages or to attach a file to an e-mail message
- The ability to transfer a file directly from your file area to that of another user

ISPs also offer online file storage, but it tends to be simpler and faster to transfer files as e-mail attachments, so there is no interim storage facility other than that used to store incoming e-mail messages until you retrieve them. Other means of online storage and access on ISPs are normally more trouble than they are worth.

E-MAIL

The rules for transferring files via e-mail with ISPs and online services differ from those that apply to BBSs. For openers, the file-size limit for e-mail messages is often several times that of BBS e-mail systems, so transferring large documents is no problem. (Check specific online services' help systems for details on message size limitations. If your document is larger than the service's mail system allows, you'll have to transfer the document via whatever options are available for nontext file transfer. Nontext file storage and transfer areas usually have no set limits on file size.)

Upload options for text files to be e-mailed can vary. On systems with private file areas that accommodate e-mailing files stored in that area, I recommend that you upload the file to the file area and e-mail it from there. Once you've uploaded a file, you usually have to go to the system's e-mail menu to send it.

On some systems, you can do an ASCII upload directly into a message that is open for text entry, but this is much slower than uploading to the file area by any protocol. (Message area buffers are usually small and/or slow because they are designed for keyboard input. When you upload to an open message, you may have to deal with time delays and/or turnaround characters.)

On the whole, however, it is best to send any file as an attached file with an e-mail message, or to copy it into the message.

TRANSFERRING NON-TEXT FILES

As with BBSs, it is not a good idea to send a nontext file via an online service's e-mail system. Message headers and display controls can corrupt your data or program file, and the file will be output in ASCII format in any event.

There are a few exceptions to this where the only way to transfer a nontext file to another user privately is via a special mail utility on the system.

As noted previously, a few online services allow you to move a file directly from your private file area to that of another user. To me, this is by far the most efficient way to privately transfer nontext files online. Once a file is in your private file area, you not only have your choice of download options but also a copy in storage that you can redownload or forward at any time. (This isn't a bad option for text files, either, as it delivers a file with no headers—and you'll usually want to remove mail headers from important documents after you download them.) Very few systems offer this service, unfortunately.

PUBLIC FILE TRANSFERS

Although private areas offer downloads for various types of data, public file transfers are most often conducted via databases, which serve as central repositories for files accessible to the online public. Applications for public file transfers include advertising, general distribution of factual information or commentary, sharing creative efforts, and distribution of public domain or shareware software. Public file areas are a better choice than individual, private distribution.

Naturally, you can download (via file capture) anything displayed on your screen as well.

BBS Uploads and Downloads

Very few BBSs accommodate file transfer for public messages beyond ASCII file transfer (à la the BBSs e-mail file capture technique I described earlier), so we'll focus on BBS databases here. The average BBS provides access to databases in one of two ways. Smaller BBSs offer access via a main menu selection labeled Files, Databases, or something similarly descriptive. Once you enter the database area, you'll usually find several databases, each categorized by the types of files it contains.

Specific commands vary, but at a minimum BBS databases will display file lists and let you upload and download files. Some also allow you to set the file-transfer protocol and search for specific files by name, keyword(s), and/or other criteria.

Uploading to a BBS database is usually fairly simple to do. You simply select Upload from a menu or issue an Upload command. The system takes over from there, prompting you for a file name and a brief description of the file. You are then asked to select a file-transfer protocol, after which you are prompted to begin the file transfer. You may not have to select a file-transfer protocol at upload time; some BBSs have you select a default protocol the first time you sign on.

After you've uploaded a file, it will either be placed in the database for immediate access or temporarily stored until the sysop reviews and places it in a public database.

Downloading a file from a BBS database is even simpler than uploading. All you have to do is select Download at a menu or enter a Download command, specify a protocol if requested, enter a file name, and start your system's download procedure when prompted.

Online Service and Internet Uploads and Downloads

Online services usually offer a greater range of upload and download options and protocols than BBSs as well as more public areas in which file transfer can be used. In addition to databases, files can often be transferred in message areas (including public bulletin boards). The personal file areas discussed a few pages back can often be used in public file transfers, too.

DATABASES

Databases on online services are most often found in special interest group areas, although some services offer public database areas, too. Databases in special interest group areas are organized into various categories by content, while public database areas tend to be open.

Online service databases are more sophisticated than BBS databases, offering powerful search features, detailed descriptions of files, multiple download options, and more.

DOWNLOADING DATABASE FILES

To download a file from an online service database, you usually read the file's description and then select Download at the menu or prompt that follows. Depending on the system, you may or may not be able to select a specific download protocol. Some systems allow you to save your choice of protocols as a part of your online profile, while others prompt you for a protocol each time you download a file. (Systems that store your protocol choice in a profile will usually let you override that choice at a download menu.)

When you give the download command, the system prompts you to begin your system's transfer procedure. The file is sent to your computer, and a beep and/or a status report notifies you when the transfer is complete.

UPLOADING AND DATABASE FILE SUBMISSIONS

Uploading a file to an online system database is a submission process that involves either one or two steps.

The one-step submission procedure is similar to that of uploading a file to a BBS database, though you'll probably be asked for a longer file description and some keywords that others can use to find your file during database searches.

A two-step submission requires that you first upload the file to your personal file area. Then you must submit the file at the appropriate database menu. After you enter information about the file (description, file name, keywords), the file is copied from your personal file area. (*Note*: The original file usually isn't deleted, so you'll have to remember to delete it.)

File uploads and downloads at Web sites are far simpler, thanks to the built-in features of browsers.

File Transfer Tips

A file transfer can go wrong in a number of ways, but the most common sources of trouble during file transfer include telephone line noise, bad files, and unmatched protocols. You can't anticipate every problem, but there are certain precautions and procedures you can observe to minimize the possibility of trouble during file transfer.

SETTING UP AND SIGNING ON

You should, of course, make sure your equipment is properly connected and that you have set the proper communications parameters for the system you are dialing up before you attempt to sign on to a system.

You'll want to give special attention to telephone line conditions when you first sign on. Watch for evidence of line noise in the form of garbage characters appearing on your screen, or when on the Net watch for slow response times. If it appears that you have a noisy line, sign off and redial to get a better connection. If the problem persists, wait an hour or two before attempting the file transfer.

If the weather in your area is bad, postpone the file transfer until things quiet down. Telephone line noise frequently accompanies bad weather—especially when lightning is present (and you shouldn't be using your computer during a lightning storm in any event).

Observing Protocol

Make sure you select the proper protocol when you tell the remote system you want to transfer a file. Sometimes a one-letter difference—entering an X rather than a K, for example—can result in your system trying to communicate with the remote system under the wrong protocol.

If you can't get a protocol to work with a particular system, experiment a bit with different settings. Because implementations of protocols differ slightly from system to system, you may occasionally find that modified protocols don't work. For example, two bulletin board systems that I call regularly implement Xmodem/CRC in a manner that is slightly different from the way my communications program handles it. Even though I select Xmodem/CRC when I want to upload a file and initiate an Xmodem/CRC upload at my end, my software refuses to communicate with the BBSs software. So, I have to fall back to straight Xmodem to transfer files on these systems.

If a system offers a specific protocol (like B Protocol on CompuServe), use it. You'll find it faster and more reliable than other protocols every time.

Web file transfers, as well as sending files via e-mail through an ISP, are far simpler, again thanks to built-in browser features.

Aborting a Transfer

If a transfer isn't going right, wait a few seconds before aborting it. Either your system or the remote system may correct the problem by resending bad data or may abort the transfer itself. Also, sometimes systems take a minute or two to synchronize.

If you do abort the transfer on your end, you may have to issue an additional command to the remote system to let it know you want to abort the transfer. This is usually done by sending several ^Cs or ^Xs. (The remote system will usually tell you how to abort before you initiate the transfer.) In some cases, your software may send the proper abort signal to the remote system when you tell it to abort the transfer at your end.

PUTTING AN END TO THINGS

Occasionally, either your computer or the other system will not acknowledge or recognize the fact that a binary file transfer has been completed. Even though the proper number of blocks has been transferred, the system seems to lock up. If this happens during an upload, try entering Ctrl-E at your keyboard (the end-of-transmission signal). Occasionally, the signal isn't sent or received.

CHAPTER 7

Physical Connections, Cables, and More

HOW TO MAKE MODEM AND NULL-MODEM CABLES

This chapter will help you in putting together the hardware and software for null-modem transfer, as well as for PC-to-modem connections.

You learned quite a bit about RS-232 interfaces earlier in this book, but we'll take things a few steps further here. I'll show you exactly how RS-232 cables are put together and how they work. Specifically, I'll show you how to make RS-232 cables and null-modem cables, and how to tie a DB-25 connector to a DB-9 connector.

(If you haven't done so already, I strongly recommend that you read Chapter 3 before trying to make your own RS-232 cable. Chapter 3 explains in detail the whys and hows of RS-232 communications.)

Sooner or later, you may need to make your own modem cable. If you want to transfer data directly between two computers with serial ports, you'll need what is called a null-modem cable. If you buy a modem that has a male connector rather than the standard female connector, or a computer with a male rather than a female connector, you will need a cable with the same gender connector on each end. Or, you might acquire an IBM AT-type computer with a DB-9 connector on its serial port, requiring a cable with a DB-9 connector at one end and a DB-25 connector at the other.

Now, you can go out and buy one, but you may find it expedient to make what you need yourself. Before you start shaking your head, let me point out that it is not difficult to make an RS-232 cable. All you have to do is attach two connectors to a length of cable; if you can solder or use a miniwire wrap tool, you can make a cable. Don't want to fool around with that stuff? You can use solderless connectors, if you prefer.

OK, you're thinking, "Maybe I can—but why bother?" I can give you several answers to that question:

- Making your own cable costs much less than buying one (often by a factor of eight, not counting the cost of a consultant).

- You save time—there's no searching around or waiting for "out-of-stock" items. Making an RS-232 cable takes only a few minutes.

- Finally, in keeping with this book's theme, making your own cable will add to your intuitive knowledge of how telecomputing works.

RS-232 Cable Components

The components of an RS-232 cable are a length of 24-conductor cable and two connectors.

CABLE

RS-232 cable comes in two varieties: round and flat, the latter more commonly known as ribbon cable. Ribbon cable, illustrated in Chapter 3, is used in RS-232 applications more often than round cable.

RS-232 cables are usually between three and six feet in length.

CONNECTORS

Connectors are classified by "gender," based on whether they have plugs or sockets. Connectors with plugs are male, while connectors with sockets are female. (Both plugs and sockets are referred to as pins.)

Connectors are available in two varieties: solder-type and solderless. Wires from the ribbon cable are soldered (or attached using a wire wrap tool) to metal pins that extend to the rear of their plugs or sockets on solder-type connectors.

Solderless connectors are set up to accept ribbon cable in a slot. Pressing two halves of the connector closed causes a tiny spike to be driven into each wire.

Connections

The vast majority of asynchronous communications applications use only eight or nine pins out of the 25 pins in the RS-232C standard (connecting pin 1 is optional in many applications, leaving eight pins in use), as shown in Table 7.1.

Table 7.1 Standard RS-232 Pin Assignment	
Pin	**Assignment**
1	Equipment ground
2	Transmit data
3	Receive data
4	Request to send
5	Clear to send
6	Data set ready
7	Signal ground
8	Carrier detect
20	Data terminal ready

The pin assignments in Table 7.1 result in a connection like that illustrated in the diagram in Figure 7.1.

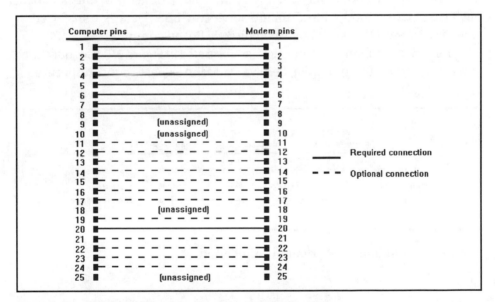

Figure 7.1   Typical RS-232 connector/cable hookup

Making a Standard RS-232 Cable

Making a standard RS-232 cable is fairly uncomplicated. All that is required is that pins 1 through 8 and pin 20 on each connector be directly connected to their counterparts on the other connector. In other words, a wire should connect pin 1 on Connector A with pin 1 on Connector B, pin 2 on Connector A with pin 2 on Connector B, etc., as in Figure 7.1.

Some systems also require that pin 22 (Ring Indicator) on the connectors be connected, mainly because of software operating parameters. If pin 22 is connected, pin 1 may not be used. (Consult your system's software and hardware manuals for details on pin-connection requirements.)

Making a Null-Modem Cable

If you have two computers in one location (say, a Macintosh and an IBM PC), and need to transfer data between them, there are several ways to do it. If both have serial ports, you might use your modem to upload the data from one computer to an online service or BBS, then download it with the other computer. Or you might pay to have the data converted from one format to another or send it as an e-mail attachment.

However, these options are time-consuming. Both machines already have what it takes to communicate with one another: serial ports. All you need to do is link them directly, substituting what is called a null-modem cable for modems and telephone lines. In any event, such a direct link transfers data far faster than a modem and online service or BBS: Data is transferred at speeds of up to 115,000 bps between directly linked computers.

A minimal null-modem connection (as illustrated in Figure 7.2) uses only three pins: 2, 3, and 7—Transmit Data, Receive Data, and Signal Ground, respectively.

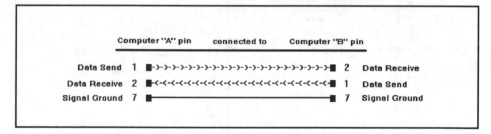

Figure 7.2 Minimal null-modem connection

The connections between pins 2 and 3 are reversed—i.e., pin 2 on Connector A is connected to pin 3 on Connector B, while pin 3 is connected to pin 2. This is so that each computer's Transmit Data pin is hooked directly to the other's Receive Data pin—the logic is (I hope) obvious.

Pin 7 on Connector A is connected directly to Connector B's pin 7. Its function is to provide an electrical ground for the signals.

Because of the operational requirements of many RS-232 ports and communications programs, the typical null-modem cable uses the nine basic pins mentioned earlier (either 1 through 8 and 20; or 2 through 8, 20, and 22).

These pins are not connected in exactly the same manner as they are in a normal RS-232 computer-to-modem cable, however. For openers, only two pins are connected to their counterparts: 1 and 7. The other pins are reversed and/or jumped, as shown in Figure 7.3

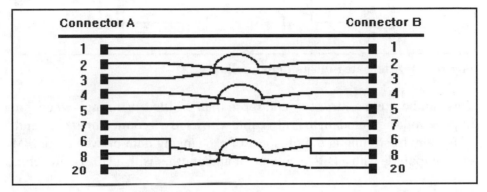

Figure 7.3 Typical null-modem connection

The connections between pins 2 and 3 are reversed; i.e., Connector A's pin 2 is connected to Connector B's pin 3, while Connector A's pin 3 is connected to Connector B's pin 2. This way, each computer's data-send and data-receive lines are always open.

Pins 4 and 5 are likewise reversed, resulting in each computer seeing a constant Ready signal from the other when checking whether it's OK to send data.

Pins 6 and 20 are reversed to fool the computer into thinking it is properly connected to a modem that has established a telephone connection with another computer. Pin 8 on each computer is jumped to pin 6 to simulate a carrier signal. (Without it, the computer's software would think that the carrier had been lost, and disconnect.) The voltage from pin 20 sets pins 6 and 8 to a level that appears to the host system to indicate a proper connection. (See Chapter 3 for more detailed information on what each of these pins does.)

Some systems may use the configuration shown in Figure 7.4, in which pins 4, 5, and 8 are jumped to one another on their respective connectors to provide the appropriate signal levels to fool the serial port and software into thinking a modem is at work.

Cross-Connecting a DB-9 with a DB-25 Connector

If you have an IBM AT, a PC clone or near-clone of the AT, or any of a number of aftermarket serial cards for the IBM PC and compatibles, you will find that your serial port has a DB-9 connector rather than a DB-25 connector.

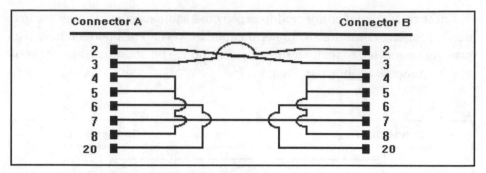

Figure 7.4   Alternate null-modem hookup

This can be quite a surprise—and more than a little frustrating—when you unpack your new modem to find a cable with a DB-25 connector at each end.

Equally frustrating is the prospect of exchanging data between one IBM PC/compatible with a DB-25 connector and another with a DB-9 connector.

WHY DB-9?

I'm uncertain as to why certain serial ports use a DB-9 connector. The DB-9's existence appears to be the result of some arbitrary decisions; there aren't really any advantages or disadvantages to using a DB-9 connector that are worth mentioning.

The DB-9 plug is possible because, as I mentioned earlier, only 8 or 9 of the 25 available pins on an RS-232 port are used during asynchronous modem communication. Its pin assignments are as shown in Table 7.2.

Table 7.2 RS-232C DB-9 Pin Assignment	
Pin	**Assignment**
1	Carrier detect
2	Receive data
3	Transmit data
4	Data terminal ready
5	Signal ground
6	Data set ready
7	Request to send
8	Clear to send
9	Ring indicator

You may have noticed that the numbers of DB-9 pin assignments are different from those for DB-25 pin assignments. This is another unfathomable occurrence, because most of the numbers could certainly be matched. In any event, Table 7.3 lists the DB-9 pin assignments and their DB-25 counterparts:

Table 7.3 DB-9 and DB-25 Pin Assignment		
DB-9 Pin	**DB-25 Pin**	**Assignment/Function**
1	8	Carrier detect
2	3	Receive data
3	2	Transmit data
4	20	Data terminal ready
5	7	Signal ground
6	6	Data set ready
7	4	Request to send
8	5	Clear to send
20	22	Ring indicator

On IBM AT-type serial cards, Equipment Ground (DB-25 pin 1) isn't used. However, the IBM serial port does require that Carrier Detect (DB-25 pin 8, DB-9 pin 1) be used. And Ring indicator (DB-25 pin 22) is sometimes used by MS-DOS communications software, so it is used in the DB-9 connector (designated pin 9).

Making the Connection

To properly connect a DB-9 with a DB-25 connector, wire the pins as shown in Figure 7.5 (DB-9 pin 1 to DB-25 pin 8, etc.).

Figure 7.5 DB-25 to DB-9 connection

The basic idea is to connect the pins per their assignments, rather than going by their numbers, although you will use the numbers imprinted on the connectors to identify the pins.

DB-9 Null-Modem Cables

Both DB-9 to DB-25 and DB-9 to DB-9 null-modem cables can be constructed, following the pin-assignment requirements I discussed for DB-25 null-modem cables. Again, go by pin assignments in determining which pins are directly connected to their counterparts, which are reversed, and which are jumped.

A DB-9 to DB-25 null-modem cable would be wired in one of the configurations shown in Figure 7.6.

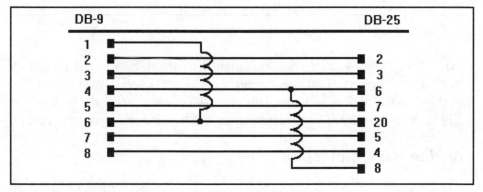

Figure 7.6   DB-9 to DB-25 null-modem cable wiring configurations

A DB-9 to DB-9 null-modem cable would be wired in one of the configurations shown in Figure 7.7.

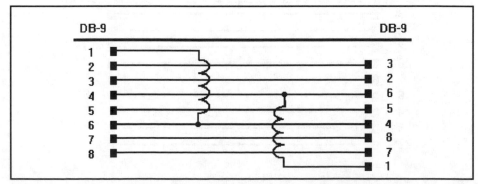

Figure 7.7   DB-9 to DB-9 null-modem cable wiring configurations

SPECIAL NOTES ON VARIATIONS IN PIN ASSIGNMENTS

A possible reason for making your own cable that I didn't mention earlier is to connect two computers that aren't designed to interface—say, an old Radio Shack Model 100 (which uses a DB-25 connector at its serial port) with a Radio Shack Color Computer (which uses a DIN connector—see the section "Other Connectors" below). Cables just aren't made for many such esoteric linkups.

Extreme caution should be exercised when attempting a connection of this type, simply because connector pin assignments (and sometimes the connectors themselves) can vary quite a bit.

Other Configurations

While the RS-232C pin assignments for DB-25 connectors discussed here and in Chapter 3 prevail with the majority of systems, you will encounter systems that differ in which pins are used. For example, while Apple's Super Serial Card uses a DB-25 connector, 10 pins are used (see Table 7.4).

Table 7.4 An Alternate Serial Connector Layout	
Pin	**Assignment**
1	Equipment ground
2	Transmit data
3	Receive data
4	Request to send
5	Clear to send
6	Data set ready
7	Signal ground
8	Carrier detect
19	Secondary clear to send
20	Data terminal ready

That configuration isn't too strange, as it makes use of RS-232C pin assignments for a DB-25 connector. But certain older modems, on the other hand, use a DB-9 connector with the pin assignments shown in Table 7.5.

I'll leave it as an exercise for you to work out how you might wire a cable and connectors to connect the Apple serial port to a modem using a DB-9 connector. It should be simple enough; as I've stressed previously, the important thing is to get the pins connected based on their assignments.

Table 7.5 Alternate Modem Connector Layout	
Pin	**Assignment**
2	Data set ready
3	Signal ground
4	Signal ground
5	Receive data
6	Data terminal ready
7	Carrier detect
8	Equipment ground
9	Transmit data

Other Connectors

A few machines don't use a DB connector at all. Certain computers (and modems) use what is called a DIN plug—a round connector with four, five, or eight pins—to connect with the serial port.

This may seem confusing at first, but it's not, once you understand the pin assignments. For example, the five-pin DIN connector used with Apple serial ports has the assignments shown in Table 7.6.

Table 7.6 Alternate Modem Connector Layout	
Pin	**Assignment**
1	Data terminal ready
2	Transmit data
3	Signal ground
4	Receive data
5	Data set ready

Wiring this kind of connector to a DB-25 connector should be fairly straightforward—again, if you understand the pin assignments at each end of the connection.

Other Standards

On some machines, you will find connectors that look familiar but which do not use the RS-232C standard. For example, serial ports on the original Mac 128 and 512K machines use a DB-9 connector—but the pin assignments are based on the RS-422 standard (see Table 7.7).

Table 7.7 RS-422 Standard Pin Assignments	
Pin	Assignment
1	Equipment ground
2	+5V
3	Signal ground
4	Transmit data
5	Transmit data
6	+12V
7	Handshake
8	Receive data
9	Receive data

These are clearly different from the pin assignments used by standard PC DB-9 connectors.

Cautions

Obviously, you should know the pin assignments for the computer and the pcripheral (or other computer) that you intend to connect with before you try to make a connecting cable. If you connect the wrong pins, you will at the very least experience a failure, and you may well damage the equipment.

You'll also want to make certain that the voltage levels used by each system are the same. (You'll normally run into this problem only when differing standards—such as RS-232C vs. RS-422—are in effect with the computers and/or peripherals in question.)

Providing information on all the serial communications standards and variants in use is certainly beyond the scope of this book—or any single book, for that matter. You will find hardware and software documentation, as well as books of tremendous help in tracking down the information you need to connect the serial ports of "alien" devices. It doesn't hurt to ask someone who knows, either. If you can't find the pin assignments for your computer(s) and/or peripheral in their documentation, by all means contact the equipment manufacturer or a knowledgeable computer technician.

NOTES ON NULL-MODEM TRANSFERS

There are certain software considerations to keep in mind when conducting a null-modem transfer between two computers. At the top of the list is the fact that you should use the same software package with each machine (assuming the computers use the same operating system). Whether or not you use the same program on both computers, be sure that both computers' parameters match, and select the same file-transfer protocol when you transfer files.

You won't use dial commands to initiate a connection between two computers connected by a null-modem cable. Most programs should be set to what is called the direct-connect mode; this is usually a menu selection designed for accommodating situations when your modem has already initiated a connection with another system, which is the net effect of using a null-modem cable. If the null-modem connection is established before the programs are booted, some of the more intelligent programs will sense a connection and move immediately into direct-connect mode.

Some programs require you to set up one machine as the host (in the answer mode) and the other as the caller. If the software package you buy has a good manual, it will tell you exactly how to set up the software for a null-modem transfer. If not, experiment with direct-connect, answer, and call modes.

Finally, as has been noted before, the precaution of using an archiving program to pack binary data or program files to safeguard against Xmodem or other padding should be observed for null-modem transfers.

CHAPTER 8

The Internet Defined: What It Is, What It Isn't, and What It Offers

The Internet is the most common application for PC/modem combinations nowadays, so it is appropriate that this book include a chapter about the Internet.

Whether or not you've been on the Internet, you probably have quite a few questions about it. This chapter shows you a bit about what the Internet is, what it isn't, what it offers, and how to access it.

INTERNET BASICS

A simple description of the Internet might go like this: "Tens of thousands of computers at locations around the world, each interlinked with the other, providing access to all interlinked computers and their files to anyone who has access to any one of these computers." This description is accurate, but it's too quick, too easy. So, let's take a closer look at the basic structure of the Internet.

Note: If you are Internet savvy, you may want to skip the rest of this chapter—although you may find the section in this chapter on the history of the Internet ("A Brief Descriptive History of the Internet") of interest.

First, you need to understand that the Internet is no single entity, nor is it a consumer online service like America Online or CompuServe. For that matter, neither are online services the Internet. However, online services can connect with the Internet. I mention this because sometimes those new to the online world confuse online services and "the Internet," which is easy to do, because the Internet holds endless potential for confusion.

The Internet is particularly confusing if you are unfamiliar with the terminology used to discuss it. You won't be among that group by the time you finish reading this chapter; you'll know more about Internet terminology and the Internet itself.

Basic Elements: Resources and Links

The Internet has two major elements—*resources* and *communications links* (which make the resources available to other computers).

There are several varieties of resources, the most important of which are *data resources*. Data resources consist of millions of data, text, and program files stored on tens of thousands of computers on the Internet worldwide. These resources are the main reason many computer users access the Internet. Data resources make up much of the surface content of the Internet—that is, what many perceive as being the Internet: text in Usenet newsgroups and/or the text and graphics displayed on-screen as *Web pages*.

Not incidentally, Web pages are the result of data and program files being transmitted to your computer. See the following section, "The Internet: Bringing It All Together," for details.

Data resources may be stored in any of several ways on computers hosting Web sites—on hard drives, in RAM, or by other means. How the data is stored is immaterial; the important thing is that Internet data resources are available to anyone who has access to the Internet.

The storage media, along with the computers on which the data is stored, and associated communications hardware and software, represent still more resources—in this case *hardware* and *software resources*.

After resources, the other major element of the Internet is its system of *communications links*. These links interconnect thousands of computers and help modem-equipped computer users access the data resources stored on those computers. Communications links consist of conventional telephone lines, high-speed data lines designed to carry only computer data, satellite and microwave relay links, modems, cable-TV links, and other components—including the computers on which Internet resources are stored.

These communications links provide a means whereby individual computers on the Internet are *networked*—simultaneously interconnected and sharing data resources—hence, the frequent reference to the Internet as a *network* of computers, any of which can be accessed at any time by any other computer on the network. In a sense, these communications links are resources, too.

(Interestingly, some computers linked to the Internet are themselves a part of networks, in the form of several PCs linked by a local area network, or LAN. Other computers that make up the Internet include mainframes, minicomputers, and individual PCs.)

Cumulatively then, data resources, the computers on which data are stored, and the links that interconnect the Internet's computers with other computers, *are* the Internet. Your perception of the data received from these resources completes the picture.

If the overall image here seems fuzzy, don't let it bother you; the Internet is more than a bit fuzzy both in concept and in reality. But it is not incomprehensible.

The Internet: Bringing It All Together

To better visualize just how the Internet functions, consider what happens when you are connected with a remote computer system—an online service, for example, or a computer bulletin board system (BBS). When you dial up another system, you have varying access to and control over that system. The commands you issue to view messages, download files, and so on cause programs on the host machine to perform certain actions. (Defined in detail in the section headed "Clients, Servers, and Hosts" later in this chapter, a *host machine* is any computer you dial up and connect with via modem.)

In a sense, you are like a *remote terminal*, issuing commands and sending/receiving data—an extension of the online service or BBS computer to which you are connected. (A remote terminal is a device connected to a computer by direct lines or telephone lines. Sometimes called a dumb terminal, a remote terminal may consist of a keyboard and monitor, and perhaps a printer or other peripheral, but it is not a computer. Rather, it is used to operate the computer to which it is connected, from a remote location, and it performs no other functions. Using a remote terminal is like being at the main keyboard of the computer to which it is connected.)

Something similar happens when you connect with a computer on the Internet, although your access and the range of commands are comparatively limited. Basically, you can request to see certain files (text and graphics) and, in the case of *applets*, run programs. Applets are mini-programs transmitted to your PC.

You request files by telling your Web browser to "go to" or "open" a specific Web page, or by clicking on a *hyperlink*, which does the same thing. When you take either action, the remote computer—the one with the page you want to see—sends data to your computer. Your Web browser translates the data into images and text on your computer's screen.

The data sent to you—and your request for it—may be routed through a number of other computers on the Internet before you see it. However, as far as you and your computer are concerned, you are connected to and communicating with only one computer. Thus, the entire web of interconnected computers can be said to be "transparent." Not incidentally, because this web of interconnected computers is worldwide, it is often referred to as the *World Wide Web*, or *WWW*.

Now imagine this: Tens of thousands of mainframes, minicomputers, and supercomputers around the world, all containing data and programs you can access. These computers, at different locations or sites, are linked to all the other computers by an extended network of connections. Every site linked by this network is as accessible as every other site. Not only are all the sites connected, but they are connected in more than one way (in the web-like structure), and also relay information between other computer systems and sites.

What Is a Site?

I should note here that a *site* is a computer or group of computers accessible via the Internet. Somewhat confusingly, the word site is also used to refer to the set of resources on a computer at a particular location that is accessible via the Internet. For example, you can access Chrysler Corporation product and other information on the World Wide Web at **http://www.chrysler corp.com**. Collectively, the product and promotional information presented is known as Chrysler's product information site. Thus, another way to think of a site is as a collection of related information files.

Each site has a unique address called a *URL*. The address **http://www.chryslercorp.com** in the preceding paragraph is an example of a URL. URL is short for Uniform Resource Locator, which is the function of the addressing system of the Web. The name is appropriate because it provides a uniform protocol for locating resources (files) on the Web.

As you will learn in this chapter, all navigation on the Web is based on URLs. You'll take a closer look at URLs in a bit, but for now consider a URL to be a site's address.

(*Note*: Internet addresses are preceded by http, which is short for Hypertext Transport Protocol. This prefix may be thought of as a command to your Web browser to connect with the World Wide Web and see the location or file following http. There are other prefixes, such as one that tells the browser to look for the file on your hard drive, which will be discussed in the section headed, "URLS: The Key to Navigating the Web.")

Some sites *are* networks, and some sites are part of other networks, existing simultaneously on the Internet and on other networks. (There are other networks, something worth mentioning in this context. In fact, connecting other networks to the Internet was a major source of growth for the Internet in the early 1990s. So, the Internet also is a network of networks.)

The World Wide Web

This is the element of the Internet that most newer modem users, as well as those who have never been online, think of as the Internet. This view is understandable because the Web gets the most media (TV, radio, newspaper, and magazine) coverage. The coverage and the interest of new users are, in turn, understandable because the World Wide Web is the most "glamorous" of all Internet elements. (All elements that are real, that is; many misconceptions about what the Internet and the Web are and offer have been fostered by film, novels, and the more sensationalistic press.)

The word glamorous is somewhat appropriate because, compared with other elements of the Internet, the Web offers glamour on several levels. There are Web sites that offer not only text, but text in colors, as well as graphics and photographs, sound, and even video, and also the previously mentioned applets.

A Pragmatic Overview of the Web

There are many ways to look at the Web. Perhaps the most straightforward viewpoint is to consider the Web as made up of millions of computer files. Data and program files are the essence of the Web; all else is the means by which you locate and retrieve files.

These millions of files are accessible, but you must know how to get to them. Later in this section, you'll look at how to navigate the World Wide Web to find files.

Once transmitted to your computer, as described in "The Internet: Bringing it All Together," Web files are put to use. If you have a Web browser capable of interpreting the files and presenting the result on your computer screen (and, in some instances, through your computer's speakers), your system presents the information contained in the Web-retrieved files as it was intended to appear.

Of course, you do not perceive all the chains of file search, retrieval, transmission, and interpretation. Rather, you see only the information that makes its way to your screen. And this is what the Web is all about—visual and audio information, in new forms and through new media and, sometimes, with new content.

DOCUMENTS, PAGES, HYPERTEXT, AND HYPERLINKS

Files at Web sites are organized into documents, each of which has one or more pages. The usage of the word document derives from the fact that, on the early Web, documents in the form of text files were the most-commonly accessible files.

The moniker stuck and is used with reference to even today's Web pages, many of which have multimedia content. (Binary files—typically graphic or program files—are also often called "documents." For a more detailed discussion of binary data, please see Chapter 11, "Internet Data Formats and Conversion.") Most references to the Web actually allude to these documents or individual pages within documents.

HOME PAGES

Note that the terms document and page are often used interchangeably, with page most often used to mean document. The first page of a document is always referred to as a site's or document's *home page*. If you navigate to a site without specifying a page, the home page is displayed. This is the default or index page for that site, which Web surfers consider the main or opening page.

In common use today, however, the term home page is often taken to mean an entire document carried on behalf of an individual, commercial, or other entity at a Web site. Therefore, Information Today, Inc.'s entire Web site (**http://www.infotoday.com**) is often referred to as the corporation's home page. Figure 8.1 shows the opening page at that Web site. (You will notice that various elements of Netscape here and elsewhere are missing, such as the button bar. This is also true of Microsoft Internet Explorer in various illustrations. I turn off the button bar and sometimes the location and other browser elements in order to display as much of the Web page as possible on the screen. So, don't be concerned if you don't see the exact same thing on your screen; it's just that we're running with different operating parameters.)

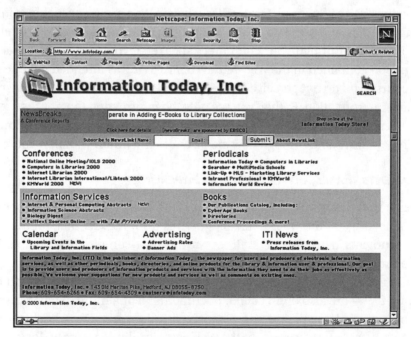

Figure 8.1   Information Today's home page

A given site on the Web usually contains more than one document or page. The Information Today, Inc. Web site, for example, hosts a publications catalog at **http://www.infotoday.com/catalog/**, which itself has numerous pages.

Viewed another way, adding the **/catalog** element of the URL **http://www. onlineinc.com/catalog** is asking to access a subdirectory on the **infotoday** server, named **/catalog**. Rather than a directory of that subdirectory, however, you see the default page (or home page) for the catalog, as shown in Figure 8.2.

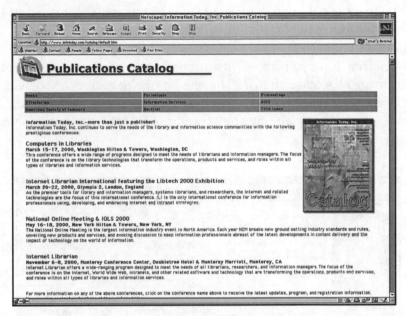

Figure 8.2 Information Today's online publications catalog

PAGE SIZES AND ROLES

However you may refer to them, Web pages vary by size (the number of kilobytes transmitted for a page) and display length (the number of computer screens required to display one page in its entirety). Depending on the layout and how much text or other material it contains, a page can require several computer screens to display it. A Web page may be designed to scroll vertically or horizontally, and Web browsers accommodate both designs.

Because of their inherent flexibility, Web sites may play many roles: Data forms, e-mail, search tools and lists, file transfers, newsgroups, and even telnet may be found at Web sites.

HTML: The Language of the Web

Web pages are written in a simple, high-level language that Web browsers can understand and process known as *hypertext markup language* (or *HTML*). Because of this, Web pages are sometimes referred to as *hypertext pages*.

Typically, the first file transmitted to your computer when you open or go to a Web page is an HTML file. Your Web browser interprets the HTML commands contained in a page to display the data it contains and data from other files, if any, as a Web page.

Text on a Web page is usually embedded, or included, in the HTML document that makes up the page. Other data may be transmitted as separate files. This includes, but is not limited to, graphic images (typically binary .JPG or .GIF files), additional text, binary data for sound files or video, and mini-programs referred to as *applets*. As mentioned earlier, binary files are often graphic image files. Since almost all images on Web pages are .JPG or .GIF format, these are the types of binary files you are most likely to encounter.

Figure 8.3 shows a Web page (left), and the HTML code used to generate it (right).

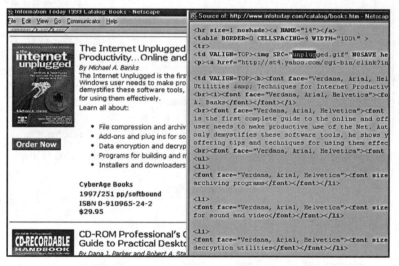

Figure 8.3   A portion of a Web page, as displayed with a browser (left), and in its HTML form (right)

Typically, the initial HTML code or page is transmitted first, which causes your browser to display the embedded text as instructed by *formatting codes* included in the HTML page. (Formatting codes are contained within the greater-than/lessor-than symbols you see in the example in Figure 8.3. For example, <b> means, "Display all the text following this symbol in boldface," and </b> means, "Stop displaying in boldface.") The coding system is like typesetting—at least where text display is concerned. HTML files are designated by the file name extensions .HTM or .HTML. Other codes specify additional layout elements, such as the location of graphics on the page and special elements like *links* to other pages.

Graphic images come next, again, transmitted as separate files. Commands embedded in the HTML document instruct your browser where and how to display images.

(*Note*: For additional how-to and reference information about the HTML language and its applications, visit **http://www.ncsa.uiuc.edu/General/ Internet/WWW/HTMLPrimer.html**. This site is sponsored by the National Center for Supercomputer Applications.)

Thus, a typical Web page is composed of several files. The text HTML file is the foundation of every Web page—the basic element. Other text or binary files may follow, depending on the page's content.

HYPERLINKS

An important coding element in HTML documents is the *hyperlink*. A hyperlink is a means of linking the current document to another Web page or to a binary file. Linked pages or files may be other documents at the current Web site, or they may be at another site entirely. The function of a hyperlink is to have another Web page, or a specific file, transmitted to your computer.

Hyperlinks may be textual or graphical in nature. A text hyperlink is usually distinguished by the fact that it is displayed as underlined, like this. A hyperlink may also be a different color from surrounding text, and hyperlinks you have already visited are usually another color still.

When you pass the mouse pointer or cursor over a hyperlink, the cursor becomes a pointing finger. Also, the URL to which the hyperlink connects is displayed in the browser's status line, at the lower left of the display.

Users can access a page connected by a hyperlink by clicking on the hyperlink itself. Therefore, it can be said that a hyperlink is a means by which a document page, or any element within a page, can be linked to other pages, files, or even other sites. The hyperlinked structure of the Web is the key to its magic; any one element of a Web site or page can be linked directly to absolutely any other element.

As implied a few lines back, some hyperlinks are embedded in graphic images (called *clickable graphics* or *image maps*). You can identify image maps by their labeling and by the fact that the cursor becomes a pointing finger when passed over them, indicating a hyperlink. As with text hyperlinks, the URL to which an image map leads or the coordinates of the image itself are displayed in your browser's status line when the mouse cursor passes over the image map, as shown in Figure 8.4.

Figure 8.4   A World Wide Web page with hyperlinks and image maps

As previously stated, a hyperlink can be a continuation of the current Web page (another page or supplementary material such as images, sounds, and so forth), a page from a different document at the same site, or a page at a different site. For example, many Web sites contain reference lists, which are really links that connect to pages at other sites.

Hyperlinks to other sites are often creative, adding features to pages such as the current time from the U.S. Naval Observatory. (To do this, you add the URL **http://tycho.usno.navy.mil:80/what.html** to a page as a hyperlink.)

Hyperlinks may also run programs on the host machine or at another remote computer. An example of running a program that's not a part of the Web page in question is the Web counter, which tracks and displays the number of people who have accessed a Web page. This counter is actually a link to a program running on the host computer or another machine (not on your PC). The program actually tracks of the number of visits to or *hits* on that Web page. It then transmits the results to a designated location on the Web page each time it is run.

Interestingly, the lists that Web search engines compile and present are also just lists of hyperlinks. The list is compiled by a search program that runs on the host computer, and the URLs, or addresses, are inserted as hyperlinks in the HTML document you receive.

FILES FOR IMAGES AND ADD-ON PROGRAMS

As previously stated, graphic images come next, transmitted as separate files. Commands embedded in the HTML document tell your browser where and how to display images, which typically have extensions of .JPG or .GIF.

Following the HTML code and text files, and any graphics files, there may be binary files in any of several forms and formats. These files might include special image types, video or animation, sound and midi files, fonts, and specially formatted data (such as a spreadsheet). These kinds of data might be handled by your browser but more often, they are handed over to *add-on programs*. Add-ons, also known as *plug-ins* and *helper applications*, are programs stored on your hard disk that your browser can activate when it encounters specific types of data.

Knowing when to run such programs—also referred to as *spawning*—is your browser's job. A browser can recognize specific types of data by file name extensions, and, based on the browser's setup, it then runs a specific program and feeds the incoming data to it. Everything else is either turned over to an add-on program, saved to disk, or, in the case of unrecognized file types, canceled.

Most browsers can be set up to use a specific add-on when it sees a particular type of data coming in. Audio files in the RealAudio format, for example, identified by the extensions .RA or .RAM, are played with the RealAudio Player program—provided that you have the program on your hard drive and that your browser knows where to find it. Your browser also must know the extensions for RealAudio data. This is a set-up item, specified from within your browser's Options or Preferences menu. Most browsers come set up to recognize most of the more popular add-on programs' data extensions.

It's worth noting here that you must obtain many of these add-ons; your browser probably does not come with them. It has certain built-in capabilities, but these do not provide all the extra features that add-ons provide. Also, some add-ons may perform certain tasks better than your browser's built-in capabilities.

Fortunately, most add-ons either are free or are shareware, which you can download at a variety of Web sites or online services.

A DESCRIPTIVE HISTORY OF THE INTERNET

The Internet's beginnings lie in a U.S. Department of Defense research program. The goal was to design computer networks that could survive a nuclear attack. Even in the 1960s, more than a little sensitive and critical data flowed through the nation's infant computer networks. The project was ARPAnet, an acronym for the Advanced Research Projects Agency Network.

(ARPAnet is sometimes referred to as DARPAnet, an acronym that includes the word Defense.)

Packet-switching networks were a major element of the Internet. A given data file or data group could be divided into many packets, or units, of information, each containing a portion of the file. Each data packet also contained information as to its destination and how it fit with other packets. Data packets would be reassembled by the receiving system's communications program.

Along the way, data packets could be routed via available paths that included going through various computers on the Internet. This kind of routing required that each computer be able to communicate with every other computer on the network, at any time, which was how the network was designed: to provide, in effect, simultaneous links among all computers on the network.

Depending on whether a given computer site on the network was too busy (or, in the worst-case scenario, taken out by a nuclear strike), the same route might not be available for all the data packets, which was fine because the data packets did not have to use the same route. As long as the data packets carried information as to their destinations, any one route was the same as the next; no one path for data was *the* critical route. Any computer on the network could reroute data packets as required for them to arrive at their destinations.

Also created by this project were certain basic network communications and control protocols, known as *Transmission Control Protocol/Internet Protocol* or *TCP/IP*. You'll see TCP/IP bandied about quite a bit in references to the Internet, but you don't need to understand it thoroughly. Just know that it refers to a set of rules by which computers linked to the Internet communicate and handle the data they're carrying. TCP/IP also (in part) defines the Internet, because a computer cannot be a part of the Internet unless it communicates by using these protocols.

(*Note*: In case you are curious, TCP is the protocol in charge of making sure that data packets get to the appropriate destinations. IP is the address protocol, used to assign a destination, or address, to data packets. Addresses from IP are used by TCP to route each data packet.)

The ARPAnet became immensely popular, and, as more and more interconnections developed, the user base grew tremendously. Eventually, commercial computer sites began hooking into the network, in addition to the educational, scientific, and government computer sites that formed its base. As the network continued to grow and evolve, its military component became a separate entity, MILNET (for MILitary NETwork), and the Internet as we know it today began to take shape.

The National Science Foundation (NSF) promoted the growth of the civilian Internet throughout the 1980s, in part with its joining a network of supercomputers to the Internet. As the Internet continued to grow, international links using Internet communications protocols were forged. By the end of the decade, commercial as well as government, education, and scientific organizations were setting up sites on the Internet. For some time, commercial entities had been using the Internet for e-mail communication and for research. Today, the overwhelming majority of new sites on the Internet are commercial.

In 1989, researchers at the European Organization for Nuclear Research (or CERN, which is the acronym for the organization's name in French) created a worldwide network of several supercomputers to facilitate access to data by physicists and other scientists using the Internet. This network quickly evolved into the massive Internet adjunct, the World Wide Web. The Web is the sophisticated system previously described. Its page-oriented documents teem with hypertext links, and today's technology adds graphics, sound, and even video at some sites for a true multimedia network.

As noted previously, the World Wide Web *is* the Internet to many observers and users. But as you will learn, the Web is only one of many resources available on the Internet.

BUT HOW DOES IT ALL WORK?

As noted, the Internet is a globe-spanning network, with a backbone of interlinks among some 40,000 computers. There is a structure to the sites and their interconnections, but it frequently changes—despite which, any computer on the Internet can communicate with any other computer on the Net. The Internet is set up so that data is typically routed over the fastest links— which may or may not be the shortest geographical route.

The Internet's geography usually has little to do with physical locations. Instead, the Internet routes connections by using a dedicated address format. Specifically, each site has a 32-bit numeric address that tells all other systems on the Internet how to contact it. In human terms, these numeric addresses are the "xxxxx.com," "xxxxx.edu," and similar addresses we use to navigate.

(*Note*: A 32-bit address is known as an *IP address* that looks like this: **192.80.63.253**.)

We deal with IP addresses in more meaningful human terms, thanks to *DNS* (*Domain Name Service.*) DNS is a protocol used by computers on the Internet to translate IP addresses. Thus, a 32-bit address takes the form of a text address, like **http://www.bix.com**. This address is also known as *Fully Qualified Domain Name.*

Data packets transmitted from one computer to another are sent through the routes that are easiest to take and eventually arrive at their intended destinations.

This process is transparent to you, the Internet user, thanks to Internet Protocol addressing and Transmission Control Protocol that routes the data.

URLs: The Key to Navigating the Web

I referred to Web addresses a number of times, always in this format: **http://www.xxxxxx.com**. This type of address is called a URL, as you know.

Consider the process of using a URL as analogous to directing your computer to a file on your hard disk—which, by the way, is something you can do, although the command to your Internet browser would be something like **file:///c:/myfiles/chapter1.htm**.

Navigating the Web by using URLs is an expansion of finding a file on a disk. (Remember my discussion of the World Wide Web as a series of files on computers at various Internet sites?) The difference is that the file can exist on any computer on the Internet network.

Many URLs include a file name so you can go directly to a specific file. The addressing system follows UNIX conventions. (UNIX was an early computer operating system that still has its adherents today. It was used on all types of computers—mainframe, Apple, PC, minis, and so on—which is probably why so much of the Internet uses UNIX-based routing.) An address indicates the site (server/computer), any directories involved, and the file to retrieve. If no file is specified, you go to the site in question, and its home page or index page is retrieved and displayed.

You must direct your browser to go outside your machine to browse the Web by using a prefix to tell it to connect to the Internet. The special protocol you use is *http*, or *Hypertext Transport Protocol*, hence the prefix "http" in a URL.

The front slashes in the address are, again, a UNIX convention. The name that follows **http://** is the site, followed by the name of the server and the file path on the server in question.

(The **http://** prefix tells your browser to find the URL on the World Wide Web. To find a file on your system, enter the **file://** prefix. To make a connection through an ftp server, you use the prefix **ftp://**. A telnet connection is indicated by **telnet://**.)

Putting all this together, if you wanted to retrieve a document named **pretend.html** in a directory named **fiction** at a fictional site called **ficcion**, you would use this URL: **http://www.ficcion.com/fiction/pretend.html**.

Note that you will find many, many documents with the file name extension **.html**; this is the extension of hypertext documents that use the HTML language. Your PC, being restricted to three-letter file name extensions, uses the extension **.htm** for HTML files. Some servers do the same.

By the way, the first part of the site name alludes to its network type. In our fictional example, **www** means this is a World Wide Web site.

Web-Browser Access to Usenet Newsgroups

To use your Web browser to access a Usenet newsgroup, in the Web Page box simply type **news:** followed by the name of the newsgroup. (You do not need to include the http:// prefix.) Therefore, to view the rec.autos.antique newsgroup, you type **news:rec.autos.antique**.

The actual computer name makes up the second part of the name. The final part is the *domain identifier* (sometimes called the *domain name*). This indicates the type of operation at that site. In this example, **.com** means "commercial," which is one of six domain names:

- .com—Commercial site, operated by a company or corporation, such as **compuserve.com** or **microsoft.com**

- .gov—Sites sponsored by governmental agencies, such as **white house.gov** and **epa.gov**

- .edu—Educational institutions, such as **muohio.edu**

- .mil—Military site, such as the U.S. Naval Observatory mentioned previously

- .org—Organization, usually a nonprofit or something that doesn't fit in another category

- .sci—Scientific or research site

Some sites carry geographical suffixes as part of their domain names, like .uk for a site in the U.K. (These are sometimes used in the U.S., the suffix being .us.) There may also be a colon and a number (like this: **:80**) appended to some site names; this is merely a designator for a given port on the computer at that location.

Incidentally, if you have the numeric IP address for a computer on the Internet, you can use it as easily as you use the domain name. For example, rather than entering **http://www.bix.com** to go to the BIX Web site, you can enter the IP address **192.80.63.253** in place of **www.bix.com**.

Note: If you know the file or document you want to access from a Web site, you can add this to the address, preceded by a slash, as in the following example, where the fictional commercial server **zxrb.com** contains the file **mike.html** in its root directory: **http://www.zxrb.com/mike.html**.

Typing this URL takes you directly to the page contained in **mike.html**, without having to view the main page of **zxrb.com**.

With all Internet sites linked full time with all other computers on the Internet, moving data to a given address is no different than moving it to any other address on the Internet.

Clients, Servers, and Hosts

Before you get rolling with these applications, you'll encounter three important terms in nearly every discussion of Internet resources and applications. I mention them here because they are sometimes used in ways that can confuse their respective meanings. The terms are client, server, and host.

A *client* is, strictly speaking, a program that communicates with another computer to obtain access to files or programs. In the overall vernacular of the Internet, it has come to mean the computer that is communicating with another computer system to access its resources.

A *server* is a computer system or program that provides resources on a network. A server is often referred to by the kind of resource it provides. Examples are mail server (accepts, sends, and receives e-mail) and news server (carries Usenet newsgroups). Web server and Internet server are sometimes confusing usages; either can mean a system that offers access to the World Wide Web or the Internet, or a system that has Web or Internet resources (such as Web pages). The simple rule for servers is this: A server provides resources, and the client connects with the server to access those resources, be they files, hyperlinks, access to other systems, or other information.

The term *host* is often used synonymously with the term server. More often, however, it refers to any system you dial up for any reason. It is logical either way: If you are dialing into a system to use resources, it is your host. If the system is enabling your access to other systems, in the manner of an Internet service provider (or ISP), it is your host, enabling your activities on the Internet or wherever it may take you.

WHAT DOES THE INTERNET HAVE TO OFFER?

I previously described the Internet as "... a set of resources, in the form of millions of files and programs on tens of thousands of computers." This description is valid, but what exactly are these resources?

When you get to the bottom line, files and applications are the foundation of all computing. The uses to which they are put are the real resources. Internet resources are no different; there are several categories of applications that make up the major Internet resources:

- E-mail
- Usenet newsgroups
- The World Wide Web
- Ftp (file-transfer protocol)
- Telnet
- The Internet itself

The following sections explore each category of Internet resources. These resources reside on the computers at various sites. As you may imagine, millions upon millions of files reside on the computers at the more than 40,000 Internet sites that currently exist—with more being added daily!

E-Mail

Internet e-mail is something of a wonder, considering what can be done with it. Millions of Internet, online service, and BBS users at tens of thousands of sites worldwide can exchange unlimited messages, with the delivery of most mail taking place within minutes—if not seconds—of sending it. It can do all this, and at a very low price. The cost of sending a typical e-mail message of two screen pages ranges from nothing to perhaps 50 cents—that upper range is the cost of time spent online typing the message on a service with high per-minute rates.

E-mail was one of the first Internet elements to surface in "mainstream" telecomputing. E-mail among Internet sites has been available from the beginning, but Internet e-mail exchange with commercial online services and BBSs is relatively recent. Commercial online service users recognized the advantages of Internet e-mail access almost as soon as their respective services made it available. There was no charge beyond their online connect time (minimal with off-line e-mail composition), and mail delivery was almost as fast as an online service's internal mail service.

Because e-mail could go to, as well as from, a commercial online service, users quickly discovered that they not only could stay in touch with Internet sites, but also with friends and associates on other commercial online services. (CompuServe pioneered this area, being the first commercial online service to offer Internet e-mail service, along with several other direct e-mail links, including MCI Mail, X.400 connections, and more.)

Today, all commercial online services—whether consumer, business, or specialty services—have Internet e-mail access.

Internet e-mail was most commercial online service users' first exposure to the Internet. Long before many had heard of Usenet newsgroups, Web pages, or other elements of today's Internet, they were using Internet e-mail to communicate with those on other services and at Internet sites.

Internet e-mail is simple to send. The address consists of the recipient's user name and the name of the online service or Internet site where the recipient has an account, entered in a simple format. The Internet takes care of routing and delivering the message. Other than that, mail composition and actually sending it goes pretty much like sending internal e-mail. Internet mail that you receive appears in your e-mail inbox, just like e-mail from other sources. (Internet sites follow the naming conventions discussed in the preceding section, headed "But How Does It All Work?")

Depending on your Internet service provider—particularly if it is an online service—there may be special addressing protocols to follow for sending e-mail to other sites on the Internet. Refer to your ISP's online help or manual for more information.

It is also worth noting that many World Wide Web pages contain mail hyperlinks, which can be used to send mail. When you click a Web page's mail hyperlink, a form for an e-mail message pops up. The message is already addressed, with your e-mail address and the sender's. Type the message, press Send, and your mail is sent. (This is true if your Web browser is set up with a designated mail server, your user ID, and a return address.)

Such a link is often known as a *mailto* because it makes use of the HTML command **mailto:userid@system.com** (where **userid@system.com** is the e-mail recipient's address).

Usenet Newsgroups

You probably heard about Usenet and newsgroups before you heard about anything else about the Internet. Commercial online services such as CompuServe began carrying, or providing, Usenet newsgroups early on because there was a large demand for them—particularly with groups involving special interests.

What Is Usenet?

But just what is Usenet? Is it another network, like the Internet? Not at all: The name Usenet is an acronym for USEr NETwork, but Usenet is more a set of rules for—and a way to—organize newsgroups. It has no specific location, and it exists both on and off the Internet.

Newsgroups are just extended simple message bases that contain messages arranged by subject and organized into *threads*. Threads are messages that are linked, by subtopic and/or a chain of posts and replies. Figure 8.5 shows some newsgroup listings.

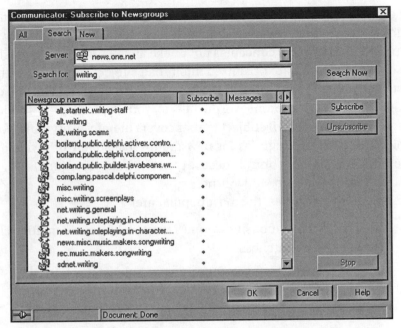

Figure 8.5   A typical listing of Usenet newsgroups

Newsgroups are like the message bases or bulletin boards on computer BBSs and online services, in that they contain messages grouped by subject and thread. However, the similarity ends here with most of them because anyone can post anything they want in the majority of newsgroups. So, prepare to wade through a lot of extraneous commentary and diatribes.

The better newsgroups do not have this problem because they have moderators who track and weed out extraneous and irrelevant messages—and users. Moderated newsgroups, however, are in the minority.

All newsgroup messages are referred to as *articles*. So, when a system menu that presents Usenet newsgroups refers to articles, it means messages.

Most ISPs (whether they are actual ISPs or commercial online services) offer all public newsgroups. (A few newsgroups, such as those devoted to a specific system and its users, are available only if you are a user on the system in question.)

In practice, you determine which newsgroups to read, and your ISP's newsreader system takes care of bringing in new messages in those newsgroups, displaying them on demand, and tracking which messages you've already read.

The typical Usenet newsgroup server copies in all messages frequently, and distributes replies and new messages posted to newsgroups to all other newsgroup servers. The whole concept is not unlike an open-ended chain letter.

Usenet newsgroups are organized into broad subject categories with endless subcategories. These categories are worth exploring, and you will quickly learn which have content worthwhile to you (typically, the moderated newsgroups). The range of subject matter covers literally everything!

The basic subject categories for newsgroups available worldwide are alt, bionet, bit, biz, comp, control, decus, general, gnu, ieee, junk, k12, misc, news, rec, sci, soc, talk, to, and vmsnet.

Among these categories, the most popular are:

- biz—Discussions of business topics (presently, mostly multilevel marketing, or MLM, pitches!)
- comp—Discussions of computer-related subjects
- misc—Topics that don't quite fit anywhere else
- news—Topics having to do with newsgroups
- rec—Recreation and related subjects
- sci—Science, from archaeology to zoology
- soc—Social subjects, including cultural mishmashes
- talk—Discussions/debate/argument on controversial themes

Newsgroups branch into subcategories and specific topics and subtopics, which are readily identified by their names. For example, a newsgroup named **alt.autos.antique** contains discussions about antique cars. The newsgroup is in the **alt** category, under the subject of **autos**, and focuses on the topic of **antique**. The material covered by one newsgroup may overlap another. For example, **alt.autos.antique** has some similarity to **rec.autos.antique**.

There are also introductory, regional, special, and local newsgroups (such as **compuserve** on CompuServe, **aol** on AOL, and **netcom** on Netcom)—not to mention some foreign (especially German) newsgroups. In all, there are nearly 20,000 newsgroups.

CODED TRANSMISSIONS AND BINARY FILES VIA USENET

The majority of newsgroups carry only text, but some are used to provide binary files for transfer. These files require that you use special software that translates files containing token seven-bit ASCII characters into their original binary forms. (ASCII, an abbreviation for American Standard for Computer Information Interchange, is a standard electronic format for textual data. ASCII format guarantees that characters—letters, numerals, and symbols—are represented within computers and during data transmission and storage in an agreed-upon electronic format called the ASCII code. This enables computers to exchange data. I discuss this and related data format elements in detail in Chapter 11, "Internet Data Formats and Conversion.")

This tokenizing, or encoding, of files is necessary because eight-bit files cannot be carried in Usenet's text-only messages.

(*Note*: In case you haven't read Chapter 3, you should know that seven-bit ASCII characters are those generated by your keyboard's typewriter keys, that is, the letters of the alphabet, numerals, and punctuation marks commonly used in communication. These are called seven-bit because the groups of electronic impulses used to represent a given character in transmission or storage requires only seven data bits. There are 128 of these seven-bit ASCII characters.

Eight-bit characters—also known as *binary characters*—are the control, graphic, and other characters used internally by your computer to store programs and certain types of data. As you might guess, they are called eight bit because eight data bits are required to represent one of these characters.

See Chapter 3, along with Chapter 11, for more detailed explanations of computer data formats.)

This capability means that images, PKZIP files, and other eight-bit data files can be transmitted via newsgroup messages. Because there is an upper limit to newsgroup message size (50 KB in all cases), more than one message is often used to transmit a file. When this is the case, headers are included in the messages containing the file that the decoding software uses to put the message contents together.

Among the better programs of this type is Wincode. This program handles both encoding and decoding files for transmission via Usenet newsgroups, using what is known as a *MIME* (or *Multipurpose Internet Mail Extension*) type of encoding.

As detailed in Chapter 11, MIME is a process of encoding data files (most often eight-bit data files). The characters that comprise the data are replaced by token seven-bit characters, which are the only sorts of characters that can be handled by Usenet. They are then transmitted as seven-bit messages. The software takes care of the encoding and decoding for you.

Such programs also can be used to e-mail binary files as seven-bit ASCII text files. WinZip is also a fine tool for decoding binary newsgroup and e-mail files.

Some online services, including AOL and CompuServe, provide Usenet front ends. Among other things, these front ends can decode certain ASCII-coded binary files transmitted as Usenet newsgroup messages. This feature saves you the trouble of decoding or translating an ASCII-coded binary file; the front end decodes and stores the file in its original format for you.

Ftp

Ftp is an acronym for *file-transfer protocol*, which refers to the Internet's special file-transfer protocol. As with other areas involving the Internet, special protocols are involved in transferring files (text or binary), and special software is required.

Special sites are required for ftp as well. You can access ftp through almost any site that offers it, but it must be open to you. Most ftp sites allow you to sign on as an anonymous user, with a standard ID and password. This is given to you before you sign on, which means that you do not need an account with the site in question. Many ftp sites do not require a password. However, because ftp sites are frequently busy, they may have restricted hours of access or may be available to only a certain number of users at a time.

File offerings at ftp sites vary. They offer everything that can be put into a file: text, graphic images, photos, data files, and on and on.

When you log on at an ftp site, you see directory and file listings, as shown in Figure 8.6.

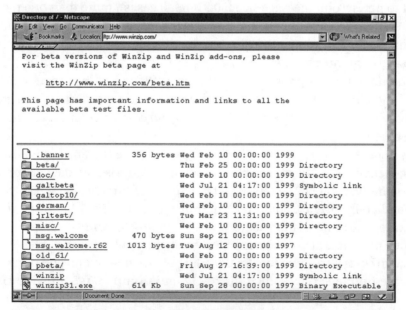

Figure 8.6 An example of ftp site directories

These listings represent files available for download. Select the file(s) you want to download, and they will be transmitted to you over the Internet using Internet file-transfer protocol.

HTML pages can be made to deliver files—which of course they do by transferring a file whenever a graphic, for example, is included in a Web page. Pages also can be set up to access a site via ftp, eliminating the need to enter the ftp address or to go through a complex selection process. This is how file-transfer protocol is made available at some World Wide Web sites. This is the case with the WinZip site (**http://www.winzip.com**). Figure 8.7 shows you what this kind of resource offering at a Web site looks like.

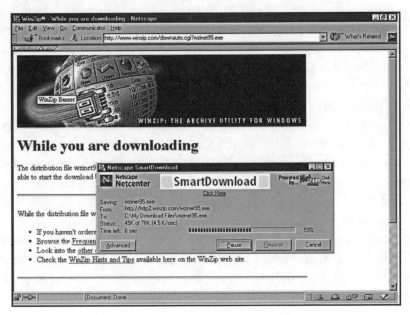

Figure 8.7   A file transfer in progress at an ftp WWW site

With these kinds of Web pages, you simply click a download button or other hypertext link to receive a file. Your Web browser software and the Web server take care of the rest. In time, file transfer via HTML front ends at Web sites may well supersede ftp as a separate entity.

Note: To get to an ftp site by using a Web browser, you enter **ftp://** followed by **ftp** and the name of the site, like **ftp://ftp.cdrom.com**, or you enter it like this for a numeric IP address: **ftp://123.456.7.890**.

(Alternately, you can use **file://** rather than **ftp://** at the beginning of the URL.)

If you know the directory and file name you want to reach, you can add these using slashes to separate directory names.

Telnet

The Internet's major function is to transfer data, and it does this well—so well, in fact, that you can sign on to certain computers on the Internet (those that are accessible in this way) by using the Internet in the manner of a packet-switching network, like Tymnet. This is done using telnet, which is a terminal-emulation communications protocol.

You must know the site's telnet address, which, when entered, takes you to the service's logon prompt. From here, you normally must have an account with the service, so you can supply your user ID and password.

Using telnet is convenient at times, in that you don't have to hang up and make a new connection if you want to check in with your account on an online service or other computer. It also may cost less than using a commercial packet-switching network. (Some online services charge less for access via telnet than via packet-switching networks). On the other hand, money that you save may be negated by your ISP's rates for telnet use.

Note that a telnet connection can handle any online activities the online service provides—reading online text, transferring files, sending and receiving e-mail on the service to which you are connected, real-time conversation, and so on. However, you must sign on in standard terminal mode. Also, because you are putting a long and involved chain of connections between you and the connection, you will notice a distinct slowdown in response time and service.

You can also use telnet with a Web browser, provided that it is properly configured. The URL format is **telnet://**, followed by the site's address in numeric or plain English. Examples are **telnet://site.name** or **telnet//123.456.7.890**.

The Internet as a Resource

The Internet itself is a resource. The physical Internet of computers, connections, and support hardware, along with the software that maintains the connections and handles data, actually *is* the Internet. What I have just discussed are applications for the Internet.

But, in a roundabout way, the Internet is also its own application. File storage and data transmission and reception are elements that without which neither the Internet nor the other Internet applications could exist.

The Internet's viability as a resource depends in large part on its capability to carry data from one point to another—which it was designed to do even under the most adverse conditions, and which it will always be able to do.

Summary

This too-brief introduction to the Internet has been to help you learn what the Internet is and how it works, with a slight emphasis on the World Wide Web—that being the most popular element of the Internet.

You now should understand the various elements of the Internet and understand how to access many of its resources by using your Web browser. You also should have a solid feel for what the Internet is, in terms of its structure and resources.

CHAPTER 9

Getting on the Net:
Selecting a Browser and an ISP

The purpose of this chapter is to acquaint you with the factors that affect your choice of most of the Internet's tools—a *Web browser* and an *Internet Service Provider* (ISP).

Most of you already have a Web browser and an ISP. But, are your browser and ISP providing optimum functionality and service for your online applications? Maybe, or maybe not. This chapter helps you evaluate each.

The first part of this chapter focuses on Web browsers—mainly Netscape Navigator and Microsoft Internet Explorer. As you will learn, these two browsers are not the only viable choices available, but they are the most practical.

The second part of this chapter provides information about ISPs. It is intended to help you decide whether you want to use an online service (such as AOL or CompuServe) to access the Internet, or a dedicated Internet access service (such as Mindspring).

The intent in both sections is to provide the information you need to make intelligent choices for the most important Internet tools. These choices, of course, should be based on your preferences, needs, and working habits.

Even if you already have a Web browser and an ISP, don't skip this chapter. You may find something that works better than your current setup. Finding what works better—or best—is what this chapter is all about. So, please approach this chapter with an open mind, and don't worry about what is labeled as "best" by other users, co-workers, or magazines. Those sources can't tell you what's best for your needs, because there is no absolute best. There is only what works for you, and what doesn't work for you. So, if something looks interesting, try it out; it may turn out to be your personal best!

WEB BROWSERS: AN OVERVIEW

As you may expect, Web browsers didn't exist before the advent of the World Wide Web. They weren't needed. But, while they are a fairly new type of software, Web browsers are far from primitive. Competition and the general state of computer technology makes it possible for Web browsers to enjoy a much faster evolution than most kinds of software.

Also, the demand for better browsers and the ever-increasing extension of Web capabilities made it necessary for browsers to reach a high state of sophistication quickly.

Interpreting HTML code was the main function of early Web browsers. Most browser features existed to support this function—the capability to connect with and navigate the World Wide Web included.

It wasn't long before other features were suddenly necessary, or at least convenient. These features include bookmark files to store commands to navigate to specific sites, more sophisticated file-handing capabilities, and a lot of other features that are standard in today's browsers.

The most important of these additional features were mail composition, sending, and delivery; Usenet newsgroup access; and ftp (file-transfer protocol) capabilities. Some features were previously handled by other programs, as was dialing up and connecting with an Internet link.

Demand and competition resulted in these and many other features and capabilities being added to various Web browsers—thus, the evolution of Web browser programs began. This evolution continues today, with new capabilities being added to keep pace with new Internet technology.

Obviously, which browser you use is a vital consideration. This is also the first of the Two Great Internet Debates. Deciding which browser is best has become an emotionally charged pastime for many on the Web. The overwhelming majority of Internet users are polarized on the subject, but each has the same opinion: The best browser is the one he or she uses.

Ironically, however, there are only two good choices among all the browsers available for Windows users—Netscape Navigator and Microsoft Internet Explorer. I'll explain why this is so in a few pages, but first, look at some Web browser basics.

Browser Functions

All browsers have certain basic functions in common. These include:

- Connecting with the Web through PPP and/or SLIP connections
- Navigating the Web and your system via http, ftp, and local system file-retrieval operations, as well as links on retrieved Web pages

■ Translating/interpreting HTML codes to display pages appropriately (It is important, of course, that your browser handle the latest version of HTML.)

■ Displaying GIF and JPEG images

These functions—Web connection, navigation, and page and image display—are the primary reason Web browsers exist. All browsers have these functions. How a browser presents itself and the degree of refinement and sophistication of its user interface are the main differences between one browser and another...

...until, that is, you start looking at features that are tied to the way other people use the Web, specifically the user interface and certain features that are often termed bells and whistles.

Browser Features: The Extras

The better Web browsers feature a number of extra features. Some simplify the Web. Others enhance it. Here's a listing of the more important browser features, not in order of importance:

■ Additional local navigation controls that let you move through a list of Web pages you've already accessed during a given online session. (These include Backward and Forward buttons and a cumulative list of pages visited during the current session, which you can use to navigate back to those pages.)

■ A file-access system that lets you open local files (on your hard drive) and save files from the Web, including HTML pages, image files, and other types of files

■ A helper program feature that starts a specified program when/if a certain file type is received from the Web (For example, if a .WAV file is transmitted from a Web site, your browser should be able to start a program that can play .WAV audio files. You should be able to specify programs to be used beyond what is already set up, and be able to add new file types and applications to the list.)

■ The capability to use plug-in programs (Plug-ins are utilities that extend a browser's capabilities, about which Chapter 8 has more to say. Ideally, a browser should be able to use plug-ins designed for a competing browser, but this is not always true.)

- If you need it, multiple language support—the ability to handle special characters you will find at some foreign-language Web sites, for example, Kanji characters at Japanese-language sites

- Again, if you have a need for this, a foreign-language version of the browser (All the menus, prompts, and so on are in the language of choice.)

- A changeable list of frequently visited Web sites that you can use to navigate to Web sites quickly (This feature is often referred to as a *bookmark*, or *hotlist.*)

- User-specifiable sizes for the RAM and disk caches used to store elements of Web pages you've visited (These caches store pages and elements of pages so they can be quickly reloaded from your disk if you revisit them, rather than having to wait for them to be transmitted again.)

- E-mail capability (enabling you to send messages to other users while online with the browser), including specifying the system to handle your e-mail (typically the STMP server), your return e-mail address, and so on

- Usenet newsgroup retrieval and posting capability (includes allowing you to specify the server that will handle newsgroup traffic for you)

- Ftp and telnet capability (with servers, as specified by you)

- Flexibility in changing operating parameters, such as whether or not graphic images are loaded with a Web page (important when speed is a consideration), fonts used to display text, and so on

- The capability to run programs in the Java, JavaScript, VB Script, and/or ActiveX languages (These programs are the development tools/languages responsible for the ubiquitous applets found on so many Web sites. This feature is either built-in to your browser or may be added with plug-ins.)

- Controllable security features (including those described in a few paragraphs, in the section "Special Notes on Security Features")

Additional features include full compliance with the current version of HTML (normally built into the latest version of every browser), special HTML extensions to permit the viewing of additional content and/or format at a Web site, and special Web sites that support and enhance the browser in question.

Beyond all this, you will want a user interface that you find efficient and pleasing. You also will probably want a user interface that you can alter, as being able to turn toolbars, buttons, and windows on or off is helpful.

Figure 9.1 shows the major elements of a browser user interface, along with other elements.

Figure 9.1 The anatomy of a Web browser

Special Notes on Security Features

The biggest concern for most users on the Web today is security. There are several approaches to Web security, including:

- Protecting data you send over the Internet from being intercepted and observed, and/or tampered with, by a third party—This is accomplished on more than one level. The simplest protection is a warning dialogue that appears when you opt to send text data to a Web site that is not secure. More complex protection techniques involve certificates (which are described in a few paragraphs).

- Using a digital certificate to ensure that you are communicating with a specific Web site and not an impostor—This procedure can also verify or authenticate a Web site's security, or lack of security.

- Identifying yourself to a Web site with a certificate—This approach protects against anyone else accessing data at that site that is specific to you.

- Protecting yourself against virus-infected software or data files, and/or other unwanted data—This can be accomplished by restricting the sorts of software that can be downloaded from a Web site and run on your computer.

- The capability to restrict access to Web sites with specific content

- Password protection to restrict access to a browser

- Control over whether or not your browser accepts cookies, either on an ask-first or a yes/no basis—Cookies are information that some Web sites store on your hard disk, and which others can retrieve later. You can use this feature to help identify you to a Web site, as well as to gather information about your Web activities, and more.

For additional information on security features, see Chapter 11, "Internet Data Formats and Conversion."

NOTES ON *IRC* AND *TELNET*

One feature that few browsers support directly is *Internet Relay Chat*, or *IRC*. IRC is a way of chatting real time via the Internet, kind of like talking on the telephone but you type and read rather than speak and listen. You almost always have to obtain additional software for IRC. You will learn more about this software in later chapters.

Telnet is another Internet feature that you will probably have to go beyond your Web browser to implement. Telnet enables connecting with specific computers on the Net directly—including online services.

Which Browser Should I Use?

As I noted previously, there are two viable choices in PC Web browsers, both available as Windows programs, of course. These are Microsoft Internet Explorer (better-known simply as Explorer), and Netscape Navigator (also known as Netscape.) Your choices boil down to these two not so much because they are the best products available, but rather the market—Internet users and Web page developers—more than any other factor decided which browsers "almost everyone" is using.

Note that a few ISPs provide you with a browser. However, you do not necessarily have to use that browser. Given that a PPP link exists once you sign on to an ISP (be it an independent ISP or an online service), most browsers can link up with the Internet, no problem. So, you are not confined to one Web browser, even when using an ISP that gives you one.

BROWSER WARS!

How, you may wonder, did it come down to a choice between Netscape and Explorer? This happened mainly by word-of-mouth and force of numbers.

(It also helped that Microsoft gives away Explorer for free, figuring to profit by sales of add-ons and support. This is not unlike the late 19th-century strategy of King C. Gillette, who gave away his new invention, the safety razor, knowing that those who had the razor would be buying blades from him.)

In the earliest days of the Web, most were using NCSA Mosaic, or some knockoff thereof. (Mosaic is the original WWW browser for the PC-using masses. It is available for download at **http://www.ncsa.uiuc.edu/SDG/ Software/WinMosaic/index.html**.)

When other browsers began to appear, Internet users had choices. And, as often happens with software in a competitive environment—even free software—one browser gained a word-of-mouth edge over the others.

This browser is Netscape. If you have browsed the Web for any length of time, you have noticed that many Web pages are labeled "Netscape-enhanced" and carry the Netscape logo. These pages take advantage of certain Netscape features that extend HTML and enable additional display elements. When viewed with a browser other than Netscape, those additional page elements aren't visible. Worse, text and graphics that are visible may not look "right." Columns and other blocks of text, for example, may be run-on.

Today, there are similarly enhanced pages for Explorer. Although it is a relative latecomer, Explorer has managed to capture a good portion of the market for various reasons. And, like Netscape, it has a great deal of word-of-mouth support, largely because it is from Microsoft. (Of course, there are those who do not use Explorer simply because it is a Microsoft product.)

Also, competition has resulted in quite a bit of evolution of the products and supporting technologies. The latter include the *Java* programming language and applets for Netscape, and a similar development system called *ActiveX* for programs that can run within Explorer Web pages.

Other factors affect the popularity of each browser, as you will learn in a few pages. But, you may wonder, which browser has the most users and supporters? This question is easy to answer: Netscape has the clear edge. As of second quarter 2000, Netscape was used by around 60 percent of all Windows-based Internet users. However, Explorer is gaining fast, with perhaps half the number of users enjoyed by Netscape.

The numbers of users for both browsers are increased by the fact that AOL, CompuServe, and others give away special versions of one or the other with their front-end software utilities.

WHICH BROWSER IS BEST?

Even with the field narrowed down to two choices, it's not easy to answer the question, "Which is the best Web browser?" (or, more properly, "Which is the better of the two?")

As previously implied, best is a relative term. You will certainly prefer one over the other, for several personal reasons. And you will probably like some of the features of your second choice, and wish they were included in the browser you prefer.

As for which browser you will prefer, the answer probably is the first one you used. Computer users tend to regard the first program they use for any length of time as the one all others must measure up to. This is true of any type of application, and even of online services and other ISPs.

Of course, the real issue here is not so much how many people use which browser but the number of Web sites optimized or enhanced for use with one browser or the other. A related consideration is exactly how much you miss not using a browser that fits a given Web site. Both of those considerations are variable.

At present, Netscape-enhanced Web pages seem to outnumber those dedicated to Internet Explorer. However, Netscape and Explorer each accommodate more of the other's features with every new version. So, the days of Web sites completely dedicated to either browser may eventually end.

What will remain important, however, are each browser's control, command, and menu structures; how specific features (like bookmarks) are set up; and other elements endemic to each, including their respective look and feel. More than anything else, these aspects are what determine most users' choices in browsers.

To a lesser extent, Web sites that enhance a browser have some effect on decisions—but you normally do not know about these sites unless you have the browser in question. If you are curious about these, read on—and visit both Netscape's and Explorer's Web sites. (The respective URLs are **http://home.netscape.com** and **http://www.microsoft.com/ie**.)

The overview descriptions of Netscape and Explorer that follow may help you evaluate each and decide which will be your primary browser.

Meanwhile, you may want to do as I do: Use both! While I spend much more time online with Netscape, I have found it expedient to use Explorer to visit Microsoft Web sites and other Explorer-enhanced Web sites. (Also, since I use both CompuServe and AOL, it is good to have some knowledge of Explorer, since they both offer it as their default, or primary, Web browser. The same is true of the Prodigy Internet Service.)

In the end, you may choose one browser over the other simply because you like it better.

Netscape Navigator

Before Netscape, browsers were fairly basic. You could connect with the Internet, call files, interpret HTML commands, display graphics, and handle other basic tasks. By the time Netscape came along, HTML itself had not advanced much further than enabling browsers to fetch and display HTML files and a few images, anyway.

Netscape's big attractions included—but weren't limited to—new HTML capabilities that were exclusive to Netscape, that it could be obtained for free or with a price for the registered version that wasn't bad, and that it was a fresh alternative to what little else was available.

Mostly, however, Netscape's early success was a case of coming along at just the right time. Merely offering an alternative to what was then available was as much to Netscape's benefit as anything else. Hundreds of thousands of Internet users jumped on the Netscape bandwagon in a very short time.

With so many users enamored of Netscape, it wasn't long before a new phenomenon hit the Web. Netscape users who had Web sites made sure that their sites supported special Netscape features that extended beyond the HTML standard. Before long, a near majority of Web sites were custom-tailored for optimal viewing using Netscape. (You still see this today, of course—the Netscape logo on a Web site's first page, along with a statement that the site is "Netscape enhanced" or "optimized for Netscape.")

This enhancing meant that the Web site wouldn't look "right" unless you were using Netscape. The difference might be as simple as not being able to see certain text formatting (created by using text-format commands unique to Netscape), or as complex as not being able to access several pages at once by virtue of the use of Netscape's frames feature. Indeed, some browsers still crash when they hit a Web page that's enhanced for Netscape—even older versions of Netscape. (To be fair, the same crash can happen with pages that are optimized for Explorer.) At the least, you may miss some important features, such as using forms.

As Netscape progressed (as previously stated, it's now up to version 4.7, the version bundled with Netscape Communicator), more and more new features were added, and it is now at a point where you cannot view some Web sites at all unless you use Netscape—the latest version! (Never mind that this limitation may reduce the potential audience for such a Web site; the majority of folks who create Web sites that are Netscape-only either don't know any better, or are for reasons of their own determined that Netscape is the absolute *best* for everyone.)

One of the biggest of these kinds of lockouts that Netscape developed was the Java programming language. This language creates mini-applications, also known as applets, which can run within an HTML Web page. JavaScript is a simpler approach to the same thing; both have in common the fact that they take some of the load off a Web site server by running on the client receiving the host Web page. They also have in common their basis in enabling the user and page elements, actions, and events to interact. That is, if you select an object (image, hyperlink, color, or whatever) on a Web page, certain things may happen (such as a sound or video file being played) that would not happen otherwise. Such an event may in turn lead to other events or bring other objects to the page.

These are programs that, originally, only Netscape could interpret and run. So, if you wanted to run Java applets found at various Web sites, you had to have Netscape—or a browser that was at least somewhat compatible with Java. (Some applets have been known to lock up or crash browsers.) Fortunately for many, Explorer introduced the capability to run Java and JavaScript applets. (Also fortunately, the advent of Java resulted in the competitive development of Explorer's ActiveX technology.)

Finally, Netscape has worked to have ISPs offer or adopt Netscape as their official Web browser. This usually means that the ISP makes it easier to set up Netscape with their service—and may bundle it for new members, and/or design their Web sites for optimal viewing when using Netscape. They may also offer technical support for Netscape and for any other browser they support.

NETSCAPE NAVIGATOR FEATURES: AN OVERVIEW

As shown in Figure 9.2, Netscape presents a fairly uncomplicated face to the world.

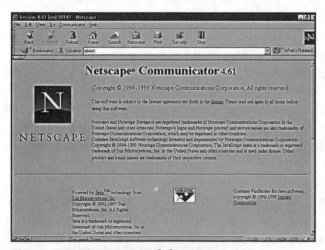

Figure 9.2   Netscape Web browser

Netscape's uncomplicated theme isn't echoed by its features, however. Netscape offers almost everything you might want in a browser, and some features that you may not know you want until you try them.

For example, take a look at the user interface. All the most frequently used controls are right in front of you, on the toolbar. The same goes for information about the current URL. The bottom-of-the-screen status bar provides information about in-progress activities (like connecting with and downloading a Web page), the URL associated with a hyperlink when the mouse cursor passes over it, and even a one-line text message from properly set up Web pages.

Fortunately, you can turn off most of these displays to show more of a Web page. This feature is handy because, unfortunately, Netscape doesn't offer what is sometimes known as a kiosk mode. Kiosk is a display mode that fills the entire screen with a Web page—no borders, no controls, or anything else from the browser. It's a great feature, particularly when you are dealing with long pages that have large graphics or image maps. In kiosk mode, you can put the maximum portion of a page on your screen, reducing the need to scroll up and down.

Otherwise, Netscape offers most of the browser features discussed previously, although it tends to be a bit lighter on security features than Explorer. Netscape provides simple warnings when you are about to send data to a server that is not secure (with or without a form), and when you are entering or leaving a secure server. Netscape also offers passwords and personal and site certificates for authenticating purposes. It supports security protocols SS2 and SS3, but not PCT—an emerging protocol.

Netscape can also warn you when a Web site is about to pass you a *cookie*, and give you the option of accepting it or not. (A cookie is information written to your hard drive by a Web site. Among other purposes, this is used to identify you on later visits.)

To run ActiveX and Shockwave applications, you have to add *plug-ins*. (This capability could become a built-in Netscape feature in the near future.)

Speaking of plug-ins, one of Netscape's more interesting features is its Installed Plug-ins registry. This makes it extremely easy to quickly survey which plug-ins you have. Select About Plug-ins on Netscape's Help menu, and you get a list of plug-ins, complete with information as to type and drive/directory locations.

Some additional bells and whistles include a drag-and-drop feature that makes it quick and easy to store or add the current URL to your bookmark list, a bookmark list that you can customize, and a command and menu structure that makes more sense to me than Explorer's.

Netscape originated *frames*, which is the ability to display several more or less mini-Web pages within one page. (Figure 9.3 illustrates this.) So, as you might expect, it does an excellent job of handling pages with frames.

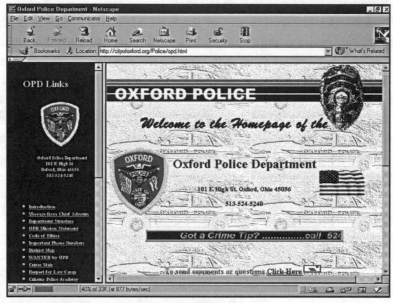

Figure 9.3   Netscape frames on a Web page

Although frames initially slowed down Web page loading tremendously for most users, the latest version of Netscape seems to have eliminated this problem.

Figure 9.3 shows another Netscape feature, one of Netscape's several online enhancements. This particular enhancement, called a PowerStart page, lets you set up an online home page with your choice of a number of categorized links. The PowerStart page can be set as your default personal home page, which is the page to which your browser goes first when you link with the Internet. Link categories include general news, sports, technology news, weather, finance, reference, and more. There's even an optional notepad, which stays live on your home page whenever you're online. You can save the contents to disk and access them the next time you're online. Other options include a calendar and a calculator. This is a great enhancement to Netscape, and probably the best of its type.

Additional enhancements for Netscape include a download page for plugins and free trial access to some pay Web sites, mainly publications and information services. The latter is for those who register their copies of Netscape online. (Select Registration Information on Netscape's Help menu.)

Netscape gets a minus in the area of online help. Its online help is literally online, meaning you have to go to Netscape's Web site to view it. A fairly comprehensive (though at times obtuse) online manual, release notes, FAQs, and more are available via the Help menu, which enters the requisite URL to get to the help feature of your choice. It would be far better to have duplicated all this off-line. A megabyte or so of standard Windows Help files wouldn't have hurt a bit. (I suspect that some of the Netscape folks were perhaps overly enamored of the "cuteness" of having all the online help for a Web browser actually on the Web. It sure makes getting help difficult—especially if the help you need is on how to get online!)

Netscape's mail and Usenet newsgroup features are a bit easier to use and slightly more powerful than Explorer's, largely due to the fact that Netscape has had more experience with these applications. However, Explorer's do-it-different-from-Netscape approach figures here, too.

That's the quick look at Netscape features. I strongly recommend that you try it for yourself. To get more info on Netscape features, visit **http://home.netscape.com**, download a copy, and take it for a test drive. Or you can buy Netscape from almost any software retailer. (If you sign up with CompuServe, DELPHI, Prodigy, or any of a number of independent ISPs, you may receive Netscape at no cost.)

Microsoft Internet Explorer

Originally designed for use only with Microsoft's online service, the Microsoft Network (MSN), Microsoft Internet Explorer began life as a fairly simple Web browser. Explorer had no really new and exciting features when it was introduced, but it didn't have to because it was intended for one market—MSN members.

Things changed rapidly late in 1995, though, as the market's focus left online services and zoomed in on the Web. It wasn't long before Microsoft made the decision to put Explorer out as direct competition for Netscape and other browsers.

This step required drastic improvements to Explorer. At the same time the program was undergoing improvement, Microsoft began pushing it as *the* browser to have. Quite a few Internet users went along with this idea, thanks to Microsoft's reputation. Also, Microsoft was able to get it included with certain products. Eventually Explorer reached the point where it was the number-two browser. And that's where it remains; as of 2000, Netscape pretty much dominated the market, with Explorer in second place.

Obviously, Microsoft brought its Internet Explorer to the game rather late, but the company is making up for lost time in two ways. First, it's following Netscape's strategy of adding features exclusive to its own browser. There are many add-on programs and utilities (ActiveX, mainly) that work only with

Internet Explorer. Indeed, Microsoft's main tactic in this area is to develop plug-ins that work better—or only—with Internet Explorer.

Microsoft's second strategy is to put its Internet Explorer in the hands of as many people as possible. This strategy was easily accomplished by adding it to Windows 95, where it is a part of the newer interlinking of applications and the Web. But Microsoft hasn't stopped there. Many ISPs and some online services (including AOL, CompuServe, the Microsoft Network, and Prodigy Internet) feature Explorer as their browser of choice. That of course means the ISPs make Explorer easier to use with their services. They provide extensive support for Explorer, design their Web sites to work best with Explorer, and—last, but certainly not least—they give Explorer with software to new members.

However, not all the major ISPs are going with Explorer. CompuServe and Prodigy Internet, while favoring Internet Explorer in its front-end software, allow users to choose between Internet Explorer and Netscape. Another major online service, DELPHI, provides Netscape, along with a suite of Internet software. Some larger national ISPs provide Netscape to new users, as do smaller regional and local ISPs.

(*Note*: Not incidentally, the embracing of one browser or another by online services and ISPs does not mean that you are locked into that browser. You usually can run a second browser easily enough; simply start it after you log in to your ISP. As I write this, I am running *three* browsers: I'm logged on to AOL, which comes with a version of Explorer built-in, and I have that running. In order to better investigate some Explorer updates, I started Explorer, it latched on to the PPP connection provided by AOL, and navigated as I directed it. A few minutes later, I wanted to compare a Netscape site with its counterpart in Explorer, so I started Netscape. It, too, hooked up with the Net via AOL's PPP connection.

(Of course, this took up well over 8 MB of memory. So don't try this at home unless you have at lease 16 MB of RAM.)

Still, Explorer may catch up. Marketing, rather than word-of-mouth brought it farther faster than Netscape. Its new technology is sure to take advantage of Explorer's existing momentum and take it still farther. ActiveX and the built-in capabilities to handle Shockwave and Java have helped Explorer claim market territory that Netscape had not previously considered.

MICROSOFT INTERNET EXPLORER FEATURES: AN OVERVIEW

As was said for Netscape, Explorer boasts all the major features discussed previously in this chapter. However, its user interface seems a little less friendly to me. (Perhaps you find it otherwise, which is fine; such judgments are largely a matter of taste.) Figure 9.4 shows MSIE's main screen.

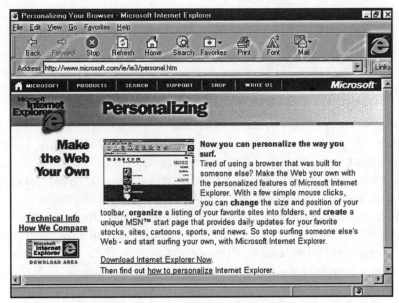

Figure 9.4 The Microsoft Internet Explorer Web browser

Explorer really came into its own, feature-wise, with version 3.0. Introduced late in 1996, this version rolled out ActiveX and Java capabilities, and the ability to handle Netscape frames (albeit noticeably slower than Netscape).

ActiveX generated the most excitement. This language caught everyone off guard, at a time when Java was the hottest thing going as far as the Internet was concerned.

Another plus is the fact that Explorer originated the semiautomatic downloads of necessary applications from Web sites. (Go to a site that offers features that require a plug-in, and you're queried as to whether you want to download that tool.)

Explorer 3.0 scooped Netscape in two other feature areas—security and help. Explorer has security features and options galore. The typical setups for certificates are there—personal and site—and there's an additional certificate category called Publishers. Cryptography protocols are supported, and you have the option to tell Explorer to not save secure pages to disk. Password protection of some settings is also available. However, some of these security elements are difficult to find (a symptom of what I feel is Explorer's relatively poorly designed user interface).

SSL2, SSL3, and PCT security protocols are supported, and you can disable downloading and running active content, ActiveX, and Java programs.

As with Netscape, you can have Explorer warn you before accepting cookies (giving you the option of whether or not to do so), and provide other warnings regarding the state of security of a site.

Explorer has a unique feature known as Content Advisor that lets you lock out access to Web sites based on language, nudity, sex, or violence. In addition to locking out children from questionable sites, it can be used to ensure that employees don't spend all their online time exploring the more salacious corners of the Web. (Look for this feature to appear in other browsers and to grow more elaborate as the Internet evolves.)

As for Explorer's help features, many are online in the traditional sense of Windows Help files, as well as online at Microsoft's Web site. This is an improvement over Netscape's approach to online help! The Windows Help is well written, and misses very few areas where you would have questions. The only weak areas occur when the Help authors assume that you know more than you really do—such as when they refer to MIME program types.

On-the-Internet help focuses on online support and on a special interactive Web Tutorial that provides introductory and intermediate information about the Internet. The only improvement on this help system would be to duplicate the Web Tutorial in Windows Help files. (It would go faster that way.) Online and on-the-Internet help features are all on the browser's Help menu, along with some Microsoft sites, including a gateway to several search engines.

Another online enhancement is the Microsoft Custom Page. This is tied to MSN, and is a means of setting up a personal home page as the first page you go to when you link to the Internet, with links of your choice. As with Netscape's PowerStart page, the Microsoft Custom Page is entirely user defined and features links by category and a set of personal links. Microsoft also provides a download page for Explorer plug-ins.

Finally, in the realm of online add-ons and enhancements, registered users get free-trial access to value-added services and publications.

Explorer's mail and newsgroup applications, as indicated in previous sections, are not on a par with Netscape's. They will get the job done, however.

The rest of Explorer's features match up with Netscape's fairly well. The only other area in which Explorer lags behind Netscape is a seemingly minor matter, but one important to those of us who have used browsers for any length of time. This is Microsoft's insistence on referring to hyperlinks as shortcuts. This is more than annoying, actually; it runs counter to accepted and common usage, and will create a lot of confusion on the part of both new users and old hands. No doubt, this comes from Microsoft's insistence on doing it their own way. (The term harks back to Windows 95, where it originated as another name for a start-up command.)

Its few minuses and my opinion of the user interface aside, I do recommend that you give Internet Explorer a try. You can download it at **http://www.microsoft.com/ie**.

Explorer is, after all, completely free. A special version of the utility is an integral part of AOL, CompuServe, and Prodigy Internet software, and a number of independent ISPs provide Explorer to new members, as well. And of course the full version is supplied to members of the Microsoft Network (MSN).

A FEW OF THE REST

As you might imagine, there are relatively few other browsers worth considering. As Netscape and Explorer continue to compete, one will always best the other in some small feature or other. However, in terms of important features, I expect both will give you what you need.

A discussion of Web browsers would not be complete, however, without pointing to some additional browsers that are worth your consideration.

Back Where It All Began ...

NCSA Mosaic (shown in Figure 9.5) is always worth trying out if you are interested in examining alternate browsers. The National Center for Supercomputer Applications (the original developer of Mosaic) continues to evolve the program, and it is interesting to see where it is going.

Figure 9.5 The NCSA Mosaic Web browser

You will find the latest version of NCSA Mosaic, along with all the information you can use about it, plus support software, at the NCSA Mosaic home page. The URL is **http://www.ncsa.uiuc.edu/SDG/Software/WinMosaic/index.html**. Mosaic is free.

Other Commercial Web Browsers?

While NCSA Mosaic and Microsoft Internet Explorer are free, and you can at least try Netscape for free (as a fully functional version), there are other commercial Web browsers. Most offer little for the additional cost. (They're typically double Netscape's price.) Considering that Netscape is an 8-megabyte (or larger) download, purchasing the program on CD may be a good idea.

ISP-Specific Web Browsers

A few ISPs provide their own Web browsers. Most of these are online services that were integrating Internet services into their offerings several years ago. They quickly moved to add Web browsers and the PPP connections to support them. A few, like AOL, started with browsers of their own design. Today, however, online services offer Netscape and/or Explorer as their Web browser. (In the case of Explorer, a special limited version is incorporated into some online services' front-end software utilities.)

Independent ISPs are in much the same situation. Almost none provide Web browsers of their own design, though; most offer Netscape or Explorer, and a very few of them offer other browsers.

EARTHLINK'S BROWSER: A CUSTOM CHOICE

Typical of browsers in the ISP-specific category is that used by Earthlink (formerly Mindspring). Earthlink offers a slightly customized version of Microsoft Internet Explorer. Customizing usually involves altering the browser's appearance so that it displays the name of the company for which it is customized. Customizing may also involve any or all of the following:

- Presetting dialup/connection parameters on your system
- Providing a customized list of bookmarks
- Setting the browser's "Home" button to a specified Web page (usually, the home page of the company for whom the browser was customized)
- Setting the browser's properties or operating parameters to suit the browser's application
- Presetting other elements, such as which Newsgroups you should access
- Altering the browser's appearance significantly
- Including special add-ons and/or plug-ins

AOL's Web Browser

AOL's original Web browser was one of its own design. It wasn't bad, but it wasn't the best. Today, AOL offers a special version of Microsoft Internet Explorer. Like all earlier AOL Web browsers, it is an integral part of the AOL front-end software.

It is somewhat limited in functions, as shown in Figure 9.7, but not as limited as you might think.

Figure 9.7   The AOL version of Internet Explorer

As you can see, Explorer's familiar toolbar is missing, as are some Explorer features. But a surprising number are included, belying the simple-looking interface. As for the buttons that are there, there are the standard navigation buttons and one labeled Search that has a "hardwired" URL that takes you to AOL's Web search site. Home goes to an AOL site, too. The Prefs button goes to browser options for setup.

Available Explorer features include all standard browser operations: ActiveX and Java capability; full security features (including certificates and cookies); content advisor; and standard controls for graphics, sound, and which programs can be downloaded and run from the Web.

There's also a Favorite Places list (a.k.a. bookmark list) and a means to navigate to sites already visited during a session.

Finally, some sites will download add-ons for Explorer to the AOL browser and set them up. You have the option to accept or reject such downloads.

This is not a bad browser for getting onto the Internet. If you use AOL for your ISP, though, you will eventually want to switch to using Netscape or the full version of Explorer.

AOL also offers browser-independent access to Usenet newsgroups, ftp, and gopher services.

CompuServe and the Internet

CompuServe's built-in version of Microsoft Internet Explorer is a little more limited in some ways than that used by AOL. A quick tour of its features will explain what I mean.

Referring to Figure 9.8, the buttons at the top of the browser window are more for CompuServe than for the Web. Three are for navigation: the left and right arrows for backward and forward, and the Reload/Stop button. (The latter is shown as Reload here, but when a page is loading it changes to Stop.)

The Main Menu and What's New buttons are for CompuServe services. The Find button brings up a dialogue that you can use to search CompuServe or the Internet. The Page window beneath the menu labels at top left acts both as a location display and as a means of revisiting pages. It drops down to display a list of all URLs recently visited, from which you can select a URL to open. The Go button allows you to enter the URL of a Web site or CompuServe area to visit.

A Favorite Places feature allows you to bookmark not only CompuServe products and services but also URLs.

Set-up features are limited, almost nonexistent. So, you won't be able to set security levels, toggle pictures and sounds off and on, and so forth.

Figure 9.8   CompuServe's version of Internet Explorer

The operation of this version of Explorer is not quite seamless, but it is smooth enough. Here again, the goal is to give the user the impression that CompuServe and the Internet are all one big entity.

Like AOL, CompuServe offers browser-independent Internet services, including ftp, Usenet newsgroups, and telnet.

BROWSING THE WEB WITH PRODIGY INTERNET

Prodigy Internet (an offshoot of the Prodigy online service) offers a special version of Internet Explorer as well.

Unlike CompuServe and AOL, Prodigy Internet did not limit its version of Explorer. It is a bit more like the stand-alone version.

INTERNET SERVICE PROVIDERS

Because you are reading this book, it's a safe bet that you already have an ISP—after all, you are online. However, there may be a better ISP for you. Hence, this section of the chapter provides information you can use to select and judge ISPs.

In the old days (a decade ago), Internet users depended on connections with educational institutions or government entities for Internet links. There were virtually no Internet service providers (ISPs). There was nowhere near enough demand to make providing links a commercially viable proposition. Also, there were vague injunctions against anything commercial touching the Net.

That was before the World Wide Web and before the Internet was drafted as a mass e-mail carrier. The majority of the online world used commercial online services. As the Web evolved and online services began offering Internet e-mail links, awareness of the Internet grew. With this awareness came a demand for the Internet.

At first, the primary demand was for Usenet, with e-mail links to existing Internet sites not far behind. Most commercial online services were able to satisfy the demand. Usenet feeds were set up, and each tied into the Internet for e-mail.

There was still the Web, though. At first a near-abstract element of the internet, the Web almost overnight became something of a famous entity, thanks in large part to publicity in the computer and mainstream media.

All the attention focused on the Web generated a greater demand for full Internet access. As is common, consumer demand was met by commercial entities. Thus commercial ISPs were born.

The first ISPs were independent—that is, they were created for the sole purpose of providing Internet and World Wide Web access. Unlike commercial online services, they generally did not provide content in the form of information services.

Commercial online services were fairly quick to recognize the demand for Internet connections. They met this first with the aforementioned e-mail and Usenet links. But it was not long before they recognized the fact that they could provide the Internet and the Web in their entirety to their members. After all, what were those entities but still more online content? So, online services became ISPs.

So, today we have two sorts of ISPs. The first sort is the independent Internet service provider, existing solely to provide Internet connections. Well, not exactly; many independent ISPs now offer content of their own, in one way or another. It's a way of competing against other independent ISPs and the online services. An example is Earthlink.

The second sort of ISP is the commercial online service. These are a rather small group, consisting of AOL, CompuServe, DELPHI Internet Services, MSN, and Prodigy Internet. Each of these is becoming increasingly involved in the Internet. All have added Internet information services (forums, reference and research tools, and the like) to their range of products and services. Also, most of the online services have evolved front ends that attempt to make their existing services a part of the Internet, and vice versa.

If this seems like an identity crisis, that's because it is. Independent ISPs and online services exist in a highly competitive market. To stay competitive, each has been forced to take on some of the attributes of the other. Look for this trend to continue; in a few years the major ISPs will be online services that have succeeded in blending and melding their conventional services with the Internet, and independent ISPs will have successfully mixed value-added information content with Internet access.

All of which brings us to the second of the Two Great Internet Debates: independent ISP or online service?

Independent ISP or Online Service?

As with Web browsers, which ISP you should use is the subject of intense emotional debate between permanently polarized viewpoints. One viewpoint is that online services should not be ISPs, and that independent ISPs are somehow better. The other viewpoint is that it doesn't matter; use the sort of ISP (and the specific ISP) that best meets your needs.

My viewpoint is the latter debate. As with anything, you should use what works best for you.

If your online applications do not extend beyond sending and receiving e-mail, browsing Web sites, and accessing Usenet newsgroups, an independent ISP will work for you.

If you have other needs or expectations about being online, you need to compare the content offered by online services with the content of the Internet at large. Which service truly meets your needs? Also, which do you find easiest to use?

This is not an easy question to answer. As noted previously, independent ISPs provide some content, but they offer nowhere near the content of the online services, which have been building their offerings for many years.

CONTENT, CONTENT, AND MORE CONTENT

What is "content"? On online services, content consists of information resources, ranging from encyclopedias to magazines to reference works and directories; people resources, in the form of special-interest groups and forums; news, weather, and financial information from trusted sources; online shopping services; magazines; exclusive columnists, consultants, and entertainment features.

There is also online product support, that is, manufacturer support for computer hardware and software products. Online services are the better choice over ISPs when it comes to product support services, at least where rapidity of response and file resources are concerned.

Most categories of online service content are available to some extent on the Web. And, unlike online services, the Web doesn't charge for access.

But, what form does the Web content take, and how far does it go? Also, just how reliable is information on the Internet?

In my experience, some of the Web's content is not as reliable as we wish, because so much of it is put up by amateurs who do it for no direct return. Thus, many, many Web sites have no incentive to take pains to get things right. Find an error in online information and point it out, and you're as likely to get "What do you expect for free?" as "Thanks, I'll change that" as a reply.

Commercial Web sites tend to provide better information. They exist as a part of a commercial enterprise and are anything but a hobby. They are either promoting or directly selling products, and the information provided can be construed as reflecting the quality of their products, or at least their image. Commercial sites have the incentive—and the means—to provide accurate information, most of the time. (One way to judge the probable accuracy of a Web site's information is to see when it was last updated. If this information is not placed on the site's home page, try viewing the source code with your browser to see if a date is embedded there.)

Now, take a look at who is providing information on the Web. You'll see Web sites for many well-known corporations and publishers as well as government agencies, but just as many Web sites in a given category are put together by amateurs.

In contrast, some information products on online services are constructed and offered as products for sale. Others are included with the online services' normal charges. Either way, the emphasis is on quality because, unlike the Web, online services are delivering products for a price. Because of this, information on online services is likely to be more complete, more accurate, and more in-depth. This isn't always true, but it is true enough to matter.

So, in choosing whether the Web's content or what a commercial online service offers is better for your needs, you must judge by the type of information you seek.

Also, you will find that online services offer information products and services that are not available on the Web. These include things like CompuServe's Phone*File and Biz*File directories and its D&B databases, and service-specific forums, publications, and reference works found on AOL, CompuServe, DELPHI, MSN, and Prodigy.

Also, regarding the relative quality of information on online services and the Web, consider this: It is time-consuming and costly to compile information. Few people or organizations do so in order to give away the information; in fact, the information industry comprises a large segment of our economy. Therefore, you will often find the more valuable information where you must pay for it, whether it's on an online service or at a Web site that requires you to pay.

SPECIAL SERVICES

There is another service category where online services shine more than the Internet. I call this the special services category. Special services on online services include e-mail features, real-time conversation (or chatting), and such things as outgoing fax and hard-copy mail.

If you have heavy and complex e-mail requirements, CompuServe and AOL are perhaps your best bet. However, with such add-on programs as Eudora or Pegasus, you can have almost all the features that online service e-mail offers.

Real-time communication is a bit more difficult for the Internet to match. While Internet Relay Chat is growing in popularity thanks to its general addictiveness, the technology is relatively poor—relative to that offered by the online services, that is. Of course, with online service chat areas, you have one less layer of communications links between you and others. Communication is routed from you to the online service's host computers, then directly to others in the conversations. IRC communication goes through another entire link—the Internet—after leaving your Internet host. So, it's usually faster, less clunky, and cleaner to use an online service for real-time conversation.

Specialty e-mail services, including sending e-mail to fax addresses and even having it printed out and mailed to recipients for you, are another class of services you will find for free on the Internet; however, sites offering such services can quickly disappear.

Remember, too, that many online services offer special Internet services. AOL has a decent interface for Usenet newsgroups that enables searching, reading, and posting. AOL also has ftp capability built into its software.

CompuServe also offers Usenet and ftp services. Even more, it has a really good telnet service.

DELPHI includes among its offerings Usenet newsgroups, placed among its SIGs as appropriate by topic.

Finally, remember that all online services offer Internet mail, Internet support, and information services.

Cost

Cost of service is the element about which the proponents of independent ISPs argue the loudest. Coming from a time when just dialing in to an online service cost as much as 30 cents per minute, I don't see what all the fuss is about. Everything online looks like a bargain to me. Still, cost is an important element and we'll examine it here.

In recent history, independent ISPs have traditionally charged a flat monthly rate for unlimited access. Online services at the same time were charging X dollars for Y hours of access per month, with additional hours billed at a couple of dollars each. And, a few premium products on the online services (business information, primarily) incur additional charges.

Today, the price structures are leveling out. The extra charges for premium information services remain, but online services are meeting the demand for economical Internet access by offering access at a competitive rate. Some charge separately for access to their traditional services, and some don't.

No matter how the billing goes, the best value in the online world is the perceived value. That is, if you have no need for the extra products and services provided by online services, you will perceive no value in their being available. Thus, you should go for the more straightforward and conventional Internet access offered by an independent ISP.

If, however, you needed access to those online service extras, the value of using an online service increases. The value-added elements of those extras would probably make the online service seem like a bargain.

EASE OF ACCESS AND CONNECTIVITY

It is a given that you want to use a local telephone number to access the Internet. You do not want to have to dial long distance to access the Internet; access should be free of extra cost and free of interference.

From the viewpoint of telephone connections for your computer and modem, there are three approaches to linking up with the Internet that don't involve long-distance connections. These are local ISPs, public packet-switching networks, and private packet-switching networks. With each, there are varying potential effects on the speed and quality of your connection.

Dealing with a local ISP is simple enough. You dial a local number, your modem talks to their modem, and you're on—using the ISP's PPP or SLIP connection to the Internet. The quality of the connection between you and the ISP is good. However, smaller ISPs do not have as high a quality of links with the Internet as large, national ISPs. Thus, a local ISP with a heavy load can get bogged down and slow down. You may even encounter a situation where all dial-in ports are busy and you can't log on.

With national or regional online service providers—either commercial online services or independent ISPs—packet-switching networks come into play. Simply described, a packet-switching network (PSN) is a special kind of data link between your computer and the ISP's computers. You dial a local number, and data is routed through a network of computers and data-link equipment to its destination. As with the Internet, packet-switching networks use more than one path to deliver data.

Without packet-switching networks, which use leased-line telephone connections that aren't charged a per-minute rate, you would not be able to dial locally into an ISP that was not in your area. There is a cost for network service, but it is relatively small per user, and it is built into an ISP's charges. Thus, packet-switching networks are invisible to us both in terms of how they make connections and in their cost.

There are two kinds of packet-switching networks—public and private. Public networks are those used by anyone; Tymnet and SprintNet are the largest. Private packet-switching networks are those used exclusively by the ISPs they serve. AOL and CompuServe operate private networks. (You can, however, access AOL and CompuServe via a public network if there is no local number for their private networks.)

What's the difference? Quality! Private networks are set up for one purpose, and they do that job very well. Public networks, on the other hand, carry traffic for hundreds of different customers in addition to the ISP you may be using it to access. This traffic can mean delays in routing data, which translates into slower connections for you. The number of users on a public network can affect the speed, too.

All of these factors come down to the following guidelines:

- If a local ISP has a reliable and high-quality connection with the Internet, go with it.

- If the local ISP's connections are not the best, go with a large national or regional provider.

- If you go with a large provider, choose one that offers its own private packet-switching network over one that uses a public packet-switching network.

Note that the ISPs that provide software are those most likely to offer the greatest ease in connectivity. They will have set up all of their systems to work best with the software they provide.

Software

The software an ISP provides, or the lack of it, may be an important consideration in your choice.

Most of the larger ISPs—independent and online services alike—provide Netscape or Explorer to new members. Some, like DELPHI, provide a suite of software that includes a browser like Netscape, e-mail software like Eudora, and a group of utilities and add-ons—all quite useful. Be sure to find out what software is offered, keeping in mind that the ISP will normally offer technical services and help for that software.

Several of the online services—AOL, CompuServe, MSN (for Windows 95/98 and 2000 users only), and Prodigy—provide software front ends that you must use to access their services. It's a good idea to learn as much about these as possible. Better yet, give them a trial run by taking advantage of free trial membership offers. You will have to use their software to dial up and connect with them before you link up with the Internet. So, it's a good idea to sign up with a service that provides software you can live with. (*Note*: CompuServe is the only service among these that offers more than one front end.)

A very few independent ISPs offer custom software. Earthlink has custom versions of Netscape and MSIE. Here again, you want to take the software into consideration before making a final decision.

Putting It All Together

As you have undoubtedly gathered, choosing an ISP is not the simplest task in the world. There are no hard and fast rules because so many subjective requirements—and tastes—are involved.

Because this is the case, I suggest that you eliminate as many potential ISPs as possible on the basis of content and services (or lack of these), ease of use and connectivity, cost, and software. Check out the remaining ISPs by taking advantage of free trial memberships. It is possible to get a good feel for a service in just a couple of hours. And the process of trying out different services will help you determine your needs.

If you're already online, you are in an excellent position to evaluate ISPs. You already know what you want and need, and you know what's possible. Go for it!

CHAPTER 10

Browser Utilities, Shareware, and More

This chapter introduces some important concepts, specifically the several categories of software used with browsers. I'll also introduce you to shareware, and we'll examine some considerations involved in installing Internet software.

If you are a longtime PC user, you may find some of the information in this chapter familiar. So, you may wish to skip the section on shareware, freeware, and commercial software ("Categories: Commercial Software, Freeware, and Shareware"). But, I do urge you to read the discussion on copyright that leads off that section.

You should also look over the sections "Getting the Words Right" and "Utility Programs." These will ensure that you have a good working knowledge of the terms and concepts used to describe various types of application and utility software.

Finally, even if you have installed your share of new software, at least scan the section "Software Installation and Setup."

GETTING THE WORDS RIGHT

Computing has always had a problem with words. Computer professionals and users alike tend to toss words around indiscriminately, certain that, if nothing else, you'll "know what they mean." For example, software goes by several names. There is "software," of course, and "programs," and even "software programs," which is redundant. And do not forget the currently popular "applications."

All that's probably simple enough, but how about "utilities"? For a full discussion of utilities, read on.

Utility Programs

Most of you probably consider a utility to be a program that performs functions in DOS or that debugs or analyzes code for programmers, but this view is too narrow (although utilities do exist for DOS and for programmers). If you consider a utility to be any small, specialized program, you are on the right track. Although today's utilities aren't necessarily small, a good working definition of a utility might be a specialized program.

Utility Software Defined

More accurately, a *utility* is a specialized program that helps or enhances another program. Depending on the tasks required, a utility may perform its job while the program for which it works is running, or the utility may run on its own.

An example of a utility that performs a specific function while running in concert with another program is a spelling checker, especially one that checks spelling as you type. Also in this category of the co-running utility are *components* that can be added to browsers: Java applets, Netscape plug-ins, and ActiveX controls.

A utility that adds to, enhances, or performs functions for another program without the other program running is sometimes called a stand-alone utility. Stand-alone utilities most often alter or enhance data files so they can be used by another program. Utilities that run "unplugged" from the Internet, such as those that convert data from one format to another (graphics or text), fit the bill here, and so do the archiving programs (PKZIP, ARC, etc.).

Categories: Commercial Software, Freeware, and Shareware

This section addresses still more computer nomenclature, specifically the terms used to describe how software is distributed: *commercial software, freeware, demoware*, and *shareware*. There are also a few notes on copyright with regard to software distribution.

COMMERCIAL SOFTWARE

In conventional software marketing, you purchase a program from a publisher or a retailer. A licensing agreement among the packaging clearly spells out your rights and limitations for using the software, and you're in business, agreeing to the terms of use by default. You get to use the software as long as you want, under these terms.

But this is not the only way software is marketed. A surprisingly large number of the most important PC utilities (and applications) are marketed under terms of temporary, extendible licensing. Still other software is provided completely free of cost, but only if you agree to specific terms of use.

These approaches to marketing are known as shareware and freely licensed software (or freeware), respectively. If you have doubts as to the meaning of either, or if you think that you are free to do with freeware as you desire, read on.

FREEWARE

Very little software labeled "free" is completely free. Although free software costs nothing, some restrictions apply. The licenses for individual programs detail (often in the extreme) what you may and may not do with the program.

The basic restrictions are simple: Although you can use a free program as you want for its intended purpose, you cannot alter it in any way, nor can you sell it or include it with other items for sale. The creator/provider of the program retains complete ownership of all copies in use. Other restrictions may or may not involve copying and sharing the program.

In all, you can't really complain about such restrictions because they don't really limit your use of the program. And it costs you nothing (except for the cost of downloading it). The restrictions protect the owner's copyright and ensure that he or she gets credit for the program's creation.

And what does the software creator get in return? Credit for the program, for one thing. Also, some free programs exist to support commercial Web sites. Such Web sites may sell products or promote products that require the use of the program in question (as is the case with some Netscape plug-ins).

Still other free programs introduce and support other products. Microsoft Internet Explorer exists largely for this purpose. So do many plug-ins for Netscape.

As you can see, this is a great way to market other products: Give the user a program that lets him or her use other programs, for which you charge.

Whatever the return for the software creator, you are granted the right to use the software all you want—but only if you agree to and abide by the terms and restrictions the copyright holder places on you.

Basically, you are safe if you download or otherwise obtain and use the software from the copyright holder. Anything beyond that is outside the terms of the user agreement. This includes selling it on disk, offering it for download at a Web site without permission, altering it with a promotional message and distributing it that way, or anything not specified in the agreement.

Free software costs nothing, and you can use it all you want. Now, look at another type of software that might be construed as free, but isn't.

TAKING A TEST DRIVE WITH DEMOWARE

A popular approach to marketing anything is to put the product in the hands of the consumer. Software publishers have used this approach since the mid-1980s with what is known as demoware. A demoware program is a partially functioning version of an application (a word processor that doesn't print or save files, for instance). These are typically provided free, by download or on disk. The theory is that users will like the demo so much they will buy the program.

A different approach to giving the user a test drive is to give him the complete, fully functional program. Along with this comes a licensing agreement that binds the user to paying for the program if he likes it and continues to use it. Netscape Navigator is distributed on this basis. You are granted a temporary license to use the program for 30 days. After that, you must register the program by paying a license fee (unless you meet certain of Netscape's criteria for a free license).

This concept is somewhat similar to shareware (explained in the following section), but the software is not made available in the same way—indiscriminately distributed online, on disk by mail, hand-to-hand, and so on. Netscape controls completely how the Navigator program is distributed, including the licensing of "official download sites" for Navigator.

Netscape Navigator was distributed in this way, along with commercial packaged versions containing the same product. This approach was unique, and it proved tremendously successful for Netscape. Very few programs use this technique, however.

SHAREWARE

Shareware is a way to try software before you buy it. It is both a marketing method and means of distribution. The term shareware derives from the fact that anyone who has the program is encouraged to "share" it with friends. This, along with placement of the software for download, ensures the largest possible distribution.

As a sales method, shareware is best described as an honor system. You use shareware at no initial cost. However, it is expected that you send a user fee to the author if you use the software on a regular basis. (Paying for the program is euphemistically known as "registering.")

"On a regular basis" usually means using a program beyond a trial period of thirty days. The user fee is sometimes called a donation, but the idea is the same: to compensate the author for his or her work.

WHY SHAREWARE?

Why do programmers market their work in this way? Shareware authors quite often cite the "try before you buy" benefit as the main reason. It gives them an edge over higher-priced software from high-powered companies who can afford to get your attention with expensive advertising. They also enjoy worldwide distribution in most instances.

Many programmers further cite the success of shareware companies like DataStorm (PROCOMM) or Nico Mak Computing, whose WinZip is a major success story, as examples of what they're emulating.

I suspect that most shareware is published as such because the authors can't get their programs published by commercial publishers. This is not surprising; there is so much good software out there—too much, in fact, to be marketed by commercial publishers. (My own opinion is that there is far too much commercial software crowding the market, anyway.)

Other programmers don't *want* to be published by commercial publishers. They may feel they can make more money by publishing their work themselves, and/or they want total control over their creative work.

Fortunately for these authors, the ease of copying files to disk and the vast network represented by online services and the Internet gives them access to distribution network.

SHAREWARE QUALITY

All of this by no means implies that shareware is of poor quality. Publishing shareware is somewhat akin to self-publishing a book, although unlike self-published books, the majority of shareware programs are of some quality. Many are of superior quality to their commercial counterparts, and many shareware products have no commercial counterparts. (WinZip—discussed in Chapter 11—is a prime example of a superior-quality program published as shareware.)

You may well wonder why some of the better shareware programs aren't published by established commercial publishers if they are so good. The answer is simple: As stated previously, commercial publishers already have more products to choose from than they can use.

SOFTWARE INSTALLATION AND SETUP

Whether you're dealing with utilities, applications, or anything in between, installing Internet software differs little from installing other kinds of software.

In recent years, few Windows programs—whether commercial, freeware, or shareware—arrive without an installation element. The few programs that require manual installation almost always come with detailed instructions. The "read me" file (named READ.ME, README.TXT, or similar) that comes with almost all shareware programs usually contains everything you need to install and get started. So, you should have no problems with the actual installation. The potential problem areas are related to preparing for installation and properly setting up a program. These areas are briefly examined here.

Disk or Download?

From the viewpoint of installation, the major difference between most Internet software and other types of software is that you rarely install Internet software from a CD-ROM or floppy disk because most of Internet applications and utilities are available for download at Web sites. A few publishers of Internet applications and utilities make disks available on request, but if you are like most Internet users, you prefer downloads to waiting for the U.S. mail service.

So, unless you copy downloaded software to a floppy disk—which, because of their large size, cannot be done with all Internet applications—you probably will install Internet software from one directory in your hard drive to another. With this in mind, what follows are considerations to remember when downloading and installing Internet software.

Stay in Control of Your Drive

Always try to keep your hard drive and its files under control. It's easy to lose a quarter, a third, or even more of a hard drive's space to old program versions, installation files of one sort or another, forgotten data files, and so on. Because most of today's programs are megabyte-eating hogs, you really want to conserve as much hard drive space as possible, even if you have a gigabyte or more of free space.

One important way to keep disk space free is to properly "clean up" after installing downloaded programs. As you may already know, a browser download can be several megabytes in size, even when compressed. Internet utilities aren't quite as big, but when unpacked they are larger than they seem.

Be Prepared

Proper preparation makes the clean-up process easy. When you download a program from the Internet or an online service, it will reside in the directory specified by the program you're using to download it. If you're not sure where it is, check your browser or communications program's set-up parameters, as appropriate. Or, start a download; your program will ask where you want to save it. Downloads usually go into a program subdirectory named \DOWNLOAD, which is fine. Just keep track of where your downloads go.

And keep track what's in this directory. If you have downloaded software more than a couple of times, it is likely that you have a bunch of leftover files in your download directory. These files are wasting space that your system could use for other purposes. So, delete them—and follow the procedures discussed here so you won't have this problem again.

Now, *before* you install a downloaded program, put it in a special directory that you use only to hold programs you plan to install. Keep only one program in it at a time (I'll explain why directly). I use a directory named \INSTALL; the name and purpose are easy to remember.

Your program installation directory should be empty, except when you are preparing to install a program. When you are ready to install a download, copy the file from the download directory to the installation directory. (This makes two copies of the download, but don't worry; you'll remedy this duplication after installation.)

There are good reasons for installing a downloaded program file from a copy in its own directory. If something goes wrong, you still have the original download. After the program is installed, you know where to go to delete the download (both copies). If you are likely to wait to do the deletion, checking this installation directory reminds you what to delete (there, and in the download directory). It's a built-in reminder service.

If the download is a .ZIP, .ARC, or .ARJ file, or a self-extracting archive, also unpack the contents to the installation directory. (Again, see Chapter 11 for more information on these files.) This keeps all the files from the archive in a convenient spot, for simple, one-command deletion. If, however, you unpack an archived file in the download directory, you could end up driving yourself crazy figuring out which files came from the archive.

A final tip on installation: If, when you install a program, you are asked to name a destination drive and directory, you should probably use the default names provided. Even if you change the drive (for example, from C: to D:), retain the directory name. There usually is no reason to change the directory name, and you'll find that doing so can leave you confused when you read documentation or help files, which assume that you are using the default names.

Also, if you install a newer version of an existing program, changing the name of the directory can result in *two* full copies of the installed program on your disk, one old and one new. (Concerning this, it is a good idea to make back-up copies of any program data files—such as a browser's bookmark file—before you install the new version. This backing up is protection against something going wrong, and is also protection against a program overwriting existing data files when it installs a new version.)

DURING INSTALLATION

The installation process for most programs is pretty much automatic. Some do ask whether you wish to do a Full installation, as opposed to a Minimum or Optimal (a.k.a. "common") installation. You don't have to think very long on this one; just decide if you have the extra hard drive space to accommodate files that you will rarely use—which is what you will need if you select the Full installation. (These files typically include extra printer or video drivers and other things the program's creator included to accommodate unusual hardware setups or other personal requirements.)

If you don't have space to waste, Optimal or Common is usually the best choice. With this installation option, you get help and/or tutorial files that do not come with the Minimum installation. (If you are already familiar with the program, you won't need those, so Minimum would be your best choice.)

AFTER INSTALLATION

Most programs do not require setup after installation. Usually, set-up options are established during the installation, either by defaults or as the result of questions the installation program asks you.

If the program is a stand-alone utility, like browser helper applications or, for example, a graphics viewer program, it's a good idea to run it before you need it. Most applications come with example files; load these to test the application. Note where the program's data files are located and any defaults it uses for things like file types (opening or saving) and so forth. There should be defaults for every variable; if not, you are given the opportunity to set them now. If any defaults do not fit your way of working, change them.

When installing a helper application, it is a good idea to check your browser's setup for assigning files of various types to given programs. Make sure that the browser knows the application exists. (If so, the application name will appear in a list the browser keeps.)

The browser also should know which file types the application should be linked to. This is determined by the MIME type settings in the browser's setup. (See Chapter 11, "Internet Data Formats and Conversion," for more information about MIME.) To check this in Netscape Navigator, select Preferences on the Edit menu, then open Navigator and select Applications. You will see the screen shown in Figure 10.1.

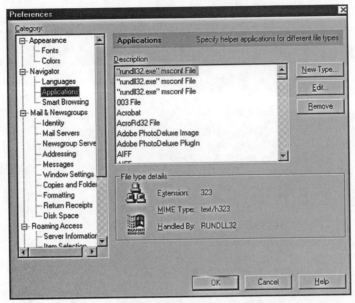

Figure 10.1   Netscape's list of helper application assignments

With Explorer, select Internet Options on the View menu, and press the Programs tab, followed by the File Types button. The screen in Figure 10.2 is displayed.

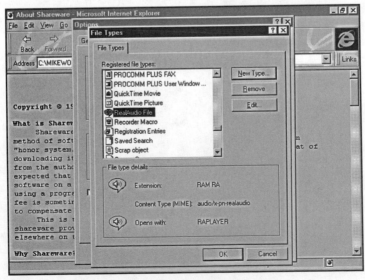

Figure 10.2   Explorer's file types listing

CHAPTER 11

Internet Data Formats and Conversion

In this chapter, you will learn about MIME data and more about binary data, including sending binary files attached to e-mail and retrieving binary files from newsgroups. This may seem confusing in some ways, but any confusion will be cleared up by a little background and some basic explanations as to exactly how computer data and files are structured, stored, and handled by your computer and the Internet.

In earlier chapters, you learned a little about data types, specifically ASCII and binary data. This chapter expands on this knowledge and explains why programs, images, and other binary data files must be transmitted in an *encoded* form.

DATA AND DATA TRANSFER ON THE INTERNET: A REVIEW

Characters in the ASCII character set are referred to as seven-bit ASCII characters because each character is composed of seven bits (that is, a group of seven zeros and ones). All modern computers use seven-bit ASCII characters, which is why they can communicate with one another over the Internet. Using the mutually agreed upon code of the ASCII character set, they share a common language.

The Internet was designed to transmit seven-bit ASCII data, largely because this was the only standard in existence at the time the Internet was developing. Also, conventional modems and other computer communications hardware demanded seven-bit characters.

Decades later, this system continues to serve data communications needs, but only if the data transmitted is composed of seven-bit characters, which means you can easily transmit textual data over the Internet and in e-mail. This is because text messages and other documents are composed exclusively of the first 128 characters in the ASCII table (the letters, numerals, and symbols that your keyboard can produce on-screen, plus a number of control characters computers use to communicate with one another during the course of data transfer).

Unfortunately, much of modern computer data is also composed of eight-bit characters, also known as binary characters or binary data.

Binary Transmission Protocols

Because computers on the Internet communicate using only seven-bit characters, it's easy to see that attempting to transmit eight-bit characters can foul things up.

Eight-bit characters being transmitted can be ignored, or they may be truncated and converted to seven-bit characters. Either way, data is corrupted. Also, data files of the type discussed here may contain certain seven-bit control characters that are intended to represent something else. The receiving system perceives these characters as commands, which completely garbles a transmission.

You can get around this incompatibility in two ways. First, *eight-bit* or *binary transmission* protocols can be used to send eight-bit data in a symbolic form that can be transmitted over the Internet.

A *protocol* is another kind of mutually agreed upon set of rules. In this instance, both sending and receiving computers use a system that does not truncate or otherwise corrupt eight-bit data characters, which allows control characters that are part of a data file to pass through just like any other character.

These protocols are limited to direct, real-time communication—typically, as a means of uploading or downloading a binary file, whether it's a file transmitted directly from a Web page (graphic or other binary file) or via Internet ftp (just about any kind of file).

This kind of file transmission is accomplished easily enough when computers communicate in real time because they can check for errors, adjust how data is sent, and/or resend corrupted blocks of data. (This is why these kinds of protocols are often referred to as *error-checking protocols*.)

Obviously, this error checking can be time consuming. So, such intensive communication is impractical for common Internet applications, such as newsgroup and e-mail traffic—the sheer volume makes it impossible. Fortunately, these forms of communication involve only seven-bit ASCII data and require no error checking or other accommodations in the way eight-bit binary data does.

As the Internet grew, however, the demand increased for transmitting binary eight-bit data via e-mail and newgroups. Several means of encoding binary files for transmission as seven-bit ASCII data were developed for non-real-time communications, including newsgroups and e-mail. Today, one standard, *MIME*, prevails. But other techniques are still used to encode eight-bit files as seven-bit files.

MIME and Other Data-Encoding Techniques

MIME, or *Multi-purpose Internet Mail Extensions*, is the standard for encoding binary data files. Your browser uses the MIME standard to determine what kinds of files it is receiving. (This is why it's a good idea to know a little bit about what MIME and other types of encoding are about. When you go to your browser's File Types setting, you need to know what you're dealing with in order to tell it how to handle incoming data.)

There are several MIME file types, including audio, image, video, text, and application (executable programs).

Each has additional subtypes for specific data types or applications. There are, for example, subtypes for .GIF and .JPG images under the "image" type. There are also subtypes for handling data types for most major PC programs. (Look at the File Type listings in your browser's set-up window; you will see many familiar programs listed under "Mime/Data Type.")

The MIME types and subtypes in part specify how a binary file is encoded. Your browser recognizes file types by the encoding technique used and/or the file name extension of an incoming file. You also can define new data types, specifying the file name extension to identify the file type and the application program needed to use it.

LEARNING WHICH MIME TYPE IS WHICH...

It will pay you to spend a little time with your browser's MIME/File types listing, seeing what sorts of programs are dedicated to what kinds of files.

Open the list on your browser. (Netscape users: Select General Preferences on the Options menu, and press the Helpers tab. Explorer users: Select Options on the View menu, then press the Programs tab followed by the File Types button.) You will see a list of file types along with a description for each, and its extension and the program used with it.

Some e-mail programs also let you do this. You can go so far as to embed lines in a message that start a given program. For example, you can put a URL in an e-mail message so that when the recipient clicks it, the recipient's browser is launched. (This kind of feature is limited, however, for use with a few of the top e-mail programs, such as Eudora, Pegasus, and BeyondMail.)

Again, MIME is the prevailing standard for any eight-bit file transfer, but other encoding techniques are used in sending e-mail and posting newsgroup messages. These techniques include UUENCODE, Base 64, and BinHex.

No matter which encoding process you use, eight-bit data characters are replaced by token seven-bit characters. Then they are transmitted as seven-bit messages. Special software handles the encoding and decoding.

If you send and receive binary files in or with Internet text messages, you need to know a bit about these MIME types. As you will learn, you do not necessarily need to know everything about encoding and decoding because your e-mail program may handle the encoding for you. But it helps to understand what happens in the background.

As noted, binary data is encoded by using token seven-bit characters to represent the actual eight-bit characters. A typical encoded file looks something like the data shown in Figure 11.1.

```
--PART.BOUNDARY.0.571.emout17.mail.aol.com.849482978
Content-ID: <0_571_849482978@emout17.mail.aol.com.75379>
Content-type: text/plain

This is a test with an attached file.  The headers above are for this
text message.  The headers below are for the Base 64-encoded file that
follows

--PART.BOUNDARY.0.571.emout17.mail.aol.com.849482978
Content-ID: <0_571_849482978@emout17.mail.aol.com.75380>
Content-type: application/octet-stream;
        name="SCHEDULE.DOC"
Content-Transfer-Encoding: base64

0M8R4KGxGuEAAAAAAAAAAAAAAAAAAAPgADAP7/CQAGAAAAAAAAAAAAABAAAAQAAAAA
AAAAEAAAAgAAAAEAAAD+////AAAAAAAAAAD///////////////////////////////
///////////////////////////////////////////////////////////////
AAAAAAAAAAAAAAAAAWAAEBAQAAAAIAAAD/////AAAAAAAAAAAAAAAAAAAAAAAACAobvF
zNW7AYChu9HM1bsBAAAAAAAAAAAAAAAQAAAP7///8DAAAABAAAAUAAAAGAAAABwAAAgA
AAAJAAAACgAAAAsAAAAMAAAADQAAAA4AAAAPAAAAEAAAABEAAAASAAAAEwAAABQAAAAUAAAA
FgAAABcAAAAYAAAAGQAAABoAAAAbAAAAHAAAAB0AAAAeAAAAHwAAACAAAAAsAAAAIgAAACMA
AAAkAAAAJQAAACYAAAAnAAAAKAAAACkAAAAqAAAAKwAAAP7///8tAAAALgAAAC8AAAAwAAAA
MQAAADIAAAAzAAAANAAAADUAAAA2AAAANwAAADgAAAA5AAAAOgAAADsAAAA8AAAAPQAAAD4A
AAA/AAAAQAAAAEEAAABCAAAAQwAAAEQAAABFAAAARgAAAEcAAABIAAAASQAAAEoAAABLAAAA
AAAAAAAAAAAAAAAWAAEBAQAAAAIAAAD/////AAAAAAAAAAAAAAAAAAAAAAAACAobvF
```

Figure 11.1 A portion of a Base 64-encoded message

This file was originally Microsoft Word for Windows text. I translated it to Base 64 encoding using a helper program called Wincode. I then copied the resulting text file into an AOL e-mail message and sent it. (Figure 11.1 shows about one-tenth of the entire file.)

As you see, all the characters used are seven-bit ASCII. Based on the MIME file type and sub-type ("application/octet-stream" in a message header) and the encoding type (also named in a message header), an unencoding program knows how to rebuild this group of seven-bit characters into an eight-bit binary file that exactly matches the original data file.

A UUENCODED binary file looks slightly different, with less header information, as shown in Figure 11.2.

```
This is a test, E-mailing a UUENCODED 8-bit file as a 7-bit
text file.

_=_
_=_ Part 001 of 001 of file sh.zip
_=_

begin 666 sh.zip
M4$L#!!?0````('%&*U<B'E%Z)7J`<`````>``',`````4U-H9611U;;&%9&&9]C[5E?
M;?!M)&9^UDS;;9M/TX,I1.&X:UER/:U+;B9TU<#*#2.[32^Q+%E.XJO(F?!CC'^/E
MUKN^W773/%T1DN(A)QT22'<2$A3IT)U%'7!`&>7'\>3F$F$$$J0(HLL#L&@>BBBL0M2%"'5
M!^^!H%,,,,,>=;;8=;?#&^/G%M&8&T'!?!B[|^'G#W#SL]]\^U^FF&UM7ZQ,V<_#[V')W]/?@@L'@++[
M[MUR'(ZYY''D37-H8)B3@YN]0]@;U]\WB[<?X@[.%?@X[#(#[ASU0?::#?#,X#@Z).;?@3R*#@(
M2F[90P P,Y(F./XM QM[?::I^^$^SUR77P`%:[3??%@&^%X@?!N#QR+ &&\.J_0%F^+;-[@
M))=AZ'!W\^@^L[351352)UFR[KKY[$$$$@(HM[2$$#P[]]F=[=[?====]]&$[6]@UTP=$GC
M'MI'^'M.#$\N;?Ho75m.!N07SM====[_]7R$7C[WF[F]U>>,]!MD9$P]%2^JN!N&Z<((C~]u####U#^S%e@75?^W%$[6[_F
M#X]Z4WF?-__90/$_B7^_]\WU![P'^^@3]\$\N%;;;;#""'#'"'9\#9S#__#_#Y*>)\L(^0[x&%/^A11
M#[L>)(?P<?#!S\!/%/@@#2\!P[P%PXX#`?GX2>]"!^&&SX#@[/@\I\"GB//][[#A^D=X<><P#
M'`L-@@@'/:)P`'\$$&#^&`GP`'O@@417_:_#____#9x_X+,#_3>X@^9PL'\\U00BZ)!.U``G^!M<8<+[^4]88]
M!8?l1`%$#++P[P^W^??/?#$];%[#\\M^W!$[QT8[/'???.[+B+!IPY:X![B?X\Lo]>5Ha[<^#,[7#[[?B?B-Qc
M*x?i1?R%-G>$$@&'P^-F/A[C$Si,M7\+MO@'XQ@%I@N''n'#>N=N#=44&[###[[#[@^F*R[,W-$[D+;=L\*H[=SH%4%<@
```

Figure 11.2 A UUENCODED MIME file

I mentioned that I copied the file into an AOL e-mail message; you can just as easily copy a file like this one into any e-mail system. And you can enter a plain-English message to the recipient before the beginning of the encoded file without corrupting the data the encoded file contains.

Also, with some services such as AOL and certain dedicated Internet e-mail programs (such as BeyondMail, Eudora, or Pegasus) you can specify that the file be attached to an e-mail message. Figure 11.3 shows how this is done with Pegasus. Note that you can specify both the type of data (in this case, the Microsoft Word document) and the type of encoding to use.

How an attached file comes through on the other end depends on whether you use an e-mail program that can handle encoding and decoding on its own or a text-only e-mail program or system. I sent the example file shown in Figure 11.1 as an attached file from AOL to an ID on CompuServe. It came through as illustrated, with a brief text message that I typed preceding the encoded portion.

When I sent the UUENCODED message in Figure 11.2 to AOL and to a dedicated ISP using Eudora, I received each as a separate file—the encoded portion of each message came through separate from the text message preceding it. AOL's e-mail system recognizes MIME data in a message. Plus, it decodes the UUENCODED data and places it in a file that is downloaded separately from the text message that precedes it. The same features are true with a dedicated e-mail program such as Eudora.

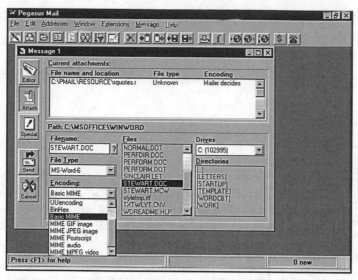

Figure 11.3   Preparing to send a binary document as an attached file with Pegasus, an e-mail program

As for how I handled the message that arrived in CompuServe mail (which does *not* separate MIME data), it was simple enough. I copied the entire message to an open Notepad and then saved it as a text file. Then I opened the file with an *unencoding program*, and the unencoding program saved it as its original file type—MS WORD—with the proper extension for that file type. Now I can access the file with Word just as I can access any other Word file. The unencoding program sorted the encoded data within the message and acted only on the encoded data.

SENDING FILES LARGER THAN THE LIMIT

On some systems, there is a limit to the size of a file you can send as a part of or attached to an e-mail message. (For example, CompuServe has a limit of 50,000 characters.) When using a system with a limit, one way around the problem is to use PKZIP or WinZip to compress the file.

If this doesn't do the trick, and you are dealing with a text or data file that can be sent in two segments then easily reassembled at the other end, send the file in two parts.

ENCODING/UNENCODING PROGRAMS

Unless you are using an e-mail program or an online service that handles all encoding and unencoding of MIME data, you need a program to perform these tasks on your files.

The best Windows programs for handling MIME encoding and decoding are WinZip and Wincode. WinZip is the better of the two for the way I work. Its capabilities as a MIME utility are not really played up, but it is an extremely easy-to-use program, and you have the added bonus of WinZip's primary functions as an archive manager.

Wincode is a *dedicated program* (a program written for a single, defined purpose) that provides some worthwhile special features. It is, however, a little more difficult to use than WinZip. The following sections give you a quick rundown on each program so that you can decide which one will best serve your needs.

You may also find a program called Information Transfer Professional (XFERPRO) of interest. XFERPRO provides a fairly fast and easy tool for creating encoded files in Windows for sending text, programs, graphics, and other files via Internet e-mail. XFERPRO, a product of Sabasoft, Inc., can be downloaded at Sabasoft's Web site (**http://www.sabasoft.com**) or at the ZD Net Software Library (**http://www.zdnet.com**).

Using WinZip with MIME Files

WinZip is the premier archive-management tool. Because it already handles specialized encoding and decoding of ZIP and other kinds of archives, it is no surprise that WinZip also takes care of MIME format data.

In fact, I used WinZip to manually encode and unencode the messages in Figures 11.1 and 11.2. The word manually is almost inappropriate, because WinZip automates almost the entire process. I only have to tell it which files to work on, as shown in Figure 11.4.

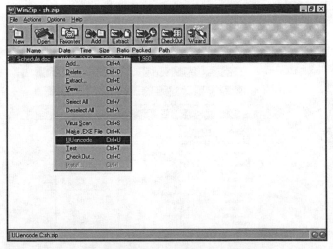

**Figure 11.4 WinZip shown as it encodes and
unencodes MIME data**

To decode an encoded file, load the file, mark it, and tell WinZip to unencode it. WinZip goes to work, unencoding the file and displaying a list of the contents. Double click the name of the file to unencode, and WinZip loads it into the application that can handle it. From here, you can edit and save the file as you desire.

Note that although WinZip will open an encoded file under any name and any extension, WinZip doesn't recognize an encoded file unless you have saved it with an extension commonly used with encoded files. These extensions are .UU, .UUE, .XXE, .BNX, .B64, or .HQX. Without one of those extensions, you will have to open the file manually. (Either type in the file's complete name, or tell WinZip to display all files in the directory—i.e., *.*.)

WinZip makes it similarly easy to encode a binary file. Simply create a new archive by using WinZip menu commands, place the desired file in it, then tell WinZip to encode the file. WinZip creates a text file similar to those shown in Figures 11.1 and 11.2. You can then copy this into a message and send it, as described previously.

Using Wincode

If you encode and decode a lot of MIME files, you may want to check out Wincode. Wincode offers several features to organize and simplify handling files.

Shown in Figure 11.5, Wincode has a businesslike interface. All the major commands are available on buttons (with graphical symbols for labels) as well as on menus. In this respect, Wincode's user interface is more accessible than WinZip's.

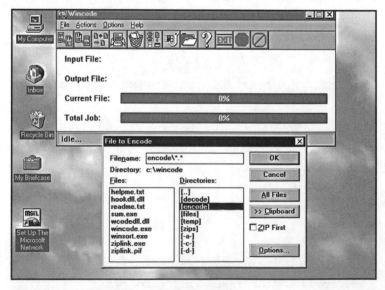

Figure 11.5 The Wincode front end

Wincode organizes incoming and outgoing files into Encoded and Decoded subdirectories, and allows you to sort files in these work directories based on various criteria. Wincode also has a feature that *concatenates*, or combines multiple files into one file. This feature is important where large binary files are transmitted in more than one part. (Multiple postings for one binary file are common in some of the "alt.binaries" Usenet newsgroups.)

Wincode is rather particular about file names. You have to be careful, for example, about the names you give to files to be encoded because Wincode recognizes file types in part by their file name extensions. If you keep this in mind, Wincode is easy to use.

Handling Binary Files in Newsgroups

The examples I have given so far are of MIME files and e-mail. Binary files in Usenet newsgroups are handled much in the same way.

Most newsgroups carry only text, but some also provide binary files for transfer. These files require that you use special software, which translates files that contain token seven-bit ASCII characters into their original binary forms. This tokenizing is necessary, of course, because eight-bit files cannot be carried in Usenet's text-only message format.

MIME-encoded newsgroup files are similar to e-mail files. As you see in Figure 11.6, they are not unlike encoded e-mail messages.

```
---------------50BC5E3027E5
Content-Type: image/gif
Content-Transfer-Encoding: base64
Content-Disposition: inline;
filename="KILB431.GIF"

R0lGODdhqwEbAfcAAAAAAIAAAACAAICAAAAAgIAAgACAg
ICAgMDAwP8AAAD/AP//AAAA//8A/wD//wAAEe7u7t3d3c
zMzLu7u6qqqpmZmYiIiHd3d2ZmZlVVVURERDMzMyIiIhE
REf//zP//mf//Zv//M///AP/M///MzP/Mmf/MZv/MM//M
AP+Z//+ZzP+Zmf+ZZv+ZM/+ZAP9m//9mzP9mmf9mZv9mM
/9mAP8z//8zzP8zmf8zZv8zM/8zAP8A//8AzP8Amf8AZv
8AM8z//8z/zMz/mcz/Zsz/M8z/AMzM/8zMmczMZsszMM8z
MAMyZ/8yZzMyZmcyZZsyzM8yZAMxm/8xzMxmmcxmZsxm
M8xmAMwz/8wzzMwzmcwzZswzM8wzAMwA/8wAzMwAmcwAZ
swAM5n//5n/zJn/mZn/Zpn/M5n/AJnM/5nMzJnMmnZnMZp
nMM5nMAJmZ/5mZzJmZZpmZM5mZAJlm/5lmzJlmmZlmZpl
mM5lmAJkz/5kzzJkzmZkzZpkzM5kzAJkA/5kAzJkAmZkkA
ZpkAM2b//2b/zGb/mWb/Zmb/M2b/AGbM/2bMzGbMmmWbMZ
mbMM2bMAGaZ/2aZzGaZmWaZZmaZM2aZAGZm/2ZmzGZmmW
ZmM2ZmAGYz/2YzzGYzmWYzZmYzM2YzAGYA/2YAzGYAmWY
AZmYAMzP//zP/zDP/mTP/ZjP/MzP/ADPM/zPMzDPMmnTPM
```

Figure 11.6   A MIME-encoded message in a Usenet newsgroup

Decoding a MIME message from a newsgroup is a simple procedure: Download it and open the message with a program that can handle unencoding, then save the unencoded file under an appropriate name. After doing so, you can use the file with the appropriate application.

DATA SECURITY AND DATA ENCRYPTION

There is great concern among Internet users about the vulnerability of transmitted data. As you know, data is transmitted over the Internet by being relayed through one and sometimes two or more computers. Because of this, there is the possibility of data in transit being viewed at any of the computers along the way. How likely this is to happen is difficult to say, but the possibility does exist.

You can deal with this potential vulnerability in several ways. The first and simplest method is to avoid sending sensitive data over the Internet—including credit card numbers. This caution makes sense, even though the reported incidence of e-mail "spying" is low.

Other approaches you can take are to use browser and Internet data-security features and, with e-mail and other sensitive document transmissions, *data encryption*. These subjects are covered in the following sections.

Browser and Internet Data Security Features

As with other aspects of the Internet, security standards cover data encryption and also keep data secure during transmission. Taking advantage of these features requires that the Web browser you use conforms to specific security standards. Both Netscape and Microsoft Internet Explorer conform to the prevailing security standards—Secure Socket Layer (SSL) and Private Communication (PCT).

Some of the most important security features are internal to browsers. These features include security certificates to authenticate your identity to a Web site, the warnings Netscape and Explorer offer when you start to send data to an unsecured Web site, and more. It's a good idea to leave these features active; even if they don't favorably affect your online activities now, there's a good chance they will in the future.

Web sites also can provide security—if your browser supports the security protocols these sites use, that is. Web site security features include security certificates that certify that they are what they represent themselves to be and are in fact *secure sites*.

CHECKING SECURITY

There are a couple of ways to check to see whether the site you are visiting is secure. With Netscape, click on the icon of a broken door key at the bottom left of the screen in the status bar. A dialogue will pop up to inform you whether any of the files you are requesting are secure. (When Netscape is receiving a secure document, the key icon is displayed unbroken.)

Explorer indicates that it is exchanging data with a secure site by displaying an icon that looks like a lock on the status bar.

Both browsers can warn you when you are doing something, like sending information via an online form, that might be a security risk. With Netscape, select Security Preferences on the Options menu, then click the General tab to enable or disable warnings about insecure sites. With Explorer, select Options on the View menu, and press the Security tab.

Finally, if a URL begins with "https://" rather than "http://" it is secure. Similarly, a Usenet newsgroup URL that begins with "snews:" instead of "news:" is a secure server.

A secure site protects the routes used by data moving to it so that credit card numbers or other sensitive data cannot be viewed en route. You still have to trust the person running the site, of course; it's analogous to giving your credit card number via voice phone over a line that is guaranteed not to be bugged. But secure sites provide some assurance that no one but you and the person to whom you are giving the sensitive information has your credit card information.

Data Encryption

Data encryption is similar to data encoding, although the intent is different. Rather than encoding data to enable it to be transmitted, you encode it so it is not recognizable. The idea, of course, is to prevent data from being understood and used by those who don't have the means of decoding it (described in the following section, "Data Decryption"). Only those to whom you provide this means of decoding the message can read it.

In practice, encryption is a process of substitution. An alternative value (also called a *token*) is substituted for designated elements of a message or other data. This is typically done on the character level. For example, the letter "r" might be replaced by "m," and other characters similarly substituted for every character in the message.

This substitution is similar to what happens when a binary file is encrypted by using UUENCODE or any other protocol—one group of characters substituted for another group of characters. The main difference here is that the goal is to make the data difficult to unscramble, except for those who have a means of *decrypting* it.

In theory, encrypted data cannot be read without a guide or reference to all the substitutions that have been made. However, a simple, non-varying pattern of character substitution is fairly easy to decode (for example, if "m" was always substituted for "r" and so on).

So, most encryption schemes vary the pattern of substitution enough so there is no recognizable pattern that can be used to decode the message.

Assuming an encryption scheme or pattern(s) is too complex to be worked out, or cracked, the only way you can read an encrypted message is with a *decryption program*, a guide to the encryption patterns used (often called a *key*), or the original encryption program.

Data Decryption

Decryption is a process of reproducing data from an encoded message based on a known code or *cipher*. The code key to decrypting encrypted data is known, appropriately enough, as the *key*.

Simply described, a key is a reference or guide that can be used to decrypt encrypted data. In effect, a key tells the user (or with computer data, the decrypting program) which symbols represent which characters, and where and how, that is, the substitutions made by the encryption program.

Keys and Encryption Software

Encryption software usually performs both decryption and encryption functions. The receiver of encoded data usually must have both the decryption key and the software.

There are several approaches to encrypting and decrypting data. Some apply to one-way data transmission, such as when you send information from a Web site using a form on a Web page. Others apply strictly to e-mail.

ONE-WAY DATA ENCRYPTION

With one-way Internet data encryption, a program at the Web site encrypts data before it is transmitted. The recipient is the only person who has the key to decipher the data. Therefore, the recipient is in control of both encryption and decryption.

E-MAIL MESSAGE ENCRYPTION

Encryption of e-mail is more conventional in that it requires that the sender can encrypt a message, and that the receiver be able to decrypt it.

You do not, of course, want to send a decryption key with the encrypted message, and you probably don't want to send it separately if there is a chance that it might be intercepted and used later to decrypt intercepted messages.

Fortunately, there is a solution. A system known as *public keys* and *private keys* was developed in the 1970s to allow encrypted messages to be sent without the sender needing to provide the recipient with a code key. Therefore, unlike older computer and non-computer encryption schemes, the sender doesn't have the decryption key with the public/private key system.

The system uses a program (the public key) that encrypts data in a way that can be decrypted only by its counterpart (the private key). The public key can be used by anyone, but only the holder of the private key (the message recipient) can decrypt a message created with the public key.

This method works particularly well for someone who needs to receive encrypted e-mail messages from many people. Overall, however, it works well in any situation where encryption is needed.

In practice, the sender needs only the recipient's public key. This setup enables the sender to use the program to encrypt a message in the required format. After it is encrypted, no one but the recipient can decode it because only the recipient has the private key.

Using encrypted e-mail files is analogous to sending a message in an envelope, as opposed to on a postcard. If this sounds like a good idea—something that anyone might want to use—read on.

Pretty Good Privacy

The header may seem facetious, but it is the name of the best public/private key encryption program going. Pretty Good Privacy is also the most widely used program of its type.

Pretty Good Privacy, or PGP for short, is the work of Phillip Zimmerman and is distributed as freeware.

In addition to creating public keys, PGP of course unencrypts messages from those who have a public key—provided the creator of the public key is the recipient. PGP also provides message authentication with *digital signatures*, also created by the PGP program.

A digital signature is a means of verifying the authenticity of an e-mail message. The message is first "hashed," which means each character is assigned a numeric value. Then a complex mathematical algorithm generates a string of numeric values that is almost impossible to duplicate or crack. The values are appended to the message as the digital signature and stored by the system that generated them for later comparison if necessary.

(The U.S. Postal Service is using such a system as a means of providing "electronic postmarks" for e-mail with its new Postal Electronic Commerce Services, or Postal ECS.)

Public keys and signature files created with PGP are text files, and resemble the following block of characters:

——BEGIN PGP PUBLIC KEY BLOCK——

Version: 2.6.2

foXwAAAQMjpgsAAAEDAMsiJK9Ah6VAXVfobv34chAeLeWxl
23OLhBEskOAc01nwbWugMgSs39/Oh7xLoU1G1ZvB7BRH8ZhvEBtcG2t5w
Pgw4m8FE7QcU3I6eWd5IFNhbGVzIDxzYcrn0hBEskBzehBEsk29Vf3QJfoXo
u39Y29VfobvtPg==
=wPgw

——END PGP PUBLIC KEY BLOCK——

With PGP, you can create your own public key and distribute it to friends, associates, and others. One way to distribute your public key is to include it after your "signature" at the end of each message. You can do this most efficiently by adding it to your sig file, which is a user-definable block of text that many e-mail programs automatically place at the ends of outgoing messages.

There also are public distribution servers for PGP public keys. Here, you can leave your public key for others and obtain others' public keys. You can find one of these servers at this URL: **http://rs.internic.net/support/wwwpks**. To download PGP, go to **http://bozo.mit.edu:9999/pgp**.

PGP for PCs is a DOS application that works on files externally from the DOS command line. You type commands while running the program in DOS, directing it to act on a file you want to encrypt or decrypt.

If you prefer an easier interface than PGP for PCs, several DOS and Windows front ends are available for PGP. A list of these programs, with links, can be found at **http://www.seattle-webworks.com/pgp/pgplinks.html**. This page also contains links to front ends for using PGP with Eudora, Pegasus, and other e-mail programs.

For more information about data security, security standards, and what various companies are doing about security on the Internet, visit RSA Data Security's Web site, at **http://www.rsa.com**. This organization is responsible for designing and implementing most of the security standards in use on the Internet. (RSA Data Security also makes available a personal online/off-line data security product called SecurPC.)

Troubleshooting
and Tips

This appendix contains advice to help you avoid and deal with online problems. Read it before you sign on to a new system and refer to it frequently; it will save you time, frustration, and money.

HOW TO AVOID ONLINE PROBLEMS
AND WHAT TO DO IF YOU HAVE A PROBLEM

If you experience a problem during sign-on or while online, don't panic. As with anything else, if you jump in and type commands at random, you'll end up confused and no further toward resolving the problem than when you started.

Being Prepared

Most online problems are not problems at all but the result of not understanding how to use a particular system. Like any other computer system, BBSs and online services normally do exactly what you tell them to do; thus, you need to understand what you are telling a system to do with each command. If possible, familiarize yourself with the service by studying its manual or command reference card. Keep these materials handy during your online sessions, too.

You'll need to understand your end of the connection, too. Before you try to dial up a BBS or online service, you should, of course, be familiar with your communications hardware and software. Spend some time with their respective manuals. (You will find it useful to keep this book handy during your online sessions, as well.)

Preventing Problems

The best solution for any problem is to solve it before you sign on. To save time you should go over the following checklist—at least mentally—before dialing. The items to check are basic and very simple, but are the most frequent source of problems.

- Check your computer. Make sure the computer's power supply and any peripherals are properly connected.

- Check your modem. Make sure your modem is properly connected to its power supply, to the computer, and to the telephone line. Read the manual accompanying your modem completely so that you understand exactly how it operates and so you know what to expect. If you are confused about or have any problems with its operations, contact the dealer from whom you purchased the modem or the modem manufacturer. And, if the modem has a power switch, turn it on.

- Check your software parameter settings. Make sure that all communications parameters are set properly for the system you are calling, as you may have changed them to accommodate another system. Are you using the proper dial-up procedure? Are the telephone number, your system ID, and password properly entered in the autologon file (if any) you intend to use?

COMMON PROBLEMS AND SOLUTIONS

Tables A.1 and A.2 list commonly encountered problems and their remedies. Take a few minutes to look them over now, so you'll have an idea of what's going on if you do encounter these problems.

Table A.1 Sign-On Troubleshooting Guide	
Trouble/Symptoms	**Remedies**
You issue dial commands, but nothing happens	■ Check your modem's power supply; make certain the modem is plugged in and turned on. ■ Check the cable between computer and modem; unplug and re-plug the DB connectors to make sure they are properly seated and making good connections. ■ Make sure the telephone cable is plugged into the modem. Or, if you

Table A.1 Sign-On Troubleshooting Guide *(continued)*

Trouble/Symptoms	Remedies
You issue dial commands, but nothing happens	are using an acoustic connector, check the fit of the acoustic cups on the handset. ■ Try to dial the phone manually to make sure it's working properly. (Look for extensions that might be off the hook, too.) ■ Check your software; make sure it is set to dial by tone or pulse, as appropriate, and that it is sending the proper modem initialization strings. ■ If you need to dial an extra digit (like 9 to get an outside line), make sure you're doing that, or check to make sure your software's doing it. ■ Make sure your modem's DIP switches are properly set (see the modem's manual). ■ Does your computer have more than one serial port? If so, check to see if the software is set for the correct port (i.e., the port to which the modem is connected—usually COM1). ■ If you have call-waiting, disable it (press *70).
Your modem dials a number, but the sound of the tones is extra loud, and nothing happens.	The sound is extra loud because the telephone line is unplugged; plug the telephone line in.
You dial up a packet-switching network, online service or ISP, and hear a slow busy signal.	The network node is temporarily busy; all available ports are in use. Hang up and try again.
You hear a fast busy signal.	This indicates a temporary overload of local telephone circuits. Hang up and try again.
The line at the other end rings, but there is no answer.	Check to see if you've dialed a wrong number. If you've dialed the correct number and the problem persists, and this is an online service or packet-switching network number, call the service's voice help or information number to report the problem.

Table A.1   Sign-On Troubleshooting Guide *(continued)*

Trouble/Symptoms	Remedies
You hear the answering tone from the system you've dialed, but your modem makes no response. (The connect tone may change after a few seconds.)	Check your modem's connections. If this does not help, turn off your computer and modem, and restart everything. If the problem persists, have your modem checked out. (If possible, try another modem; this will verify that your modem is at fault.)
The system you're calling doesn't recognize your ID and password.	The ID and password may be case-sensitive. Try re-entering your password in all caps or all lowercase letters. Also, turn on your software's local echo (duplex) so you can see what you're typing when you enter the password.
The other system answers and yours responds, but lines of garbage characters scroll up your screen, non-stop.	You have dialed up at a speed the other system can't handle. (Example: You are dialing a system that has a 24kbps modem at 56.6kbps.) Set your system to a lower speed and try again.

Table A.2   Online Troubleshooting Guide

Trouble/Symptoms	Remedies
The characters you type aren't displayed on your screen.	Change the duplex, echo, or mode setting with your communications software to "half" or "full" (whichever is the opposite of its current setting). Go to the "Setup" or "Parameters" section of the BBS or online service you're on and change the duplex setting in your online profile to "half" or "full" (the opposite of the current setting).
Everything you type is displayed twice, lliikkee tthhiiss.	Again, change your communications software's duplex, echo, or mode setting, or tell the remote system that you want the opposite of what you have.

Table A.2   Online Troubleshooting Guide *(continued)*

Trouble/Symptoms	Remedies
You hear the answering tone from the system you've dialed, but your modem makes no response. (The connect tone may change after a few seconds.)	Check your modem's connections. If this does not help, turn off your computer and modem, and restart everything. If the problem persists, have your modem checked out. (If possible, try another modem; this will verify that your modem is at fault.)
Your screen displays "garbage" text with no pattern. (Example: xxxx~xxx@~xx~@xxx.)	■ Check your speed setting. ■ If you are using a packet-switching network (public or private), you may have dialed the wrong number. ■ Make sure you've dialed the number for the speed you are using. ■ If you have to tell the system you are calling your modem speed at sign on with an identifier code, make sure you've done that. ■ If none of these work, hang up and try again; you may have a bad connection. NOTE: If you try to sign on to Tymnet with ANSI terminal emulation, you will get lots of garbage, and probably won't be able to sign on. Turn off ANSI emulation before you use Tymnet.
Your screen displays partially garbled text. (Example: Welc`@~nm@e.)	Check your parity setting. If you're on at 8 bits, change the parity setting to "None." If you're on at 7 bits, change the parity setting to "Even" or "Odd" (the opposite of what you're using).
The screen displays garbled text consisting of oddly-spaced characters, like this: ~ #@ Rr ? A@ x H @	Your data bit setting is wrong; change it to either 7 or 8.
The remote system disconnects.	■ Someone has lifted a telephone extension, and the line noise has made the modem disconnect. ■ Call-waiting knocked you off line. Disable it. ■ Has it been several minutes since you typed a command? Most systems hang up after a preset time if there is no input from you.

Table A.2   Online Troubleshooting Guide *(continued)*

Trouble/Symptoms	Remedies
The remote system disconnects. *(continued)*	You may have logged on to a system that doesn't support MNP 5, with MNP 5 activated at your end.
You type commands and control characters, but absolutely nothing happens—the remote system does not respond (what you type may or may not be echoed on your screen).	■ Have you entered a Ctrl-S? This is an almost universal "pause" signal, and will make the other system stop sending. Enter Ctrl-Q to get things moving again. ■ The remote system may be having some problems. Send a True Break character, a Ctrl-C, or a Ctrl-O to interrupt the system and get back to a menu or prompt.

Equipment Manufacturers and Vendors

For more specific information about what's available in dedicated fax machines, PC fax boards, and modems, contact the manufacturers in this listing:

DEDICATED FAX MACHINE MANUFACTURERS AND VENDORS

AT&T
   99 Jefferson Road
   Parsippany, NJ 07054

Brother International Corporation
   8 Corporate Place
   Piscataway, NJ 08855

Canon U.S.A., Inc.
   P.O. Box 3900
   Peoria, IL 61614

Citifax
   3667 Woodhead Drive
   Northbrook, IL 60062

Citizen/CBM America
   Corporation
   2999 Overland Drive
   Los Angeles, CA 90064

Fujitsu Imaging Systems
   Commerce Park
   Corporate Drive
   Danbury, CT 06810

Gestetner Corporation
   Gestetner Park
   Yonkers, NY 10703

Harris/3M Corporation
   23000 Park Lake Drive
   N.E. Atlanta, GA 30345

Hitachi America
   50 Prospect Avenue
   Tarrytown, NY 10591-4698

Konica Business Machines USA, Inc.
   500 Day Hill Road
   Windsor, CT 06095

Minolta Corporation
101 Williams Drive
Ramsey, NJ 07446

Mitsubishi Corp.
P.O. Box 6008
Cypress, CA 90630

Monroe Systems for Business The
American Way
Morris Plains, NJ 07950

Murata Business Systems, Inc.
4801 Spring Valley, Suite 108B
Dallas, TX 75244

NEC Information Systems, Inc.
8 Old Sod Farm Road
Melville, NY 11747

Olivetti U.S.A.
765 U.S. Highway 202
Somerville, NJ 08876

Olympia USA, Inc.
Box 22, Route 22
Somerville, NJ 08876

Panasonic/Panafax
10 Melville Road
Melville, NY 11747

Pitney-Bowes, Inc.
3191 Broadbridge Avenue
Stratford, CT 06497

Ricoh Corporation
5 Dedrick Place
West Caldwell, NJ 07006

Sanyo Business Systems
51 Joseph Street
Moonachie, NJ 07074

Savin Corporation
9 West Broad Street
Stamford, CT 06904

Sharp Electronics Corporation
Sharp Plaza
Mahwah, NJ 07430

Tandy Corporation
One Tandy Center
Fort Worth, TX 76102

Toshiba America, Inc.
Telecommunication Systems
Division
9740 Irvine Boulevard
Irvine, CA 92718

Xerox Corporation
P.O. Box 24
Rochester, NY 14692

Pc Fax Board
Manufacturers and Vendors

American Data Technology, Inc.
44 W. Bellvue Drive, #6
Pasadena, CA 91105

AT&T
1 Speedwell Avenue
Morristown, NJ 07920

Brooktrout Technology, Inc.
110 Cedar Street
Wellesley Hills, MA 02181

Brother International Corporation
8 Corporate Place
Piscataway, NJ 08855

DEST Corporation
1201 Cadillac Court
Milpitas, CA 95035

GammaLink
2452 Embarcadeo Way
Palo Alto, CA 94303

Hayes Microcomputer Products, Inc.
P.O. Box 105203
Atlanta, GA 30348

Intel PCEO
Mail Stop CO3-07
5200 NE Elam Young Parkway
Hillsboro, OR 97124
http://www.intel.com

Microlink International, Inc.
4064 McConnel Drive
Burady, British Columbia
V5A 3A8 Canada

Omnium Corporation
1911 Curve Crest Boulevard
Stillwater, MN 55082

Panasonic Corporation/Panasonic
Industrial Company
2 Panasonic Way
Secaucus, NJ 07094

Ricoh Corporation
5 Dedrick Place
West Caldwell, NJ 07006

Xerox Imaging Systems
1215 Terra Bella Avenue
Mountain View, CA 94043

MODEM MANUFACTURERS AND VENDORS

Anderson Jacobson, Inc.
521 Charcot Avenue
San Jose, CA 95131

AT&T
1 Speedwell Avenue
Morristown, NJ 07920

Hayes Microcomputer Products, Inc.
P.O. Box 105203
Atlanta, GA 30348

Radio Shack
300 One Tandy Center
Fort Worth, TX 76102

USRobotics
800 McCormick Boulevard
Skokie, IL 60076

Ven-Tel Modems
2121 Zanker Road
San Jose, CA 95131

ZOOM Telephonics, Inc.
207 South Street
Boston, MA 02111
617/423-1072
http://www.zoomtel.com

Glossary

Acoustic coupler. (Also acoustic modem) A type of modem that converts binary computer signals to audio signals and then transmits the signals through a telephone handset. *See direct connect modem, modem*

Analog signal. A signal that varies in a continuous manner, such as music or the voice tones carried over telephone lines. A radio or electric signal or system that uses variations in amplitude (strength) or frequency on a carrier wave to carry information. *See carrier wave, digital signal*

ASCII. Acronym for American Standard Code for Information Interchange. ASCII is a standard numeric code used by most computers for transmitting data. There are 128 standard ASCII code numbers (0 through 127), each of which is assigned to an alphanumeric character, control character, or special character. Digital computers handle data as strings of binary numbers that are digital counterparts of numbers in the ASCII code, which in turn represent certain characters. Some computers may use a modified ASCII set with an additional 128 characters, called eight-bit ASCII. *See binary, character, control character, digital*

ASCII download. A download format that requires that you open your computer's capture buffer before issuing the download command to the remote system. Some systems may display the file with a delay, Control-Z, and bell (Control-G) at the end to signal the receiving computer that the end of the file has been reached. *See buffer, capture, download, turnaround character, upload*

Asynchronous. Data transmission in which the amount of time between each bit sent may vary in a nonuniform manner. To compensate for this, each character is individually synchronized, usually through the use of start and stop bits. *See start bit, stop bit*

AT Command Set. A standardized set of commands used by most modems, so named because the command used to initiate modem operations is AT. Other commands include D for "dial," T for "use tones when dialing," and P for use "pulse dialing." Also known as the Hayes Command Set, it is based on the Heatherington Patent.

Auto answer. An option that allows a modem to detect an incoming call and answer the phone by responding with a tone that is recognizable by the calling computer—all without the use of a telephone set.

Auto dial. (Also auto-dial, autodial) An option that allows a modem to dial telephone numbers as opposed to the user dialing the telephone manually. Used to describe a modem that is capable of generating pulse-dial and/or Touch Tone (DTMF) signals without a telephone set. *See DTMF, modem*

Auto line feed. *See carriage return, line feed*

Autologon. A sign-on process whereby a computer's terminal software communicates with another computer system in a pre-arranged sign-on sequence. *See autologon file, logon*

Autologon file. A special disk file containing instructions for your computer to follow after it connects with another computer. Autologon files can usually be edited to include user IDs, passwords, etc. *See autologon, logon*

Backspace. The action of moving a cursor one or more spaces to the left (back) on the computer screen. This action is normally accomplished by sending a Control-H (an ASCII 8), which is what most computers' backspace keys send.

Baud rate. A measure of how often a signal in a communications channel makes a transition between states, states being changes in frequencies, voltage levels, or phase angles—i.e, a measure of the number of signal events per second. Baud rate is not necessarily equivalent to bits per second: Depending on the communications system, one transition of state can transmit one bit or more or less than one bit. *See bit, bits per second*

BBS. *See bulletin board system*

Bell. The Control-G (^G) character, used for the end of file during ASCII downloads on some systems and as a prompt signal on others, which causes the speaker on many computers to beep.

Bell compatible. Used to describe a modem that conforms to AT&T standards for a specified communications rate—e.g., Bell 103 for 300 bps modems and Bell 212A for 1,200 bps modems. Modems at both ends of a connection must recognize the same standards if they are to communicate successfully.

Binary. A system of counting that uses only two digits: 1 and 0. Referring to a system that uses two states (off/on, high/low, negative/positive, etc.) to represent information.

Binary file. A file that is stored in binary format using binary digits, as opposed to ASCII format. Sometimes used to refer to files stored in eight-bit ASCII format as well. *See binary*

Bisynchronous. Telecommunications in which two computers send and receive data at the same time.

Bit. Contraction of BInary digiT. The smallest unit of computer information; its value is either 0 or 1. *See binary, byte, character, data bits, stop bit*

Bit rate. *See bits per second*

Bits per second (bps). A measure of the rate of data transmission expressed as the number of data bits sent in one second. This is not necessarily the same as baud rate, nor does it represent the number of characters sent per second, as each character is composed of more than one bit. *See baud rate, bit, character, characters per second*

Block. A group of characters or bytes transmitted as a single unit. Data is typically transmitted in blocks during binary file transfer, as with Xmodem protocol. Blocks vary in size depending upon the protocol and computer systems used. *See Xmodem, error-checking protocol*

Board. Slang term for bulletin board system. Also, an area on a Web site or online service where public messages are posted. *See bulletin board system*

Bps. *See bits per second*

Break character. On some host systems and online services, a control character designated as the one to interrupt or discontinue a current operation or process. Most often, Control-C or Control-P is used as a break character. However, a true break signal consists of a 200- to 600-millisecond sustained high signal (a logical or binary 0). *See break*

Buffer. A section of a computer's RAM reserved by terminal software to temporarily store incoming data for display and/or later capture. Also, a section of a computer or modem's RAM used to temporarily store commands. *See capture*

Bulletin board system. Most often referred to as a BBS, a bulletin board system is a computer and software combination set up to receive calls and respond to commands sent by the calling computer. The average BBS offers file-transfer and message-exchange capabilities, with varying levels of sophistication of features. Most BBSs are single-user, PC-based systems. *See multi-user systems, sysop, system*

Byte. (Also data word, word) A group of bits handled by a computer as a discreet unit; a computer data character. A byte is usually composed of seven or eight bits. *See bit, character*

Capture. To store the text or other material being displayed by a remote system in your computer's RAM buffer or on disk or other media. *See buffer*

Carriage return. The signal sent by a computer's Enter or Return key; normally a Control-M, or ASCII 13. Often referred to as CR. On most systems, a carriage return moves the cursor to the left-hand side of the screen.

Carriage return and line feed. A setting, usually determined by your terminal software, that adds a linefeed (Control-J) after each carriage return sent or received, the purpose of which is to move the cursor to the left-hand side of the screen and down one line. Also referred to as CR/LF. *See carriage return*

Carrier. (Also carrier wave, carrier tone.) A tone transmitted over telephone lines that can be modulated to carry data. A carrier tone is an analog signal of constant frequency and strength. *See analog signal, modulate*

CCITT compatible. Used to describe a modem that meets one or more of the standards set by the CCITT (an international telecommunications standards committee, now known as the ITU or International Telecommunication Union). This is the standard used in western Europe and most of the rest of the world outside North America for 1,200 baud communications (so it is necessary to have a modem that recognizes the CCITT/ITU standards if you wish to access systems outside North America). The CCITT/ITU standards have of course been adopted by U.S. modem manufacturers. *See International Telecommunication Union*

Character. (Also data word, word.) A letter, number, space, punctuation mark, symbol, or control character; any piece of information that can be stored in one byte. A representation of the same coded in binary digits. *See bit, byte*

Character bits. *See data bits*

Character echo. *See echo*

Character length. (Also data word length, word length.) A communications parameter that determines the number of data bits in each character sent. Seven data bits are required for each character in the standard ASCII character set, while eight data bits are used to transfer binary and eight-bit files. *See data bits, ASCII, binary*

Character set. The characters that can be displayed, printed, stored, and/or transmitted by a particular machine. *See character*

Characters per second (cps). A measurement of the number of characters transmitted each second, based on the bps (bits per second) rate and the length of the characters being sent. *See baud rate, bits per second, character*

Command. An instruction or set of instructions that tells a program to perform a specified function or operation. Commands are either typed or selected from a menu. *See control character, menu, qualifiers*

Command mode. A software operating mode in which all keyboard or other local input is sent to the computer's communications software. *See terminal mode*

Communications link. The telephone lines and associated systems that link two systems in communications. May also include a packet-switching network.

Communications parameters. *See communications settings*

Communications port. *See port*

Communications settings. The parameter settings used by terminal software; the group of changeable settings available in a terminal program. These settings determine how your computer will communicate with another computer and include baud/bps rate, parity, duplex, character length/data bits, and number of stop bits. *See parameters, configuration*

Communications software. Dedicated software that enables and facilitates data communications. Also known as terminal software.

Conference. An interactive, real-time conversation system. Sometimes referred to as a CB simulator or chat mode. *See message, real time*

Configuration. The specific, customized arrangement of hardware, or the parameter selections and operating setup of communications software.

Connect. The point at which two computers are first connected and mutually acknowledge same. This is often indicated by the display of the word connect on your computer's screen.

Connect charges. The cost of time spent online via an ISP or a commercial online service. This is normally calculated on a per-month basis, but sometimes is calculated on a per-minute or per-call basis.

Control character. A normally nonprinting character generated by holding down the Control key and a letter key on a computer keyboard. Control characters are used on many systems to issue commands. In hardware, software, and system documentation, control characters are usually referred to as Control-X, but may sometimes be denoted as CTRL-X or ^X. *See command, control key*

Control key. A special key on your computer keyboard marked CONTROL, CTRL, Ctrl, or <CTRL>. The Control key is designated as Control, CONTROL, CTRL, or ^ in computer software and hardware documentation. The Control key is used in conjunction with other keys to send special characters as commands to a host system. *See control character*

CR. *See carriage return*

CRC. Acronym for cyclic redundancy check; a feature of certain error-checking protocols. *See Xmodem*

CR/LF. *See carriage return and line feed*

Current. Refers to a message being read or just read, or to a file being transferred. On most Web sites and online services, commands that operate on individual messages or files operate on the current message or file when no message or file is specified with the command.

Data. Information of any type. Addresses are data; so are names or groups of numbers. Data is the plural of the Latin *datum*.

Database. An organized collection of related data stored in the form of binary and/or ASCII files. Databases are usually organized into various topics and may contain text, data, and program files. The files may be searchable by various keywords and may be downloaded. *See field, file, keyword, search*

Data bits. The number of all bits sent for a single character that represent the character itself, not counting parity or stop bits; normally seven or eight bits. A communications setting. *See bit, byte, character, character length, parity checking, stop bit*

DCE. Acronym for data communications equipment. Generally, any device (such as a dial-up modem) used to establish and transfer data on a communications link. *See modem*

Data word. *See character*

Data word length. *See character length*

Default. A setting, instruction, or data used by program if no value is entered by the user. *See parameter, program*

Delete/rubout character. A special character which, on many systems, backspaces and deletes rather than backspacing and overwriting (which is the case with the backspace key). The delete/rubout character is an ASCII 127. *See backspace*

Demodulate. To recover data from a carrier wave; the opposite of modulate. *See modem, modulate*

Dial up. The process of calling one computer with another via telephone. *See sign on*

Dial-up modem. A modem designed to operate within a bps range that is effective in transmitting data via voice-grade telephone lines or other types of lines, and that uses communications parameters that are compatible with other dial-up modems and packet-switching networks. *See dial-up system, leased line modem, modem*

Dial-up system. Any ISP or online service that is designed to be accessed via voice-grade telephone lines. *See dial-up modem*

Digital. Referring to or using the binary system, particularly in storing, handling, and transmitting data. *See analog signal, binary, digital signal*

Digital signal. A discontinuous signal, identified by specific levels or values, typically on or off, 1 or 0. An electrical signal in which information is coded as a series of pulses or transitions. *See analog signal*

Direct-connect modem. A modem that connects directly to a telephone line via a modular jack. *See acoustic coupler, modem*

Directory. A summary list of available files or messages in a storage area on a Web site or online service, or a list of files stored on a disk. Directory (or Catalog) is frequently a command used to display such a summary list. *See database*

Disconnect. (Also log off, logoff, sign off.) To terminate a connection with another computer. On some systems, a command or menu selection, which causes the connection to be terminated.

Display. To print to the computer screen. On some systems, a command that prints a text file to the screen using the display format specified in your online profile and any special formatting commands provided by the host system. Also, the computer's screen or monitor. *See profile, screen, scroll*

Download. To receive data from another computer. On some systems, may be a command that initiates an ASCII or XMODEM download, or a download via another protocol. *See buffer, capture, kermit, turnaround character, Xmodem, Ymodem*

Duplex (Communications mode). In terms of a communications mode, duplex describes the ability of a data communications channel to handle two simultaneous signals; a mode that determines the direction in which data flows. Contrast with "duplex (communications parameter)."

Duplex (Communications parameter). A data communications parameter used to determine whether another computer echoes characters typed at your computer's keyboard back to your computer for display. When your system is set to full duplex (sometimes called echoplex or echo), it does not echo characters typed at its keyboard to its screen, but echoes received characters back to the screen of the system to which you are connected. When your system is set to half duplex (sometimes called non-echoplex or no echo), it echoes the characters you type to its own screen, but does not echo received characters back to the remote system. Contrast with "duplex (communications parameter)." *See full duplex, half duplex*

DTMF. Acronym for Dual Tone Modulated Frequency, which is the descriptive name for the tones used by a Touch Tone telephone.

Echo (Character echo). To repeat or redisplay. When character echo is enabled during data transmission, the receiving computer sends back characters it has received for display on the transmitting computer's screen. *See duplex, full duplex, half duplex*

Echoplex. *See full duplex*

Electronic mail. Often referred to as e-mail, electronic mail is an online message system used to deliver messages from one online user to another. E-mail files are usually private (i.e., accessible by the sender and recipient only), and often the user must go to a special online area to read e-mail. Most e-mail systems handle ASCII text files only, but some will transfer binary files intact.

Emulation. A mode of operation that enables a computer to function as if it were a specific type of terminal. Terminal emulation is an option included with some software packages. *See terminal*

Enter. To type text in a field in response to a prompt, or to create a message or text file online.

Equalization. A feature available with some modems that compensates for or adjusts to poor quality telephone lines by altering frequencies and other transmission elements.

Error-checking protocol. A file-transfer procedure in which data is transmitted in sets or groups of characters, called blocks, packets, or frames, rather than one character at a time. For the purpose of error checking, information from which the receiving system can calculate the number of bytes in each block transmitted is sent along with the block. If there is a difference between the number of bytes received and the number of bytes specified with the block, most error-checking protocol systems will cause the block to be retransmitted. Examples of transmission systems using error-checking protocol include Kermit, MNP, Xmodem, and Ymodem. *See block*

Even parity. A parity state that the parity bit assumes the value necessary (1 or 0) to make the sum of the 1s in each byte or character transmitted an even number. This is used only with an Even parity-checking scheme. *See odd parity, parity bit, parity checking*

External modem. A self-contained desktop modem connected to a computer via a serial interface cable plugged into the computer's serial or RS-232 port. An external modem can generally be used with any computer, provided the proper cable is used, and may be acoustic or direct connect.

Field. A defined area containing a fixed number of characters. Fields are found in databases as the units that make up records. Fields also follow online prompts where you are expected to enter exactly the number of characters specified (as at a date prompt) or no more than the specified number of characters (as at a password prompt). Some fields have a default value that is used if no value or character string is entered. *See default*

File. A collection of data stored as a discreet unit. A file may consist of text in ASCII format (as in a message) or text, data, or programs in binary format (as in a file stored in a database area). *See database, electronic mail, file name*

File name. The identifying label given a file. File names commonly consist of a name of up to eight letters or digits, followed by a period, followed by an extension of up to three letters or digits. Example: NAME.EXT. Other separators, such as a slash (/) may separate the name and extension on some systems. *See extension, file*

Filter. To remove unwanted characters in a transmission. This is a function of terminal software.

Flow control. A means whereby a receiving computer can signal a sending computer to pause and resume data being sent. This is normally accomplished by sending a Control-S to pause the data transmission, after which sending is resumed with Control-Q. (Control-S and Control-Q are the defaults used by most terminal programs.) Alternately, turnaround characters may be used to signal the sending system to transmit each line. The purpose of pausing data flow during a capture or download is to allow time for the data to be written to disk. *See handshaking, turnaround character, XON/OFF*

Full duplex. A parameter setting in which the system to which you are connected echoes (sends back to your screen for display) characters you type, as you type them. If your terminal software is set to full duplex, commands and other input you type will not appear on your screen unless they are echoed by the host system (which means that the other system must be set to half duplex). Also, a communications mode in which data is sent in both directions at once on a communications channel. *See duplex, echo, half duplex*

Half duplex. A parameter setting in which your system echoes (sends back to your screen for display) characters you type on your keyboard. Thus, if the host system does not echo your input for display, your terminal software must be set to half duplex. Also, a communications mode in which data can be sent in only one direction at a time on a communications channel. *See duplex, echo, full duplex, mode*

Handshaking. The mutually agreed upon method by which the rate of data transmission is controlled during an ASCII upload or download. Also, any exchange of signals used by communicating systems to establish compatible communications parameters. *See download, flow control, upload*

Hang up. *See disconnect*

Hardware. The individual or collective physical components of a computer system, including but not limited to the keyboard, monitor, disk drives, printer, and modem.

Hayes Command Set. *See AT command set*

Hayes-compatible. Describes a modem that uses all or most of the AT or Hayes Command Set. *See AT command set*

Host echo mode. *See full duplex*

Host system. The computer system receiving a call from another system. Also, a system that provides access to another online system. *See local system, originating system, remote system*

ID. (Also identifier, user ID, username.) The name or "handle" by which you identify yourself to a host system. Various information is tied to your online ID within the host system, such as your password, screen display parameters, and, in the case of commercial online services, billing information. A user ID may be a number, a name, or a series of letters and numbers. *See password*

Input. A command, value, or other data provided to a program or database by a computer user or another outside source. Normally, information entered at a prompt. *See data, default, prompt*

Initialization string. A character string that "wakes up" a modem; such a string usually precedes dialing commands. A typical modem initialization string consists of AT (for "attention").

Interface. An electronic device that facilitates communication between a computer and a peripheral device like a modem. *See port, RS-232*

Internal modem. A modem installed inside a computer, usually in the form of a printed circuit board or card.

ITU. The International Telecommunication Union, formerly the CCITT (Comité Consultatif International Téléphonique et Télégraphique), headquartered in Geneva, Switzerland. This organization sets international standards for telecommunications devices.

Kermit. A special error-checking file-transfer protocol that transfers files in variable-sized blocks. Requires "Kermit capability" on the part of your terminal software and the remote system. *See block, error-checking protocol*

Keyword. A word used to index files in databases and other information retrieval areas on some systems. The keywords attached to a file serve as references during database searches. *See database, search*

Kilobyte. A unit of computer memory, normally referring to the number of bytes in RAM or the size of a file. Equal to 1,024 bytes. *See bit, byte*

Leased-line modem. A modem designed to operate over specially conditioned, or leased, lines "leased lines" at speeds in excess of 9,600 bps. *See dial-up modem, modem*

Line feed. A signal (usually a ^J) that causes the cursor to advance one line downward on the display screen. Sometimes sent after a carriage return. *See carriage return and line feed*

Line noise. Random electrical signals, produced by malfunctioning circuit components or natural disturbances like storms, that disrupt or generate errors in data transmission.

Local echo mode. *See half duplex*

Local system. A relative term of reference that designates the system you are using; normally the call-originating system as opposed to the computer receiving the call. *See originating system, remote system*

Log in. *See sign on*

Log off. *See disconnect*

Log on. *See sign on*

Mark parity. A parity state in which the parity bit is always a digital 1. This is used only with a Mark/Space parity-checking scheme. *See parity bit, parity checking, space parity, word*

Menu level. *See prompt*

Mode. *See duplex*

Modem. A device used to translate binary signals from a computer into tone signals for transmission via telephone line, and vice versa. (From modulate-demodulate device.) *See acoustic coupler, carrier, direct-connect modem, modulate, demodulate*

Modulate. To alter some characteristic of a carrier wave or tone according to an established protocol in order to transfer information via the carrier. *See carrier, demodulate*

Multi-user system. A host computer system that can communicate with more than one computer at a time. Such a system can accommodate real-time conferencing and other features that single-user systems cannot. Virtually all online services are multi-user systems; the vast majority of BBSs are not multi-user systems. *See conference, real time*

Network. Two or more computers or terminals connected together via modems and cables or telephone lines. Also used to refer to an online service.

No echo. *See duplex, half duplex*

No parity. A parameter setting in which parity checking is not in effect. *See even parity, mark parity, parity bit, parity checking, space parity, word*

Non-echoplex. *See duplex, half duplex*

NRAM. Acronym for Non-volatile RAM. RAM that retains its contents even if its power is turned off.

Null-modem. (Also crossover cable.) A direct cable connection between two computers (normally via serial ports) for transferring data without use of a modem.

Odd parity. A parity state in which the parity bit assumes the value necessary (1 or 0) to make the sum of the 1s in each byte or character transmitted an odd number. This is used only with an odd parity-checking scheme. *See even parity, mark parity, no parity, parity bit, parity checking, space parity, word*

Off-line. A state in which a computer system is not connected with another computer.

Online. Connected with another computer; the opposite of off-line.

Online service. A commercial service that provides any or all of the following services for a fee: communication, database, information storage and retrieval, and other services. Sometimes referred to as "networks," online services are usually multi-user. Examples of online services include CompuServe, DELPHI, MCI Mail, NewsNet, and the Prodigy service.

Option. In general, a menu selection that is not a command; a choice. *See command, menu*

Originate. To initiate a call or connection between two computers.

Originating system. The computer system making a call to another computer system, as opposed to the computer system receiving a call. *See host system, local system, remote system*

Output. Information sent from a computer to its screen, a printer, a disk file, or to another computer.

Packet. *See block*

Packet switching. A method of sending information from one place to another by splitting data into "packets" or groups that are transmitted on a "space available" basis along various data links. *See block, packet-switching network*

Packet-switching network. A data communications service that transmits data from one computer system to another in the form of packets. Most packet-switching networks provide a nationwide system of local telephone numbers (called nodes) to enable users to access online services without incurring long-distance charges. DataPac, SprintNet, and Tymnet are packet-switching networks. *See block, packet switching*

Parallel communication. The simultaneous transmission of the bits (7 or 8) making up a character, using several data lines. In parallel transmission, each bit is transmitted via its own wire. *See port, serial communication*

Parameters. Settings selected by a computer user and/or included in a program that are used as established values or defaults in program operation. *See default, communications settings, program*

Parity bit. The bit designated as the check, or counting, bit during parity checking. The parity bit may be even, odd, mark, or space. *See even parity, mark parity, no parity, odd parity, parity checking, space parity, word*

Parity checking. A method of data transmission error checking in which the transmitting computer adds a bit to each character transmitted. The value of the bit is either 0 or 1, to make the total number of "1" data bits in the character even or odd; or a "mark" or "space," depending on which type of parity (Even/Odd or Mark/Space) is being used. The receiving computer then verifies the data sent via the sum of the "1" bits or the presence or absence of "1" in the parity bit slot, as necessary. Also, the terminal software setting that sets the parity checking parameters. *See data bits, even parity, mark parity, no parity, odd parity, parity bit, parity checking, space parity*

Password. A string of letters and/or numbers used to verify the identity or authorization of a user calling an online service or BBS. Use of a password prevents unauthorized use of an online ID or unauthorized use of a system. Ideally, passwords are known only to those who own the ID or account with which they are associated. *See ID*

Port. A point of connection between a computer and a peripheral device such as a modem or printer. A port consists of a special kind of connector within or on the case of a computer into which a connecting cable may be plugged. A port can be either parallel or serial, and may perform a number of functions in addition to routing data. *See RS-232*

Post. To place a public message on a BBS, usually in a message area or board area.

Profile. On BBSs and online services, a set of default parameters that the host system uses to communicate with you. A profile may contain information on display parameters (screen width, lines, and color), file-transfer protocols, prompt/menu displays, and other elements. Parameters in a profile are usually changeable, and can be temporarily reset on some systems.

Program. A set of instructions that tells a computer how to perform a defined task or tasks, and that processes commands and input in accordance with these instructions. *See command, default, input, parameter*

Protocol. The mutually agreed upon rules or settings used by two computers in data transmission.

Protocol transfer. *See error-checking protocol*

Qualifiers. Specifications or modifiers that may be added to certain commands on some systems. Qualifiers limit or direct how a command is executed. Example: Delete All (in which Delete is the command and All is the qualifier). *See command*

Remote echo. *See duplex*

Remote system. A relative term of reference designating the system you are not using; normally the system receiving the call, as opposed to the computer making the call. *See local system*

RS-232 (RS-232C). (Also RS232/RS232C.) An international standard for the electrical connection and data transmission between computer serial ports and peripherals such as modems. *See CCITT, interface, ITU, port, serial communication*

Serial communication. The sequential transmission of the bits making up a character one at a time using a single data wire. *See parallel communication, port, RS-232*

Signals. Words, codes, or sounds transmitted as variances in electrical voltage, current, and/or frequency.

Sign on. (Also log in, log on) The process or event of connecting with and identifying your computer to another computer system. Sign on typically involves sending a user ID and password to the answering system when it prompts for them.

Space parity. A parity state in which the parity bit is always a digital 0 (zero). This is used only with a Mark/Space parity-checking scheme. *See even parity, mark parity, no parity, odd parity, parity bit, parity checking, word*

Standard. An official or de facto method or set of rules generally used or followed by computer hardware and/or software.

Start bit. The first bit transmitted in the asynchronous transmission of data. The start bit (along with a stop bit or bits) frames a transmitted character. Used to synchronize the receiver with the transmitter, a start bit signals the receiving computer that a character is to be transmitted. A start bit is always a digital "1." *See asynchronous, stop bit*

Stop bit. A data bit that marks the end of a transmitted character, thus framing (with the start bit) the character. Transmission of a stop bit returns the transmission circuit to its at rest or idle state, and also provides timing information tied to the baud rate. Most terminal software packages offer the option of setting the number of stop bits to 1 or 2 (1 stop bit is the norm). Like a start bit, a stop bit is always a digital "1." *See bit, byte, data bits, character, start bit*

String. A series of letters, numbers, or symbols to be input or output as data. Strings that cannot be used as numeric operands and whose values do not vary are character strings. "Franklin Robert Adams," "555-1969," and "3-21-51" are all character strings. Strings with set numeric values are numeric strings. "451.50" and "910234" are numeric strings. *See character*

Synchronous. A form of transmission in which groups of data bits are sent at regular, uniformly timed intervals. Unlike asynchronous transmission, synchronous transmission does not require start or stop bits. *See asynchronous*

Syntax. A set of rules governing how commands, file names, or data can be entered at a prompt. *See prompt*

Sysop. Shorthand for "system operator." The person who operates a BBS or a specific area of an online service.

System. A term used to refer to any computer (and its peripherals), particularly a computer that is connected with another computer whether as a host or as an originating system.

Telecommunications. Data communication over telephone lines via computers and associated devices.

Telecomputing. In general, using a personal computer to communicate with BBSs, online services, or other personal computers.

Telex. An international telecommunications system that handles messaging to and from special Telex terminals anywhere in the world. Telex service can be accessed directly with a personal computer through Telex carriers such as Western Union and RCA, or via any of several online services that provide gateway access to Telex carriers.

Terminal. A device that displays and sometimes stores data received from another computer and that can transmit data from a keyboard or a mass storage device. A dedicated computer that is capable of performing telecommunications and related tasks only. *See emulation*

Terminal configuration. *See communications settings*

Terminal emulation. *See emulation*

Terminal mode. A software operating mode in which all keyboard or other local input is sent directly to the modem, which accepts it as commands or passes it on to a remote system as appropriate. *See command mode*

Terminal settings. *See communications settings*

Terminal software. *See communications software*

Text. Any message or file composed of standard ASCII characters. *See ASCII, character*

Text file. A file in ASCII format, as opposed to binary or binary/ASCII format. *See ASCII, binary, file, text*

Timesharing system. An antiquated term used to describe computer systems that are accessed by more than one user at a time.

Transmission rate. *See bits per second*

TTY. Short for teletypewriter or Telex. *See Telex*

Turnaround character. A preselected character or prompt for which a terminal program may wait before sending a line of text during an ASCII upload or before receiving an ASCII download. *See download, flow control, upload*

Upload. To send data to another computer. On some systems, a command that initiates a file transfer from your computer to the host system. *See download, turnaround character*

User. A term applied to someone who dials up, or uses, a BBS or online service.

Videotex. An outdated term applied to the transmission of textual data and/or text and graphics by an online information service.

Word. Another term for a group of bits used to transmit a character. *See bit, byte, character, stop bit*

Word length. *See character length*

Wxmodem. Windowed Xmodem. *See Xmodem*

X.25. A special communications protocol that enables multiple sessions on one line, available on some systems and packet-switching networks.

X.400. An intersystem e-mail standard used in transferring data between domestic and international e-mail systems.

Xmodem. A special error-checking file-transfer protocol that transfers files in blocks of 128 bytes. Requires "Xmodem capability" on the part of your terminal software and the remote system. *See block, error-checking protocol*

XON-XOFF. A standard type of flow control using Control-S to signal a sending computer to pause and Control-Q to signal the sending computer to resume sending. This is the flow control used by most systems. *See flow control*

Y-connector. (Also Y-jack.) A special connector that converts one jack (socket) into two so that two phone lines may be plugged into one receptacle.

Ymodem. A special error-checking file-transfer protocol that transfers files in blocks of 1,024 bytes. Requires "Ymodem capability" on the part of your terminal software and the remote system. *See block, error-checking protocol*

Zmodem. A special error-checking file-transfer protocol that transfers files in blocks of (usually) 512 bytes. Requires "Zmodem capability" the part of your terminal software and the remote system. *See block, error-checking protocol*

Index

More CyberAge Books
from Information Today, Inc.

net.people
The Personalities and Passions Behind the Web Sites
By Eric C. Steinert and Thomas E. Bleier

With the explosive growth of the Internet, people from all walks of life are bringing their dreams and schemes to life as Web sites. In net.people, authors Bleier and Steinert take you up close and personal with the creators of 36 of the world's most intriguing online ventures. For the first time, these entrepreneurs and visionaries share their personal stories and hard-won secrets of Webmastering. You'll learn how each of them launched a home page, increased site traffic, geared up for e-commerce, found financing, dealt with failure and success, built new relationships—and discovered that a Web site had changed their life forever.

Softbound • ISBN 0-910965-37-4 • $19.95

Super Searchers on Wall Street
Top Investment Professionals Share Their Online Research Secrets
By Amelia Kassel Edited by Reva Basch

Through her probing interviews, Amelia Kassel reveals the online secrets of 10 leading financial industry research experts. You'll learn how information professionals find and analyze market and industry data, as well as how online information is used by brokerages, stock exchanges, investment banks, and individual investors to make critical investment decisions. The Wall Street Super Searchers direct you to important sites and sources, illuminate the trends that are revolutionizing financial research, and help you use online research as part of a powerful investment strategy. As a reader bonus, a directory of top sites and sources is hyperlinked and periodically updated on the Web.

Softbound • ISBN 0-910965-42-0 • $24.95

Internet Blue Pages, 2001-2002 Edition
The Guide to Federal Government Web Sites
By Laurie Andriot

With over 1,800 Web addresses, this guide is designed to help you find any agency easily. Arranged in accordance with the US Government Manual, each entry includes the name of the agency, the Web address (URL), a brief description of the agency, and links to the agency's or subagency's home page. For helpful cross-referencing, an alphabetical agency listing and a comprehensive index for subject searching are also included. Regularly updated information and links are provided on the author's Web site.

Softbound • ISBN 0-910965-29-3 • $34.95

Great Scouts!
CyberGuides for Subject Searching on the Web
By Nora Paul and Margot Williams • Edited by Paula Hane

Great Scouts! is a cure for information overload. Authors Nora Paul (The Poynter Institute) and Margot Williams *(The Washington Post)* direct readers to the very best subject-specific, Web-based information resources. Thirty chapters cover specialized "CyberGuides" selected as the premier Internet sources of information on business, education, arts and entertainment, science and technology, health and medicine, politics and government, law, sports, and much more. With its expert advice and evaluations of information and link content, value, currency, stability, and usability, *Great Scouts!* takes you "beyond search engines"—and directly to the top sources of information for your topic. As a reader bonus, the authors are maintaining a Web page featuring updated links to all the sites covered in the book.

Softbound • ISBN 0-910965-27-7 • $24.95

Internet Business Intelligence
How to Build a Big Company System on a Small Company Budget
By David Vine

According to author David Vine, business success in the competitive, global marketplace of the 21st century will depend on a firm's ability to use information effectively—and the most successful firms will be those that harness the Internet to create and maintain a powerful information edge. In *Internet Business Intelligence,* Vine explains how any company—large or small—can build a complete, low-cost, Internet-based business intelligence system that really works.

Softbound • ISBN 0-910965-35-8 • $29.95

Design Wise
A Guide for Evaluating the Interface Design of Information Resources
By Alison J. Head

"*Design Wise* takes us beyond what's cool and what's hot and shows us what works and what doesn't."
—Elizabeth Osder
The New York Times on the Web

Knowing how to size up user-centered interface design is becoming as important for people who choose and use information resources as for those who design them. This book introduces readers to the basics of interface design and explains why a design evaluation should be tied to the use and purchase of information resources.

Softbound • ISBN 0-910965-31-5 • $29.95   Hardbound • ISBN 0-910965-39-0 • $39.95